# To Be and How to Be

# To Be and How to Be

## TRANSFORMING YOUR LIFE

### through

## SACRED THEATRE

## PEGGY RUBIN

Theosophical Publishing House
Wheaton, Illinois * Chennai, India

Quest Books
Theosophical Publishing House
P. O. Box 270
Wheaton, Illinois 60187-0270
www.questbooks.net

Cover design by Jessica Stevens, www.design-savvy.com
Text illustrations by Trish Broersma
Text design and typesetting by Wordstop Technologies (P) Ltd, Chennai, India

Page 101: Excerpt from "A Tewa Prayer," from p. 13 in *The Tewa World: Space, Time and
Becoming in Pueblo Society*, by Alfonso Ortiz. Copyright © 1969 The University of Chicago
Press. Page 159: Excerpt from "Like a Planet," by James Bertolino reprinted by permission of
the poet, Snail River, 1995, Quarterly Review of Literature, Contemporary Poetry Series. Page
193: Excerpt from "The Man Watching," by Rainer Maria Rilke from *Selected Poems of Rainer
Maria Rilke: A Translation from the German and Commentary by Robert Bly*. Copyright ©
1981 by Robert Bly. Reprinted by permission of HarperCollins Publishers. Page 232: Excerpts
from "Love after Love," from *Collected Poems 1948–1984*, by Derek Walcott. Copyright © 1986
by Derek Walcott. Reprinted by permission of Farrar, Straus and Giroux, LLC and Faber and
Faber Ltd. Page 248: Excerpt from *Fire in the Head: Shamanism and the Celtic Spirit*, by Tom
Cowan. Copyright © 1992 by Tom Cowan. Reprinted by permission of HarperCollins Publishers and Riverside Literary Agency as agents for the author. Pages 255–56: "Thanks," from *Rain
in the Trees*, by W. S. Merwin. Copyright © 1988 by W. S. Merwin. Used by permission of Alfred
A. Knopf, a division of Random House, Inc. Pages 256–57: "School Prayer," from *I Praise My
Destroyer*, by Diane Ackerman. Copyright © 1998 by Diane Ackerman. Used by permission of
Random House, Inc.

**Library of Congress Cataloging-in-Publication Data**

Rubin, Peggy.
To be and how to be: transforming your life through sacred theatre /
Peggy Rubin.—1st Quest ed.
   p.   cm.
Includes bibliographical references (p.   ) and index.
ISBN 978-0-8356-0853-4
1. Spiritual life.   2. Self realization—Religious aspects.
3. Theater—Religious aspects.   I. Title.
BL624.R74 2010
204'.3—dc22                                                                    2010001154

4   3   2   1   *   10   11   12   13   14
Printed in the United States of America

To

Jean Houston, Jodie George, Sharron Dorr

and

all the Players creating their lives as Sacred Theatre

*The soul is here for its own joy.*

—Rumi

# Contents

# Foreword

Y ou are about to enter a masterpiece so important, so radically original, so critically helpful that, frankly, at first I felt speechless to comment on it. In this book you will become a passionate player on the stage of your own life's journey. You will find new heart, new mind, new voice, and new expression. Most importantly, you will be drawn into the genius and magic of Peggy Rubin.

Peggy Rubin is a master of the once-and-future art of Sacred Theatre. A brilliant actor, teacher, scholar, and evoker of the depths of human possibilities, since 1987 she has created in her workshops a powerful modern version of using the mysteries of the theatre to open people to the art, spirit, and creativity inherent in the drama of their lives.

In this work she draws upon antecedents in the Mystery traditions. The rites of the ancient Mysteries provided powerful initiatory journeys of anguish, grief, loss, redemption, knowledge, and ecstatic union with the god or goddess. During the journey one "died" in some sense to one's old self and was reborn to a higher self or even to identification with the goddess or god. One also received special wisdom and training into deeper life and its meaning.

Often, the journey followed the story of the suffering of gods and goddesses. The training came from the goddess's representatives—as in the cult of the Triple Goddess in the Eleusinian Mysteries—in her aspect as Persephone, Demeter, and Hecate; that is, as maiden, fertile Mother, and wise old crone. This most renowned of Mysteries assured a life-changing experience as the participant witnessed the tale of Demeter losing her child Persephone to the god of death, Hades, who makes her queen of the Underworld. The grieving Demeter searches everywhere for her and, as goddess of agriculture, causes the crops to die and the world to become a wasteland. But then, aided by Hecate, a goddess of wise magic and of crossroads, Demeter is able to recover Persephone for part of the year, during which time life on earth is renewed.

We know very little of what happened during the ancient Mystery rites. However, from what can be recovered from early Christian commentaries drawn from those who sneaked in on false pretenses, we gather that, imitating Persephone, the initiate underwent a physical and symbolic night descent into the Underworld, where the initiatory experience occurred. A fragment of a work by the Greek poet Pindar says of the initiates upon their return: "Happy are they who, having beheld these things, descend beneath the Earth. They know life's end but also a new beginning from the gods."

As in those ancient Mysteries, this book provides the reader and serious practitioner an experience of the journey from one's ordinary diminished condition into extraordinary life, "a new beginning from the gods." By what means does such a transformation come about? Based on her many years as a Shakespearean and classical actor, Peggy Rubin uses the traditional theatre (and occasionally movies and television) as "a metaphor for framing and living life." Drawing from the plays and rituals of many cultures, but principally from Shakespeare, she leads you, the reader, into experiences that explore, evoke, and help resolve your most pressing and confounding issues. Everything is here: life in its incandescence and with a cast of characters that encompasses the entire human condition. You discover personae and capacities you probably never knew you had and, through the great nine powers of the theatre, glean the wisdom and practices to bring you home to the deep truths of who and what you really are. As Peggy leads you consciously to work with some of the greatest characters in human history, a rich and varied world of experience opens to you. You can feel the passions of Romeo and Juliet and wield the magical powers of Prospero. With Viola, you can exuberantly play with a complete change of identity and, with Hamlet, become a master of expression. You can experience the pride and doubt of Othello and, with Balinese sacred dancers, know the transformative value of conflict. With Oedipus, you can gain the equanimity to overcome even the cruelest fate; with Hermione and Helena, you can die and be reborn. And, ultimately, you can enjoy the gifts of the Cauldron of Plenty as they were bestowed by Dagda the Good, the Celtic god of abundance.

Within the spoken or enacted stories of the glorious plays, you can allow your life to be writ larger, the particulars of your existence finding amplification and elucidation in the universals of the greater story and the larger characters that the theatre often contains. Entering the realm of the plays and their personae, you become polyphrenic, having many more personalities and skills to draw upon, and seem to inherit a cache of experience that illumines and fortifies your own. Soon, you will discover that you, too, are a valuable character in the drama of the world soul, pushing the boundaries of your own local story and gaining the courage to be and do so much more.

Through it all, using words like wands, Peggy is there beside you, guiding, evoking, praising, and celebrating. She is, after all, a true midwife of souls, an evocateur of the divine in each person with whom she works. And what is she trying to call forth in you the reader? The genius of larval minds, carriers of new genesis as the world is getting ready to move. The ability to think in varied postures in order to stock your spiritual income so as to have the wherewithal for ethical and creative expenditures. A sufficiency of intellectual and moral passion to explore new ways of being for body, mind, and soul—and with it the ability to present the availability of an unobstructed universe both within and without. For, as Peggy shows from her vast spectrum of knowledge and experience, science is not enough, religion is not enough, art is not enough, politics and economics are surely not enough; nor is duty or action, however disinterested; nor, however sublime, is contemplation. Nothing short of everything will do. And everything is what theatre, raised to its sacred dimensions, can provide.

If you are a therapist or psychologist, you will find here luminous techniques to engage the body, mind, and heart of your clients in the journey of healing. If you are a priest, rabbi, or minister, you will discover a spiritual psychology filled with a profound order of story and practice. If you are a teacher, a consultant, or a friend, you will find new textures for the fabric of relationship. And, if you are one who really wants to make a difference, here is a trove of ways to bring new mind to bear upon old and new matters.

But what of Peggy herself? In addition to leading her own workshops in Sacred Theatre, she has been my working partner in our Mystery Schools, Social Artistry trainings, and travels for some twenty-five years. With me, working with the United Nations and other international agencies, she brings her craft and genius to developing human capacities among leaders the world over, newly empowering them to deal with the enormous challenges now facing every society. Modest to a fault and radically empathic, Peggy opens hearts and minds that had been closed by force of culture and circumstance. I consider her friendship and partnership one of the greatest gifts of my life, as, in this book, they will become in yours. Peggy Rubin is one about whom we may say that the human heart can go to the lengths of God. If those lengths lead to a theatre, all the better!

—Jean Houston
January 2010

# Acknowledgments

The best part about writing a book is writing the acknowledgments. The trouble is that the book has taken fifteen years to write, and there are so many people to thank that this part could be longer than the book itself. Nevertheless, here are a few of the people who helped the work of Sacred Theatre take shape and evolve. I am grateful to all and to each of them.

Jean Houston, the incomparable, informed me in 1987 that I was to give a presentation on Sacred Theatre at a conference in The Netherlands on Sacred Matter and therewith began my saga with this work.

The gallant, intrepid organizers of Sacred Theatre workshops abroad include: In Australia, Marian McClelland, Beverly Kryzynoski, Jenni Woodruffe, Tricia Kotai-Ewers, and Beryl Chalk (who saw potentials in the work that she transformed into a PhD from the University of Western Australia). In Jamaica, Sheila Graham and Alwyn A. Bully of UNESCO. In New Zealand, Dave and Louise Breuer and their miraculous daughter Melodie. In Russia, Tatiana Antonyan, Irina Antonyan, and the Urania Group.

Workshops in California have been sponsored by Robin Van Doren, Fran Rothman, Barbara Glazer, Judith Annette Milburn, Elaine Larson, and Penny McManigal. In Colorado, by Dianna Butler. In Illinois, by Ruthann Fowler and Sr. Joyce Kemp. In Kentucky, by Chris Kubale and Sandy Robinson. In Michigan, by Judith Allen, Sr. Esther Kennedy, Lucille McNaughton, Pat Nuznov, Anaja Raphael, Penelope Trikes, Nancy Nikolauk, and Linda Berry. In Minnesota, by Marie Burgeson and Maria Genne, whose husband Cris Anderson said at his first workshop,

# ACKNOWLEDGMENTS

"Where is the book about this?" In New Jersey, by Pat Heck and Patti Kaufman (this is the longest running and best fed: fifteen years of workshops, sometimes three a year, and all enhanced by glorious food). In South Carolina, by Carolyn Rivers; in Wyoming, by Natasha Yon. And in Oregon, by Trish Broersma, Elizabeth Austin, and Hilary Tate. These three are the Sparta Dancers (I am the fourth), long-time allies whose support and guidance keep me going.

In addition to these cherished friends, numerous others supported the long process of creating this book and the work on which it is based. A partial listing: Elizabeth Alberda, Frank Hayes, Gwynne Jennings, Denise Kester, Janice Luckenbill, Christiane Meunier, Elisabeth Rothenberger, Mary Russin, Andrea Wachter, and Laura Ann Walton.

Editorial counsel came from Brenda Rosen, Carolyn Bond, Dody Schwartz, Amy Ober, Hilary Tate, and Richard Smoley. Publicity mavens include Pat Heck and Wendy Jane Carrel, as well as Quest Book's Xochi Adame. The wonderful book title came from Phillip Salazar at Publishers Group West. My writing buddies include Gayle Frye, Lisa Nelson, and Trish Broersma. I also thank Lisa for proofreading and Trish for my website and all manner of design assistance.

My editor, the brilliant, indefatigable, and meticulous Sharron Brown Dorr, Quest Books' publishing manager, made the book's publication possible.

Among the people who made my life a venture into Sacred Theatre are my parents, Margaret and Will Nash; my aunt, Nancy Light; my sister, Mary Collins; my brothers, Bill and Neel Nash; and all my remarkable nieces and nephews. My young-life husband, George Vafiadis, led me into the arms of William Shakespeare, where I have lived happily ever since. My mid-life husband, Ben Rubin, taught me to laugh and tried to teach me to write. Many theatre teachers and directors gave my life play clarity, depth, and purpose; they include Zula Pearson (Lon Morris College); B. Iden Payne, James Moll, and Francis Hodge (University of Texas); Dimitri Rondiris (Greek National Theatre); Angus Bowmer, James Sandoe, Robert Loper, James Edmondson, Jerry Turner, and Richard Hay (Oregon Shakespeare Festival). Gratitude also

# ACKNOWLEDGMENTS

to the best boss anyone ever had, Bill Patton, and to his wife Shirley, a fellow actor from my earliest days at the Oregon Shakespeare Festival. Special friends and coworkers of my years there include Sally White, Darlene Templeton, Lois Pischel, Paul Barnes (also a favorite director), Nora Yeoman, Kit Leary, and Mary Turner, with whom I traveled the wilds of eastern Oregon and Washington as Shakespeare missionaries. And special thanks to my dear adoptive mother, Gertrude Bowmer.

Wise advisors deepened my understanding of aspects of the Powers of Sacred Theatre, including Don Campbell, Emily Devine, Bruce Lipton, Gay Luce, and David Patten. If I misinterpreted their remarks, I ask forgiveness.

Teachers in other fields have enriched the play of my life in countless ways; they include Elaine de Beauport, Donna Eden and David Feinstein, William Emerson, Karlton Terry, and Michael Meade.

Several beloved sacred players have left this great stage of the earth and I want to remember them by naming their names: Joy Craddick, Belle Douglass, Ernestine Griswold, Caroline Jerome, and Natasha Yon.

Personal help and encouragement came from Shannon Crane, who fed me a thousand meals and almost that many drinks; and Willene and Tom Gunn, who provided retreats in beautiful Montana. It was Willene's magnificent mezzo voice that lifted me during a long siege of grief. Susan Brown and her beautiful daughters, Chloe and Phoebe, have cheered my life immeasurably. Alison May took me to Burning Man and listened to the story of the book; and Jodie and Jon George have been my best friends almost all my life.

Without Jean Houston, this book would never have been started; without Jodie George, it would never have been finished; and without Sharron Dorr, it would never have been published.

Thanks, and thanks, and ever thanks.

# Prologue

Life can be experienced as a great play—sometimes a comedy, sometimes a tragedy, sometimes a satire, but always a play. A play is a story enacted by living actors before a living audience, not filmed, not recorded, but alive *now*.

Plays have been around since the earliest days of humankind. I like to think they began soon after our ancestors discovered fire. Imagine the innumerable interactions that must have taken place around its comforting warmth—painting on cave walls or rocks or the bark of trees; making music, storytelling, or dancing; teaching the young ones—all elements that comprise the essence of human culture.

Imagine also, in that ancient firelight, one of our ancestors wanting to tell us how she found honey by following bees to their hive, or how he and his cohorts chased and killed the wooly mammoth. As a group we are celebrating the honey or the great roasting haunch of meat. Telling the story excites us so much that suddenly one person leaps up and begins to enact the adventure, to tell it through the body as well as through the voice, as if it were happening in this moment. We watch, admire, question, and respond; perhaps we add music and sound. We participate in the enactment; we are changed by it and we never forget it.

Today, as always, such telling is a way of honoring and understanding our lives as a community of human beings. Stories become a mirror in which we see the great patterns and deep truths that transcend the mere facts of our individual existence. Playing the play of life is a daring adventure. It takes courage, focus, excitement, and intention not to let our life stories just happen and instead stand up to enact them with verve and delight. This book invites you to become a Player, to take the stage of life and play your story for all it is worth.

## The Theatre as Sacred

This book uses the traditional theatre as a metaphor for framing and living life. I think of it as a dialogue between us. We will be talking about how actors work as they prepare and play their roles and how their training can provide ways for us all to live more buoyantly. First, may I share some thoughts about how I believe the theatre began as a sacred act, how your life is a sacred art form, and why I call what we are doing together Sacred Theatre.

Let us return to the ancient firelight and our ancestors' celebration over the roasting meat. We can imagine the excitement as the first actor rises to enact the story of the hunt; we can almost hear the accompanying sounds and feel his listeners' enormous gratitude for the animal that gave its life to provide protein and also gave them this reason to celebrate—and, incidentally, to invent the theatre.

Wise people who ponder such things suggest that our beliefs about the soul's existence might have originated in these moments. The hunters watching the animal's life ebb away would have felt not only exaltation over this gift to the tribe, attained after immense effort and cunning, but also sorrow over its loss. They must have experienced the puzzling sorrow that afflicts us all in the awesome, undeniable presence of death. Perhaps from that mix of joy and sorrow grew the hope that death might not mean the end for this buffalo or mastodon, that an everlasting part of it had gone to reunite with the great soul of buffalo or mastodon in the unseen world. And, our ancestors may have reasoned, if such could be true for the animal, then there was hope for their own everlasting life as well.

Thus in the celebration through enacted story of the life and death of the animal and the everlasting life of its soul, a sense of the sacred may have come to be.

Fast forward many thousands of years, and we find that the idea of an eternal essence in all living beings has become a central reality in human belief. So also has grown the understanding of sacrifice as the animal or plant's gift of its life so that humans may survive. (The word *sacrifice* carries a meaning of "making sacred," or "recognizing as sacred.")

Eventually, as people conceived of a divine realm and told and enacted stories about gods and goddesses, the idea arose that some of those gods so loved us that they, too, were willing to sacrifice themselves for the well-being of humanity. The ancient Greeks expressed gratitude for the gifts of agriculture by enacting the Mysteries of the Earth Mother, Demeter, and her daughter, Persephone, who "dies" each year, descending to the Underworld for that season when winter reigns and rising again in the spring. These rituals lasted for thousands of years and gave participants a means of coming to peace with the omnipresent force that death represents.

With their experience of the year's turning and the annual gift of renewed life, the Greeks evolved a belief about the soul's life that reflected this ever-dying, ever-rising tide of time. And it wasn't just the Greeks. Across the world, wherever there is a distinct turning of the seasons, our ancestors developed beliefs and stories about what causes it. They felt or imagined forces, entities, and gods that helped account for the constantly changing process of birth, growth, development, decline, and death. The stories of the gods perhaps grew from human experiences of awe and from the praiseworthy desire to honor the mysterious processes of life, sacrifice, and the soul.

These god-centered beliefs and rituals have made their way deep into our psyches, whether or not we are aware of it. And it is this worldwide richness that has become the breeding ground for theatre.

Some twenty-five hundred years ago, at the same time the Mysteries of Demeter and Persephone were enacted in ancient Greece, formal theatre began through the retelling of another Mystery, the alchemy of the grape and the vine in the production of wine. At first it was a ceremonial event to honor the god who mysteriously embodies the vine, the grape, the wine, the drinking of the wine, and the force that drives them all. His Greek name is Dionysus, though we often call him by the name the Romans adopted, Bacchus. Because the theatre as we know it in Western civilization began with these ceremonies, Dionysus is known as the god of the theatre.

Stories, both poignant and terrifying, grew up about this god. The most painful tale, told in the Mystery traditions attributed to the poet/singer Orpheus, involved Dionysus being torn apart as a child by jealous Titans, who then ate him to hide their crime. His father, the almighty Zeus Thunderer, rescued Dionysus's heart and furiously struck the Titans with his lightning bolt. From their ashes rose human beings. Hence we humans have two natures: we are jealous destroyers and we also contain the innocent child of the god. Part of our work as sacred players is to identify and honor the essence and conflict of these two natures.

Naturally, Dionysus came to life again (as the grapevine springs back after pruning). The Greeks celebrated him annually as the ever-renewing energy of the god force. At first they wrote songs and choral odes in tribute to him; groups of young people trained for months to speak, sing, and move with the words that honored all the gods but especially Dionysus of the wine, whose sacrifice, through the crushing of the grape, gives humankind such joy and pleasure. One Hymn to Dionysus exclaims:

> You are honored
> by all the gods and by all the men who dwell upon the earth.
> Come, blessed and leaping god, and bring much joy to all.[1]

The ceremonies in Athens celebrating Dionysus slowly evolved into contests among the poets and bards, in which highly trained choruses presented such god songs through chanting and movement. Tradition holds that one fateful day some daring soul risked an innovation, imitating our ancestor around the fire who stood up to enact the story instead of simply tell it: a member of the chorus stepped away from the group and "became" the god whose song they were singing. According to Greek scholar David Sacks, "This step is traditionally credited to a shadowy genius named Thespis (circa 535 BCE), who also may have introduced the single actor's wearing of a mask to signify character."[2] Thus the first actor took the stage in celebratory gratitude to the sacred powers that make life possible, eventful, precious, and rich. In honor of that first actor, today all people in the theatre can call themselves *Thespians*; we are his soul descendants.

## BLESSED BE THE OPPOSITION

Back to our distant ancestors by the fire—surely one of them felt the urge to stand and declare, "No! It didn't happen the way *you* say. *I* was the one who threw the lucky spear." Similarly, the Greeks recognized that, in order for a story to move forward dramatically, it has to depict contending forces. This recognition gave us the words *protagonist* and *antagonist*. In the theatre the first actor is the protagonist, the leading character who champions a particular cause or point of view. The second is the antagonist, the one who declares the equivalent of a loud, clear "No!" Then the protagonist is compelled to respond, and the antagonist to respond to him, escalating the tension until a climax is reached, with the action moving to some form of resolution, followed in ancient Greek drama with a formal summing up by the chorus.

In Sacred Theatre as well, we come to recognize that conflict is just as essential in the unfolding drama of our existence. Two forces contend in ways that may be bellicose or joyful, but one always comes up against the other. Challenge and response, action and reaction, are the forces that move our lives forward, just as they do in any play. As chapter 7 explores, I believe that participating in conflict with authenticity is one way to develop the soul. By acknowledging the crucial importance

of conflict, we can lift ourselves away from our usual disheartened responses to difficult situations and begin to respond to them with freedom and even a wild joy.

And no matter how painful, bizarre, or horrendous the story may be—
onstage or off—it helps to remember that the theatre was originally
dedicated to the divine power of Dionysus and grounded in the realm
of the sacred. No matter how far the modern theatre and its children
of movies and television seem to have wandered from that sense, the
foundation of the theatre, and its infusing grace, is firmly based in
gratitude for the life-sustaining gifts of the gods. In the same way, no
matter how far our lives may seem to have wandered from the sacred,
they too are grounded in a sacred force that brings life, holds life, takes
life, and brings life again. The great play that we enact with our lives is
a sacred play whether we know it or not.

## Making a Play

For every word an actor speaks onstage, every gesture she makes, hundreds of ideas have been tried and discarded during rehearsal. And
for every person onstage there are dozens more behind the scenes,
contributing to the coherence and aliveness of the action: costumers,
stage designers, builders, prop makers, stage managers, lighting designers and controllers, ticket sellers, ushers, and house management
staff members who make life easier for everyone in attendance. I want
to acknowledge that your life also carries a huge "back story"; part of
this book's purpose is to tease out strands of that story and honor all
the people who have made it possible for your play to get to the stage
and keep on playing.

   We will accomplish this purpose in an actor's way: by asking questions and engaging fruitfully with nine forces, or powers. These nine
powers underlie all theatre work and can support your life with the
same energy and excitement that an actor feels before an eager au-

dience. Each chapter describes one of these powers and provides opportunities for training with vigor and élan.

Do you remember the fundamental questions we once learned in journalism class: Who? What? When? Where? How? Why? The powers of Sacred Theatre answer these questions this way:

**Question One**: *Who?*
**Answer**: You!
**Power**: Incarnation
You came into this life with purpose, determination, and delight, ready to act, enact, and react. You came prepared and able to play many roles. You are the star in your own life, and you are also a participating player in many other lives. Learning to embody this lifetime fully is one of the goals of the chapter on the Power of Incarnation.

**Question Two**: *What* are you doing?
**Answer**: Enacting a story
**Power**: Story
You are a living story, part of the immeasurably rich story of life on earth, and you can experience, remember, reinvent, and enjoy the multitude of ways you have participated profoundly in it. Finding your own essential story and tapping into the great story of Life on Earth are two actions that engage this power.

**Question Three**: *When* are you enacting this story on this stage?
**Answer**: In this present moment
**Power**: *Now!*
The Power of *Now!* offers an understanding of the strands of past and future held in this present moment and provides training in learning to flow easily with each successive fragment of time.

**Question Four**: *Where* are you enacting this story?
**Answer**: On the stage of life
**Power**: Place

The Power of Place provides you with a sacred stage composed of imagination, memory, reality, and recognition of the energy of the earth. This stage gives you the strength of belonging and the capacity to take a stand on behalf of your life.

**Question Five**: *How* are you enacting this story on this stage in this moment?
**Answer**: By virtue of three great creative forces
**Powers**: Expression, Point of View, and Conflict

1. The Power of Expression invites you to gain creativity through speech and movement so that your full body, voice, and intention are aligned and you are able to express the exact emotions or ideas needed to move forward.

2. The Power of Point of View focuses on the gift of being who you are, appreciating why you are the way you are, and valuing your unique way of seeing and doing, as well as on the ability to embrace other perspectives in order to shift and expand.

3. The Power of Conflict gives you again and again the opportunity to learn and to grow, and even to transform. No life, or play, can exist without this power, and the higher the conflict the better the play.

**Question Six**: *Why* are you doing all this?
**Answer**: For the love and joy of it all
**Powers:** Audience and Celebration

1. The Power of Audience is that of observer and attentive listener. All good plays are performed for and before an audience, for the purpose ultimately of celebrating life. Your individual play is performed for a sacred audience who witnesses and applauds your work. This power also enhances your awareness of the joy of being a member of the sacred audience in other people's plays.

2. The Power of Celebration is the payoff. It provides the enjoyment for which you, as a sacred player, are doing all this preparation.

*Yes!* is the word that theatre shouts aloud. No matter how poignant, painful, or tragic the events of your story may be, life demands that you—that all of us—learn to celebrate its existence in every moment.

## The Art of Dedication

As mentioned, the ancient Greek theatre festivals were dedicated to Dionysus, god of wine and ecstasy and an untamable force. This dedication on the part of actors, playwrights, sponsors, and audience involved ritual, sacrifice, and honoring. Thus all the activities of the festival were made sacred.

It behooves us as sacred players also to dedicate the experience of our lives to some force greater than we are. With that action, we consecrate our endeavor and acknowledge that we are engaged in Sacred Theatre. So now the question becomes, "To whom or to what do I dedicate my life play?"

You may have an immediate answer: "I dedicate my life play to Beauty, or to Healing, or to Holy Wisdom, or to God, or to the enlightenment of all beings." And that's perfect. However, it is energizing to consider the question more deeply, realizing that the sense of dedication can shift over time. For example, I realized at a young age that my life was suffused with a love for learning. But in my fiftieth year I met Jean Houston and learned from her of the ancient feminine principle of wisdom called the Sophia. Somehow that wisdom principle became personalized, and the Sophia gave my life renewed purpose and an underlying story to relate to and attempt to understand.

Occasionally in this book we will take a short break, as I ask you to personalize the ideas that may have come up in your reading. These breaks are headed *Pause, Please*. We are doing this work the actor's way, by asking questions; each pause will include questions to give you time and space to reflect, or write, or ask your own questions, or simply to meditate. Here is the first one:

# *Pause, Please*

Realizing that things can always change, can you now dedicate your life play to some ethical principle or divine being that is larger than your own life? It will help focus the process if you write your dedication. Here is mine:

> I, Peggy Rubin, dedicate this part of my life story to divine Sophia and all the beings from every culture who represent the power of learning and the search for wisdom. May the writing and work of this book serve these Wisdom Beings honestly and honorably, and may this work be of benefit to others.

So now, make your own dedication. Write out what you want to say today about how you wish to perform the great play of your life for some high purpose. If this is difficult to imagine, consider what you love and honor the most. People in my classes, for instance, have dedicated their life plays to their grandchildren, to beauty, to the earth's healing, or to service, as well as to their sense of the Divine.

When you have at least a draft of this dedication, I'll meet you "onstage" to talk about who you really are, as we explore the Power of Incarnation.

*. . . then there was a star danced, and under that was I born.*
—Beatrice, in Shakespeare's *Much Ado About Nothing*
(2.1.313–314)

# One

# The Power of Incarnation

**B**eatrice is Shakespeare's merriest heroine, able to see humor in all situations, laugh at herself, and delight her hearers with the swiftness of her mind. She plays with ideas as adroitly as a fencer engages in swordplay. In the words on the facing page she teasingly describes the circumstances of her birth, circumstances that perhaps gave her the gift of laughter, which is her true nature. I'm fond of this quote, not only because I am fond of Beatrice, but also because it is a metaphor for the belief that we are born in resonance with cosmic energies that help to form our own true nature.

## HERE'S THE STORY

A star danced when you were born, no matter what else may have happened. A star danced, and you embody the essence of that star. Carrying that essence, you were born into a multimillion dollar theatre production called *My Life*. This fantastic creation boasts a cast of thousands; it tells of profound love, daunting challenges, daredevil accomplishments, and heart-stirring action. It presents a unique story that will play one time only, so it is valuable and deserves applause and awe.

The Power of Incarnation invites you to become fully embodied, with your share of star power woven into your precious human flesh. This power asks you to step fully onto the stage of your life, knowing that you bring a profound gift and have a potent purpose for being alive.

All the world is your stage (as Shakespeare reminds us), and your whole life is a vast and elegant drama played upon it. You incarnate a fascinating character. You enact a powerful story through your actions and your words. You express that story through your voice, your movements, and your facial expressions. You perform actions, driven by need and desire; you respond to others and sometimes change your actions because of them.

To make this incarnation even more interesting, you enact different roles in other people's plays: best friend, teacher, student, lover, spouse. And you do so in cameos and in bit parts; as a supporting character; in a leading role; and as a chorus member, an extra, or even a member of the audience. In your own play, however, you remember that *you* are the star.

## How It Works in the Theatre

In the traditional theatre, an actor incarnates a character on a designated place called the stage. During the course of the play, we in the audience pick up dozens of clues about a character through the way she looks, sounds, and moves. These clues help us understand the person the actor is incarnating and the story we are watching.

Everything happens through the characters' words and deeds. Only rarely do we encounter a narrator, as we do in a novel, and we are never given a novel's rich behind-the-scenes understanding. In a play what you see, hear, and can discern is what you get. Most of "what we get" comes through the skills of the actors employing the Power of Incarnation.

# THE POWER OF INCARNATION

## To Be, or Not to Be . . .

That is the question:
Whether 'tis nobler in the mind to suffer
The slings and arrows of outrageous fortune,
Or to take arms against a sea of troubles,
And, by opposing, end them?
–Hamlet (3.1.58–62)

Many people assume that in this famous speech Hamlet is musing over suicide. But the great teacher/director B. Iden Payne taught that the question is not actually one of suicide, but of BEING, of how to gather our inner forces to face conflict courageously, even though we may die in the process.[1] Hence the speech is essentially about the nature of the Power of Incarnation. Am I willing to become fully embodied in the flesh and then to do what needs to be done, with a whole heart, whole mind, whole body? Or am I not?

If you are fortunate, when you are born, in a new and tender body, you make a dramatic entrance onto a stage that has been prepared with skill and attention. Your presence fills the space; just by being born, you influence the lives of everyone around you. Your rare human embodiment radically affects the other actors in your primary family play. In an ideal world you would have had parents who prayed to invite and then to welcome you here, perhaps with words like these:

### Prayer of Welcome

Come, blessed one,
out of the realms beyond space and time.
Gather your spirit, your friends, teachers and allies.
Make arrangements (some might call them contracts)
to meet and play the play together.
Are you volunteering for high service?
Have you chosen to take on flesh
in order to discover something new,
to restore something old,
to learn something interesting, or

to experience the joy of being in a body?
Whatever your reason for coming—
an excursion, a field trip, a fly-by—
Remember, you come bearing gifts, and
you are wanted here in the flesh
for who you are
in your spirit and your soul.

In the earliest days of your life that welcoming prayer may not have been spoken to you in words that you could feel or understand. But imagine that it is being spoken now by the Power of Incarnation. This power calls over and over again, with three essential messages:

The first message urges you simply *to be*. It urges you to be fully in your body now, for it is only in full embodiment that you can offer the sublime, unique gift that is your essential nature. In our discussion of this first message, we will look for the heart of this birthright of yours.

The second message urges you *to do*, to take action in alignment with your reason for being. You appeared on this great stage for a holy purpose, cast in a specific role, able to play many parts, to study the other characters performing in your play, and especially to learn how to perform your primary role so that your reason for being born can be fulfilled.

The third message urges you to stay alert to even greater possibilities of your life purpose, which may lie beyond what you can know or discern now.

It may help us to tap into the Power of Incarnation by exploring these three messages in greater detail.

## MESSAGE ONE:
## BE FULLY IN THE BODY

*Caro* (root *carn*) is Latin for "flesh." To be incarnate means to be enfleshed; we are made of meat. In his generous and helpful book, *Good Life, Good Death: Tibetan Wisdom on Reincarnation,* Rimpoche Nawang Gehlek observes that one archaic meaning of *incarn*, the root of *incarnation*, is "to cause to heal." He goes on to say, "While we live and when we die we have a chance to heal our minds."[2] Those words answered one of my long-held questions about the underlying purpose of coming into life. When we come into fleshly matter, we acknowledge that we are here to heal and be healed. *Incarnate* also implies that an energy, soul, or spirit has come into this flesh, in much the same way that a good actor "becomes," for a time, the character she is enacting. In Sacred Theatre we acknowledge that there is more to us than our fleshy tissues. Yet we also recognize that it is only through our physical bodies that our soul's true gift can be offered. Some belief systems would persuade us that the body is unnecessary for spiritual growth— indeed, that it is the root of all evil. I believe, however, that the body is absolutely necessary for the bequeathing of our gift. In fact, we cannot possibly bestow it without the power and pressure of our flesh itself. No wonder we need to be kind to it! As the Buddha said, "In this six feet of flesh I can become enlightened."

## *Pause, Please*

Read aloud the Prayer of Welcome (see pages 15–16). Feel it as if it were sounded for your soul and resounds now through your body. Can you allow yourself to believe that you are wanted here on this earth, that your flesh is holy, your gifts profound, and your purpose for being a sacred trust?

Think of a time when you felt most successful, when you were totally engaged, using everything you knew, expressing all you had to express, giving everything you had to give, and—most importantly— realizing it in the moment. You knew fully at the time that *this* is who you are, right here, right now. I believe those moments hold clues to the unique gifts you are here to offer to the world.

Now reflect about the experience, using these questions:

What was the occasion?

Who else was present?
What was your primary action?
What was your body doing?
What were you thinking?
What were you feeling?

Here's my example: Angus Bowmer was the founder and artistic director of the Oregon Shakespeare Festival, where I worked for many years. When he died, we held a memorial service in the theatre that carries his name. I was one among several privileged to speak about him. I loved him, and I respected his wife of many years as a chosen mother. I felt the weight and the honor of needing to speak well for and about him. I described his way of leading a cheer when it was time to celebrate an occasion. I read from his writings about the theatre and about acting Shakespeare. I closed my talk with words a friend had sent me, quoting Rabindranath Tagore: "Death is not putting out the light; it is blowing out the lamp because the dawn has come."

Reviewing that moment, I realized that my essential gift is about singing praise. My primary mode is in celebrating, recognizing beautiful words, being inspired and moved by them, and using language and emotion to honor the lives of others. And my capacity to sing praise comes through my love for study and learning, seeking wisdom about life in order to celebrate it.

Now, explore your own times of greatest aliveness, remembering them as if they are happening now; then harvest them for nuggets of awareness about the gifts you bring to this earth. Write the words: "In the moments I remember with the greatest satisfaction, I am _____." Fill in the blank with what you are doing, feeling, being, what is happening with your body, and who else is present. "From that awareness, I begin to see my star-essence gift as _____."

## MESSAGE TWO:
## DISCERN WHAT YOU ARE HERE TO DO

Having gleaned a sense of the great gift with which you were born, let us now talk about the importance of acting in alignment with it. Some people carry their gift for decades or even a whole lifetime without expressing it. And it's not enough simply to recognize your gift intellectually; it is essential to identify the purpose implied therein and then to operate through it. Otherwise, the gift atrophies, as would an unused muscle. As we'll learn later, that primary life purpose takes the form of an active, overarching verb.

If you are not sure of your primary purpose, one clue is to notice what your body most loves to do or when it feels most alive. If you *are* aware of your purpose but are not living into it, again, your body will provide a clue: it gets sick, it feels tired all the time, it goes numb, or you feel generally dissatisfied.

We find a tragic example of not living to one's purpose in the role of Willy Loman in Arthur Miller's *Death of a Salesman*. And we see the devastating effects this loss has on everyone around him. At the play's beginning, Willy has been a traveling salesman for many years and is tired to the bone of traveling, of having always to be pleasant and "up" in order to sell effectively. One actor who played this role to perfection is a favorite of mine, James Edmondson. In the play, Jim *became* Willy. We could see Willy in the way Jim's shoulders slumped. It was as if he had really been carrying suitcases of heavy samples to and from his old sedan, to every department store buyer in the northeastern United States for years, relentlessly forced to drive the narrow roads of New England for a brutalizing boss in a changing world and disintegrating economy. The actor transformed his body to show the truth of Willy's life—its near hopelessness, its overwhelming weariness, its loneliness—even before he had spoken a word. The moment he appeared on the stage we felt his body, his aging, his life closing in on him, and our own bodies responded in sorrow, pity, and dread.

The playwright never tells us, the way a novelist might, all the details of Willy's life before the time of the play. One flashback scene, however, does show us an incident in which he becomes estranged from his beloved son. In it, his son, in trouble at school, travels to Boston to visit Willy at a hotel and encounters him with a young woman, a secretary of a department-store buyer upon whom Willy relies for sales orders. The son experiences this liaison as a deep betrayal of the family, and his relationship with his father is forever broken.

This scene marks the beginning of Willy's disintegration and also illustrates some questions we need to ask ourselves, namely: What happens when we find ourselves stuck for too long in a role that is not aligned with our incarnational purpose? What mistakes do we make—as Willy heartbreakingly does—because we are out of attunement?

Arthur Miller, like all good playwrights, only gives us clues about Willy's true reason for being, and each of us is free to select a possible answer. My guess is that Willy is essentially a family man; he adores his young sons and his garden and needs to be at home as much as possible. His soul's gift is his loving power as a father. His soul's purpose is to offer that gift to the ones he loves: to guide, teach, and be a companion to them. But his job, his role as family provider in the only way he knows, runs counter to that purpose in taking him away for long periods of time. Herein the tragic dilemma that eventually overwhelms Willy's life.

*Death of a Salesman* is a story that strongly warns us what not to do. What follows, on the other hand, is a story about a woman who absolutely fulfills her life's incarnational gift and realizes her purpose no matter what is going on with her body.

Shortly before she died, the gifted singer Odetta gave a concert in the town where I live. Her very presence showed that she was fully incarnate in her magnificent, strong body, a body big enough to support, hold, and unleash that equally magnificent voice. However, some months before the concert she had broken her hip, and it had not yet healed. So she was thinner and, on this evening, sang from a wheelchair. Odetta had beautiful hands with long fingers, and friends remember her playing the twelve-string guitar as if she had invented it. At this performance, however, she was accompanied on the piano, and she used those glorious hands not to play her guitar but to play the air, to play the energy, to play her audience. Her voice produced the music, and her fingers amplified its majesty with exquisite grace. Even though she could no longer sing and play the way she once had, she sang and played another way, equally powerful. Odetta was born not only to make music but also to *become* music. And she used her being music to wake up the world through her singing.

## Pause, Please

To repeat, first we come into being, and we come bearing a gift. In human flesh, our gift of being weaves into and inspires our primary purpose. We thus express our gift through actions. From that weaving, through a lifetime, we *become* the gift; we *become* the purpose. That is the Power of Incarnation.

As sacred actors, we gain clues from our bodies, sometimes straightforward, sometimes metaphorical, about our reason for being. Take pen and paper and write, "My body is _____ ," and list its qualities, like sturdy or small or tall or willowy or powerful. Then, "My body loves_____," and list actions like touching others or making love or walking or hiking or swimming or climbing trees or sitting placidly or lying down or singing or all of the above. Then, "My body can _____," and list what comes: give birth, father children, cook, hunt, drive, run, sew, create beauty around me, craft wonders.

From these ways of honoring your body, begin to discern the qualities you incorporate. Is there a unifying theme, like Odetta's body was made to be music?

Similarly, can you begin to sense what it is that you are born to incorporate so fully that you have no choice but to express it? Were you born to teach, to inspire, to plant seeds, to learn, to paint, to play? Does

21

your body provide the strength, the sensory capacity, and the skills and facility to perform your incarnational task?

Now write, "My body, my experience, and my loves show me that I am born to be _____ and from my fullness of being to do _____."

For example, "My body, my experience, and my loves show me that I am born to be one who quests for learning—to sit, listen, and solidify learning in my body—and then to move with and express it in the world."

## Playing with Verbs

It is common wisdom in the theatre that a central theme carries the play, usually in the form of an active verb, and identifying that verb is the director's job. For example, if I were directing *Much Ado About Nothing*, I might see the play's essential verb as being *to lift*, as in to elevate the spirit and lighten the heart. In our lives as sacred actors, though, what defines the essential verb is our sense of our incarnational gift. If your gift is for inspiration, your basic action verb might be *to teach* or *to evoke*. If your gift is for nurturing, your basic verb might be *to mother*, or *to garden*, or *to feed* others. As I said earlier, I feel my own gift to be for praising, hence my verb is *to celebrate*. I hold my sense of both of them within the wider context of my life's dedication to Lady Wisdom; thus I have found my way over time to celebrating through learning.

Once you discern and begin to honor your gift and the potent verb implicit therein, it is vital to hold on to them as you would a lifeline. If necessity forces you to live counter to your gift, as Willy Loman felt himself to be, tragedy can ensue and unhappiness certainly does. But I believe we can always find a way to live through our gift, no matter the circumstances. And if we do, we won't feel compelled to whine or act like a victim. We can live beautifully even in the face of hardship.

For instance, I have a friend whose gift is for creating community and whose verb is *to support*. She is currently suffering from acute pain in her knees and is also recovering from a heart attack. Nevertheless, she continues to mentor and to bring her gift to vast networks of intellectuals and artists: reporting news, organizing events, and making new connections.

Another friend is engaged in support for one of her teachers, a man convicted of a brutal murder. She is gaining many allies who are striving to appeal the case and win him a new trial. In the process she is creating a Green Justice Project, which seeks to provide training and hope to prison inmates. Her gift is one of passionate commitment and her verb is *to encourage*. Meanwhile, in prison her friend refuses to despair and continues to teach, to write poetry, and to create music. Clearly his gift is for inspiration, and his verb is *to educate*.

## A Multitude of Expressions

While I believe it is true that we come here to embody one central action, it is also true that we can perform that action in a thousand ways, as Odetta played her music. The true being you are incarnating is not rigid; it doesn't have just one note. We might think of your primary verb as the arc that overreaches the whole of your life, and of all the various roles you have to play as ornaments adorning it. In the great play of life, you are constantly asked to assume different roles that allow you to explore and express your reason for being. The opportunities to play many aspects of that central role provide stimulation, variety, and creativity, as well as fertile learning.

In Shakespeare's play, for instance, Hamlet's incarnational gift is passion for exploring, and I believe his primary verb is *to seek*, as in the search for wisdom, or *to know*, in the sense of knowing the truth. But in the course of the play he serves this basic verb through many roles: trusting friend, distraught yet dutiful son, unhappy courtier, angry nephew, lover, betrayed lover, madman, hospitable companion, conspiracy seer, contrivance plotter, and vengeful prince. As such he grieves, questions, follows, commits, teases, sets traps, devises stratagems, accuses, ponders, considers, threatens, puzzles, pretends, disguises, fights, seeks vengeance, and takes other actions. Similarly, there are myriad roles that we can and should play within the context of our great role. Without such succulent variety, the world would be a dull place, indeed.

It is delightful to play many roles if you are able to hold with your belief about your primary one. Every minor part you play will inform your core person, as long as you choose to be open to that possibility. In other words, once you are attuned with your essential gift and purpose, every aspect of your life can reflect that attunement; every action can serve your great incarnational task.

An artist, whose gift is for words and whose verb is *to write* creatively, spent years playing the roles of wife, mother, housekeeper, daycare supervisor, gardener, cook, chauffeur. Sometimes these roles felt fulfilling, but often she felt nearly crazed with boredom, anger, and despair. Nevertheless, she maintained a sense of her gift and her action verb. She engaged in wordplay with her babies, her friends, her car. Too tired to read, she spun words into stories, into pictures, into poems. Everything became an occasion for her to express herself; every role taught her more about her capacity with words and imbued her with knowledge of what she needed to express in her writing. She never denied her feelings of frustration, but she did choose to explore them using her gift of words and to find ways of transforming them by writing poems.

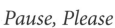

## *Pause, Please*

Reflect on the many roles you have played in life and how they inform your central gift of being and your primary verb of doing. With coloring pens, draw a beautiful arc across a piece of paper. Label the arc with the words that best describe what you are here to do. Suffuse the arc with colors that represent the great gift that you bring to the earth. The purpose is to allow you to see your through-line clearly, augmented by the beauty of your stellar gift.

On a different sheet of paper, make a list of all your roles: daughter or son, sibling, mother or father, friend, lover, student, teacher, wild one, artist, gardener, ally, guide, etc. Once the list is relatively complete, draw each role as an ornament hanging from the great arc. Make each as beautiful as you can.

Now place the arc and its ornaments within the context of the quality to which you dedicate your life play. (See the *Pause, Please* in the prologue, if you need reminding.) Do that by drawing some symbolic representation of that quality as background or support to the arc of your life.

Can you track the opportunity that each role has provided for understanding your incarnational gift and fulfilling your main purpose? Give some thought to how each has served to strengthen the quality to which your life is dedicated, and then write a few words naming the connection. I wrote, for example, "My role as English teacher (even though I felt a failure at it) taught me the power of praise as a learning tool for children; I see in retrospect that my purpose was to celebrate the students' lives in the service of Wisdom, even as I learned much about myself, and them, in the process."

# MESSAGE THREE:
## STAY OPEN TO GREATER POSSIBILITIES

Movies rely on "typecasting." Most roles are cast solely on how an actor looks and what his posture conveys. This is almost a requirement; so few lines of actual dialogue exist in a movie—so much needs to be revealed by the camera alone—that we in the audience need to get all the necessary information from our first glimpse of the character. The casting agent will search carefully to find the actor who looks and sounds exactly right for each role. Of course, a good actor, knowing the casting agent is looking for a scruffy villain, will often create a perfect characterization almost overnight and present herself at the audition, not as an actor, but as the scruffy villain. You will notice that most typecasting depends on there being a culturally-fixed, preconceived notion. In other words, typecasting is often about stereotypes.

However, there is an innovative method of casting that works against type. It happens in traditional theatre fairly often, especially when the director trusts the actor as one who knows and practices the Power of Incarnation. This casting against type keeps the audience surprised and the other actors on their toes. It is useful in plays that audiences may have seen many times, as is the case at many Shakespeare festivals. Casting a woman in a male role, as an example, stimulates people to pay new attention. Casting against type can be refreshing because it makes us look and listen again.

Working against type is also refreshing in life. It might just be possible that you, in fact, are on earth to do the *opposite* of what you appear able to do. What if you look and move like a stevedore and yet are here to incarnate the soul of gentle, tender care? What if you are a dainty dewdrop of a person yet have come to be a high-rise construction worker? We could playfully conclude that part of your purpose is to surprise people, with all the delight and teaching that such surprises bring. In any case, it is vitally important that you not abandon your own sense of self because of your appearance.

Another aspect of staying open to possibilities is to recognize that your sense of purpose may be only part of the whole story. If we ask a worker bee, for instance, about its purpose, the bee might say it is to make honey. In our larger view, though, we see the bee's purpose as pollinating the blossoms so that we may have fruit to eat.

Similarly, in the Indian epic poem, *The Ramayana*, Prince Rama believes his purpose is to be a perfect warrior prince so that he may become a good king. When he succeeds, he believes he has fulfilled that purpose, part of which is that he must protect and guide his people, including his wife. When a demon kidnaps her, Rama goes to war to win her back; and in doing so, he again believes he has fulfilled his aim. Subsequently, however, the skies open and the gods reveal him as not only Prince Rama but also an incarnation of the great god Vishnu, whose purpose is to sustain the world. As this avatar, Rama has incarnated for the sole purpose of destroying the demon; thus from a divine perspective the whole point of the kidnapping was to bring him to fulfill his true role.

From these examples, we learn that our sense of purpose might extend beyond our scope of understanding. That is, we may be in the hands of the gods. All the more reason, then, to play our role with all the fervor and enjoyment we can summon. At the same time, we need to stay open to the possibility that we are fulfilling a purpose greater than we can imagine.

---

## Pause, Please

A friend of mine tells a story about walking with Marilyn Monroe down a street in New York and observing her shrink inside herself so thoroughly that no one recognized her. Marilyn then asked her companion teasingly, "Do you want to see *Her*?" In an instant she transformed herself into the great star and immediately caused a stampede.

Marilyn's skill as an actor demonstrates the joy of surprise and the possibility of fresh perceptions that can come when we reveal our selves as different from what we appear to be. Consider how you, too, may have surprised yourself and others in this way. Is there a teaching in the surprise?

Has there been a time in your life when you thought you were doing one thing and then realized later that you were fulfilling part of another design altogether, even as the bee who thinks its purpose is to make honey but is also fulfilling the larger purpose of pollination?

It is helpful also to notice when we have shallowly judged someone on the basis of physical appearance and turned out to be wrong.

We can never know exactly what another's deep reason for being may be, but chances are it is richer and more profound than we can imagine.

## THREE SACRED PATHS OF BEING AND DOING

An ancient Hindu text, the Bhagavad Gita, offers eloquent understanding of the pathways that souls take to remember their reasons for becoming incarnate. In it, a conversation takes place on a battlefield between the magnificent warrior Arjuna and his charioteer, Krishna. Like Rama in the above story, Krishna is an incarnation of the mighty Hindu deity Vishnu, whose reason for being is to maintain the world, to keep it safe and on its own incarnational path.

Krishna describes several *yogas*, or "yolks," to link the human being back to his source, align him with his purpose, and keep him there. Of these, three speak to the Power of Incarnation for the sacred actor: Karma Yoga, the way of actively serving others; Jnana Yoga, the way of wisdom; and Bhakti Yoga, the way of devotion to god and to the god in all things. Variations exist on these themes of living to serve, living to learn, and living to love, but as general guides for remembering who we are and why we came to earth, they cover the field.

I like to think of these three yogas as divine shelters that can sustain our individual primary life verb so securely that it continually receives new sustenance and power. My gift is praising; my primary verb is *to celebrate*. But I can choose which of the great three yogas most accurately reflects this way of being and doing. When I see my verb sourced in the search for wisdom, that yoga carries a certain set of attributes that inspire and energize me. Another person whose verb is *to teach* finds particular joy in sourcing that verb in the great yoga of love, while yet a third with the verb *to nurture* may feel strengthened when she sources it in the yoga of service. Even if you don't particularly identify with any of Krishna's three yogas, seeing your primary verb in relation to one of them will help sanctify your work in the world.

## The Way of Service through Healing

I believe that the highest form of service, as Krishna conceived of it, involves healing. There is no way to prove this, but my personal conviction is that healing is a major reason for incarnating now. Remember Rimpoche Nawang Gehlek's observation that the word *incarnation* carries a root meaning that implies healing. I believe that everyone alive today, perhaps in spite of appearances, is here to heal something in one way or another. Although healing is not everybody's fundamental reason for being, each of us is required to perform some action related to it—in terms either of restoring our bodies, our spirits, and our neighborhoods or of repairing the damage humans are doing to the earth herself.

Perhaps you feel strongly that healing is your gift. If so, then your ultimate goal is to learn to embody healing itself. The one healer I know who illustrates this embodiment perfectly is Donna Eden, author of *Energy Medicine.* She has healed herself and others of debilitating illnesses and in the process become a veritable force field for well-being. As Jean Houston puts it, "Donna is so alive that she makes champagne look like warm beer."

If this is your path, the process can be made simpler, and perhaps move a little faster, when you consciously recognize such embodiment as your intention. You intend not only to be a healer, uniting your essential gift and your life purpose into one elegant, powerful role, but to do so with such determination and skill that you actually *become* healing, as Odetta *became* music. For most healers (or musicians or teachers), this is a lifelong process, but it's worth a lifetime of devotion. That is what is so precious about our existence: we can learn to become our purpose/gift in a way that only we can, thus adding a unique strand of being to the sum total of the universe's wisdom.

As an embodiment of healing, you play your role through all your experiences. You will be presented with numerous opportunities to assist others, perhaps by simply being a friend, witness, guide, or kind neighbor. More directly, you may find yourself serving the work of healing as doctor, researcher, nurse, therapist, herbalist, nutritionist, counselor, energy worker—in other words, through a variety of roles offering a variety of training and methods. As an authentically embodied healer, you seek out new knowledge and understanding as you practice your art. And as a *fully* embodied healer, you will be able to work on a large scale. Being willing to stand in the world as healing itself can help to heal family heritage, community and cultural wounds, and even national and earth-level wounds.

## THE WAY OF WISDOM

In the Bhagavad Gita, Krishna's second yoga is the path of wisdom, which in all the spiritual traditions of the world is pursued by asking the big questions: Who am I? Where did I come from? Why am I here? Where am I going? What is the meaning of it all? Arjuna's questions to Krishna are what begin the dialogue and move the story forward. This process is also the actor's way. As he incarnates a character, the actor asks the same questions, and he gratefully can learn many answers from the script. Additionally, he will propel each action and add aliveness to the scene by asking himself urgently: *What do I want in this moment?* In life, of course, we *have* no script, at least that we are aware of. But the sacred actor will nevertheless keep asking the big questions and be guided by her incarnational gift to choose the most appropriate answers. And if she is following the way of wisdom, her moment-by-moment question will be: *What do I need* to learn *in this moment?* The answer is what will keep the story of her life moving on its true course.

One of the experiences of the wisdom way is to realize that even when you are off course or denying your gift, you are still learning. Occasionally, as Willy Loman does, we may feel we must disguise our gift or delay living into its purpose in order to get along with others and just "do our job." But the perceived need to delay living fully into purpose may be precisely the device that existence provides to keep the play interesting. C. G. Jung would say that our ways of straying from the path *are* the path. In the way of wisdom, we recognize that these deviations and delays are filled with information. In the process, we can learn vast amounts about ourselves and others.

And in the tension between what we are here to do and what we think we must do, we create great drama. Take Hamlet: I believe his essential role is in the pursuit of knowledge and understanding. He is a born scholar; his is a "noble mind." But he is also a born prince, with the demands, expectations, and assumptions a royal role carries. From these two imperatives, we could imagine that his central, organizing verb is *to grow* into a scholar king. But circumstances won't have it so. **?** ♡

At the play's beginning, Hamlet's studies have been interrupted by the sudden death of his father, the king. Called home to his father's funeral, he discovers that he has not been named king as he might have expected. Instead, his uncle, his father's brother, has wooed the country's courtiers and statesmen, won the election, and been crowned king himself. In addition, he has suddenly married Hamlet's mother. Then the ghost of Hamlet's father appears, telling Hamlet that he has been murdered by this same uncle. The ghost cries out for vengeance and demands that Hamlet be the one to take it.

So now, in addition to Hamlet's contending roles of prince and scholar, a third role competes for his attention and demands immediate action—that of the avenger. While it seems that this demand would steal him away from his primary purpose of scholarship, in fact he applies the skill and means of a scholar to the situation. He asks questions; he investigates his own emotions and reactions with a scholar's cool, often ironic eye. As only a scholar would do, he remains passionately engaged in the process of studying the situation unfolding around him in all of its horror. It is this relentless pursuit of wisdom that makes Hamlet one of the best-loved characters in all of Shakespeare. We love him because, even in the most adverse of circumstances, he remains true to himself and to his primary purpose—that of learning and of expressing the truth of that learning. I love him because he shares his thoughts with us as he is thinking them. And these thoughts are profound enough to keep us happily pondering them all our lives.

## THE WAY OF LOVE

In the Bhagavad Gita, Krishna recommends the path of devotion to God as the greatest soul-level achievement of a lifetime. For me, this path has a correlate: that of being willing to see and love the god in all things and express that love through caring, compassion, and kindness.

If your gift is for loving, and your purpose is to love and then become the embodiment of love, you are on a rich path, indeed. And you are in a great tradition, one that includes poets and other artists, spiritual leaders, mystics, and ordinary people. It is a path that requires years of training, learning, and experimenting. But once you feel in your bones that to love is your true purpose, every role you play becomes a means of expressing that love. Even in the midst of feeling anger, you will know that beneath the anger is love. You will understand that the experience of anger is simply a means for your soul to learn its present limits and seek ways to transcend them. Life's teaching power rises when you recognize that, in spite of all appearances, your "failures to be loving," and what those failures teach you, comprise the exact means of your ultimately becoming love.

Even tragedies can prove your dedication to the path of love. I recently heard of a woman whose incarnational path is clearly leading her to that embodiment. A teacher, the woman lost her ten-year-old son in an automobile accident four days before Christmas. The family was in the midst of the holiday flurry, and there were already presents to and from the boy under the tree. On a snowy afternoon, he impulsively rode his sled down a sloping driveway into the wheel of an oncoming car. After his death two hours later, his mother's first concern was to comfort the young woman who had been driving the car and to reassure her that the accident was not her fault. At the funeral attended by hundreds of friends, the mother ended the ceremony by inviting everyone to sing "Joy to the World." My sense is that her gift is for affirmation and her purpose is to love. In the ensuing twenty-five years, all the love she felt for her son she has poured into her community—serving on the school board, raising money for underprivileged children, beautifying parks and buildings, and producing special cultural events.

## *Pause, Please*

Remember what you wrote earlier that gave you clues about the incarnational gift you bring and the ways you offer this gift through action. The gift you bring is what sets you on the path. Consider whether your gift and primary purpose align with any of Krishna's three noble paths: service or healing; wisdom or learning; and devotion or love. A good life includes all three, but usually one feels stronger than the others and reflects more accurately the treasures you brought into this incarnation.

Now review three actions you have taken recently that seem to represent the core of your identity. What have you done in the last day that you feel good about? What in the last week? The last year? Is there a common theme that might strengthen your understanding of your path?

Also, recall Jung's insight that our ways of straying from the path *are* the path. Have you experienced challenges that have seemed to thwart your sense of purpose? If so, can you see in retrospect how they have actually provided teachings that have *enriched* that purpose? How have these challenges taught you to be who you truly are?

Write: "The most painful experience of my life has been _____. It demanded that I _____. From it I learned _____. Because of this experience I understand that I am being asked to embody the role of _____.

## Whose Life Is It Anyway?
## Our Roles in Other People's Plays

As we relate to others, the ideal way is to hold on to our main purpose as a guide wire and then find different, surprising, and joyful ways to fulfill all the roles we play in their lives. "Keep it fresh," one of my favorite actors is always saying. To do so adequately requires playfulness, emotional range, and heartfelt generosity.

When we make assumptions about our roles in others' plays, we create some wonderful complications. Parents, for example, sometimes insist that they are the stars of their children's lives, whereas the real work of life is for the children to grow into their own plays. True, in the early years, parents are essential for getting a new life started in a healthy way. But being essential to another's play is still to be only a supporting actor. A tiny child may look to her parents as the stars of her life, but when the child becomes her own person (and that's sooner than we may realize), healthy parents learn to nurture the child so that she realizes the true star is herself.

People in love commonly cast the beloved as the star of their own play: "You take over, you are in charge. At last I've found you, the One who can make it all perfect and worthwhile." Sometimes we fall in love so that we will have an intimate costar. It's often tempting to think we should place the relationship or the family in the leading role. Usually this happens because of a lack of courage and commitment to our own lives. We mistakenly believe that purpose and meaning come only in making another person more important than we are or in serving that person totally. We neglect our own healing; we lose understanding of who we are and of our true place on the sacred stage of our lives.

A good relationship should be the star of its own play—the relationship play—and as such have a life of its own. We are active participants in that play, certainly, but our role in it is to support the relationship. We must find out what the relationship wants, what its reason for being might be, what its major qualities are, and how we might sustain it in ways that are healthy for it and for all of its participants.

Similarly, the family is the star of the family play; we participate fully but maintain our primary role in our own play. If we instead focus solely on the family as the central principle of our lives, we are likely to demand the same from others and become resentful if they do not comply. Such over-involvement sets up a murky tension that can undermine everyone's chances for healthy survival.

We want to define our roles in other people's plays clearly, acknowledging that life changes. We may go from costar to supporting player, from supporting player to having a bit part, and from there to having a cameo, or even to being an extra, just one of the crowd. We need to learn to accept such changes gracefully; otherwise, we find ourselves heartbroken, feeling out of a job and destitute, as parents who are empty nesters sometimes do. Recognizing that the role has shifted and acting accordingly is essential to living wisely. When changes occur, as they must in any living work of art, we want to be able to assess how well we have played those roles, with what delight and enchantment, and how our method of playing supports the fulfillment of our primary task.

## *Pause, Please*

Reflect on the roles you play in others' lives. For example, you are your mother's daughter (or son). How is this different from being your father's child, or being a grandchild to a grandmother, rather than to a grandfather? What subtleties of body, voice, and actions would make it clear that you were relating to one and not the other?

From this exercise, can you see how the roles you play are different within each relationship, how you change with different people? Are you the same person to your daughter as to your son? To your best friend as to your boss?

Notice, too, how you sometimes become a different person even in a stable, long-lasting relationship. This morning you are one person with your spouse, and this evening you will be another. We become different people all the time: we change, relationships change, the other person changes, often because of actions to which we have responded—while at the same time the responding has changed us.

In this whirl of evolving roles, how does each role you play tell you more about your true purpose for being in a body?

## Living Our Role despite How We Are Treated

The sacred actor, whose soul power and purpose are fully embodied in this incarnation, can hold that power and purpose through life's disasters while also remembering that those disasters are vital to the great play being enacted.

Let's say your chosen role is lover. You've come to this understanding after a lifetime of playing many different roles, loving many different ways. You've loved and sometimes thought you hated your parents; you've loved and been annoyed with animals; you've loved friends, lovers, comrades, colleagues; and you've argued with them, despised them, been furious with them, and adored them. You've loved children with an even more extravagant range of emotional possibilities. All have led you to an awareness about what love is and the deep truth that you are, to your inmost soul, a person born into this world to love.

Then you go back home to your family, perhaps, or somewhere find yourself with people who see you as you once were—as a child, maybe, experimenting as she tried to learn to love. Suddenly you find yourself being the person they perceive rather than the one you have become.

Each of us has had such an experience of becoming stuck in a role limited to others' perceptions. If, after some time away, we return to a place where people remember us in a previous role, we will find that role enveloping us again.

In Bernard Shaw's play *Pygmalion* (later the musical *My Fair Lady*) the flower girl who later is taken for a princess tells her tutor, "The difference between a lady and a flower girl is not how she behaves, but how she's treated."[3] Years ago I read of two psychological studies that seemed to demonstrate this truth. One experiment put highly educated, highly motivated young men into a psychiatric ward, where no one knew their real identities. Treated as patients, they soon began to feel like patients and demonstrate symptoms of mental illness; in short, they became like the inmates.

In another experiment, a mental patient volunteered to take a new drug as a test. Within days he changed completely, becoming engaged and outgoing and "normal." Everyone was thrilled with the drug's effects. After the patient was discharged, however, the staff found all the drugs hidden in a drawer. He had not taken any of them. But because the nurses, the doctors, and other staff members had engaged him in conversation, questioning him several times a day in order to monitor the test—in other words, because they talked with him as if he were a full person instead of a patient—he was able to come back to himself without the drugs.

Ori and Rom Brafman's fascinating book *Sway: The Irresistible Pull of Irrational Behavior* describes this phenomenon as the chameleon effect. Citing test after test in different countries, the authors say, "when we brand or label people, they take on the characteristics of the diagnosis. In psychological circles, this mirroring of expectations is known as the Pygmalion effect (describing how we take on positive traits assigned to us by someone else) and the Golem effect (describing how we take on negative traits). But let's use 'chameleon effect' as our catchall term."[4]

To maintain the truth of who we are, no matter what our circumstances, requires great strength, especially for those who have been consistently mistreated. It takes courage not to succumb to abusive behavior by becoming what we are told we are. Many people seem able to reach deep into their inner being, in spite of horrific experiences, and define themselves not as they are seen but as they truly are: soul bodies filled with power and high purpose. It is crucial, though, that the wounding be acknowledged, with the authentic incarnational power restored in a healthy way, so that the wound will not be carried forward to succeeding generations.

## INCARNATING THE ROLE YOU WANT

Bernard Shaw says, "Life isn't about finding yourself. Life is about creating yourself."

To take the lead in our own great play, we study, we review, we honor our life, and we make choices about how we intend to enact our role. Acting is about making choices—creative, life-sourcing choices. The time comes when we can choose to incarnate the role we want, playing the part we want to play.

If people can survive reasonably intact from torture, abuse, denigration, and hatred, then surely we who have had an easier hand from fortune can emerge in the middle of our lives, or earlier, with a decision: "I'm turning my role around. Until now, I've been a victim; now, I'm a lover."

You now listen with fresh ears for proof of the accuracy of your new avowed purpose as a human being. Even if you believe you have imagined that purpose, or made the whole thing up, you can make it true: play the role with all the skill you have, and it will grow into you.

One way to listen is to notice, in the light of your choosing, what your actions are. Perhaps your chosen purpose is all encompassing: to make your way home to union with all beings, or God, as many wise ones tell us is the truth for all living beings. Perhaps as you watch what you love and do, you may find that your true purpose is to play, to learn, to enchant, to teach, to grow. Or it may be simply to be, as a single flower adds to the world's beauty, so that your song of life adds to the world song of celebration. That may be all that you are here to do. And it is enough.

Please understand that when I speak of being the star of your own play, I am not talking about selfishness or even self-centeredness. I'm talking instead about your responsibility to yourself to fulfill your incarnational role. We need to remember or find that purpose and then to step onto the stage awake, aware, and loving it.

Your choice of a mission might come in images, as mine did. I once took an imaginary journey to the moment of my physical incarnation in this lifetime: I saw myself as a tiny, joy-filled sprite hopping around in the wombs of many women, reminding them of the Divine Ones' love for them. That was all I was doing, all I needed to do. But I got caught—or fell in love—with my birth parents and their incarnational purposes, so I get to spend this life learning more about joy, about love, about how to live in a body and have that body be an accurate reflection of my mission. And about how physical presence can also hold the opposite of love as part of its learning. My desire now is to be a good messenger, bringing word to all beings that they are loved—from the inside, by the Divine. Whether I succeed or fail, the image of my mission keeps me inspired, and it makes me laugh.

To embrace fully the Power of Incarnation, it is vital to choose joyfully your purpose for being. When you have a sense of it, it plays through you and becomes the primary note, the hum of your life. It grounds your every action. Then you bring its power to all the roles you play.

*God made man because He loves stories.*

—Elie Wiesel

# Two

# The Power of Story

"What are you doing here?" As just discussed, you are here to fulfill your incarnational purpose. And the way to do that is to enact a story. In this chapter we seek out the strands of the story that only you can play. You are the one who gets to say where, when, and how your true story began—the story that only you can tell. Was it at birth, or when your parents met, or when your grandparents met, or was it when human life began, or was it just yesterday? Is it part of a myth with no beginning and no end? As a sacred player, you also can decide what story you wish to enact from now on.

## THE LIFE ON EARTH STORY

Life begins (we don't know how) through some munificently elegant combination of DNA and proteins. Some precise mixture of elements forms a new union, even as our own lives began with our mother's egg and our father's sperm.

Life creates itself into billions of expressions, each of which seems to enjoy a process of what looks like growth and expansion, definition and precision, and each of which usually combines with other elements—other cells, for example—to create more of itself (or something better). An individual living entity does that for as long as it can. If it is a redwood tree, it could go on for a millennium. But all life forms seem to carry an information technology that gives way after a time.

Individual entities (a daisy, a mollusk, a human being) ultimately stop producing and reproducing, wither, deplete, and die—to who knows what new forms. Life as a whole, though, goes on.

Our own lives are just a tiny part of this great story entitled "Life on Planet Earth," which is itself a tiny part of the story of the immense universe. But even though our individual stories are only a small part of the whole, they are nevertheless an important part; and it is the job of each of us to enact them with courage and with gusto. By tapping into the vast story and finding ways of relating to it, we gain a splendid source of ideas, creativity, freshness, and vigor.

## Pause, Please

As sacred players, we are asked to invest thought and energy into these considerations:

What do I believe about the nature of the story of Life on Earth?

What is the nature of my own life story?

How does my story participate in the Life-on-Earth story?

At the moment, we will concentrate on the first question. Write a heading: "I believe that the story of life on earth is about _____." Write as much as you can about the life that swirls all around you. Make it a song or a saga; try not to leave anything out.

## In the Beginning

Hindus speak of all life as an ocean of story. As such, great stories extend into an indefinable territory beyond any clearly marked beginning and any known end. We can, however, pick up our ideas of the Earth story pretty much anywhere or any time we want. We can begin, as some astrophysicists do, with a variation of the Big Bang. Then we can follow the dramatic story of the creation of stars, our solar system, our sun, our earth, and—mysteriously, a couple of billion years ago—life.[1] Finally, we can search, as some scientists do, for the evolutionary guidance that led to our becoming human.

Human beings seek to understand beginnings and to know endings; this seeking is one of our species' most endearing characteristics. And the stories we invent about the creation of life on earth amaze and enchant us. They also teach us about the richness of the process of creation itself. Studying the creation stories of astrophysics, as well as of cultures worldwide, helps us relate our individual stories to the big story of Life on Earth.

For example, some of us experience life the Big Bang way, with sudden, unexpected flashes of illumination that spill out in waves to affect all aspects of our lives. Others travel more at evolution's pace, slowly adjusting, trimming, clearing, until at last we find ourselves made new, only to begin again the same slow process. Some of us follow the example given in the beautiful opening chapter of the Hebrew Bible, when God hovers over the deep darkness, breathes upon it, and then says, "Let there be light." We create our lives through first imagining what light (for example) might be and then using the power of words to bring it into being.

An ancient Egyptian origin story tells of Amun, who as the great goose awoke the cosmic energies of creation by cackling. This delightful image suggests that we can experience the universe as made of laughter, and when we do we enhance the process of joyful creation. Stories from Japan tell of a goddess who crafted the universe by weaving. Ancient Egyptians, again, tell of a potter god who created human beings by molding them from Nile mud. Early Indian scriptures say the whole of creation came through the sounding of the holy syllable, *Om*. Other traditions say it is all made of music. The most poignant tales involve the sacrifice of an enormous, generous-hearted being whose body is given to form the physical earth: In China, the being is a male figure, Panku. In Mesopotamia, it is the primordial mother, Tiamat. In India, it is Purusha, and in several indigenous American tribes, it is the Corn Mother.

The Iroquois speak of Sky Woman, who fell from heaven into this world, guided to the back of a giant turtle by birds whose wings cradled her falling. The turtle swam to the middle of a vast ocean. Animals offered to provide a place for her; finally the humblest of them (some versions say the muskrat) succeeded, diving so deep to the bottom of the ocean that he was able to bring a piece of earth back to the turtle. This tiny piece of earth grew and multiplied for Sky Woman so that she could have a home. Thus the earth is called Turtle Island.

One of my favorite stories is from ancient Greece. It tells of the Mother of all things who emerged from chaos and created the sea and the shore because she needed room to dance. Dance she did, until she created a wind, and from the wind a great serpent. She transformed herself into a bird and mated with the serpent, then laid an egg, around which the serpent wrapped himself until the egg was ready to split apart and allow everything to be born. This story combines many elements of the creative process, but the essential one is the dance.

Each aspect of these creation stories can reflect the ways in which we live and create. Our ancestors invented or revealed them from the deepest places in their awareness to make sense of existence. Even now, these stories can inspire us, answer our questions, and teach us about the process of living.

## *Pause, Please*

Living your life's story with vigor becomes clearer when you consider your way as a creator. Think about the times you have known yourself as most inventive. Can you relate those moments to a traditional creation story that appeals to you? Do you relate best to the dancer, the diver, the weaver, the potter, the sound maker, or the visionary who speaks, "Let there be light"? Or does your primary story involve creating new life—through lovemaking and childbirth, for example?

Make a list starting with the words, "I feel most creative when I am _____. I am here to _____." Trust what comes, and be aware that you are finding your way into the essence of the story you are here to enact. I believe that all of our plays are about creating and that our ways of creating provide the heart of the story. You might say, for instance: I am here to create through laughter; I am here to dance creation; I am here to weave (or create through my hands); I am here to create through words (to write, teach, or inspire); I am here to dive deep; I am here to create space for others; I am here to love, to offer myself in service to creation.

If, when linked with our incarnational gift and our primary purpose, we become conscious of the ways in which we approach life creatively, we will gain clues about the nature of our story. Using myself as an example again, I know I am here to sing praise and to celebrate on the path of wisdom; this statement comprises my essential gift and primary purpose. As I braid this knowledge into my favorite creation story of the cackling goose god, I sense the nature of the story I am here to enact. My purpose *to celebrate* joins with laughter as an element of creation, and my story becomes one of a person who imbibes life through joy.

As you look for this creative essence in your own story, it will unfold in its unique way as only you can play it. A true and wonderful thing is that your unique telling of your exclusive story contributes to the vigor of all the stories of Life on Earth. In addition, your tapping into the Life-on-Earth stories supports your own vitality. When you participate in life, you add to the general joy of the whole world, and the world adds to your joy in reciprocal kindness.

## GETTING THE STORY TO THE STAGE

Simply telling or hearing stories is enjoyable, but when a story becomes enacted, a wild, new energy enters. In large part, the actors revealing the story embody this energy; they bring focus, intention, awareness, resolution, diversity, suspense, release from suspense, awareness of paradox, and, most importantly, the determination to go all the way and not be impeded. They bring the fortitude to do the work that must be done until it is finished, or until they are all dead. Yet they perform with an attitude at once of élan and complete seriousness. They follow the artist Bob Rauschenberg's suggestion to performers: each thing you do is the most important thing there is, and it doesn't matter at all.[2]

Playwright Charles Mee wrote a splendid homage to Rauschenberg in his performance piece called "bobrauschenbergamerica," in which one piece demonstrated the artist's way of being perfectly: Several actors appeared in bathing suits and on roller skates, sweeping around the stage with ease and earnestness. Then they reappeared holding huge bottles of what announced itself as gin. Very seriously (as if participating in an important scientific experiment), they began to pour the gin all over the floor. When they deemed it had reached an adequate level, they removed their skates and proceeded to take running dives into the gin, as if they were swimming, over and over again. The scene made us all laugh. The actors knew what they were doing was sublimely silly, and yet the meticulous care they took in preparing the space, pouring the gin, and then splashing around in it made the whole endeavor fun to watch. I still laugh when I think of it.

This paradoxical awareness is equally important in real life: we need to "go for it" with complete earnestness and yet enjoy it with ease, delight, and at least some silliness. Nature herself seems to express this exuberance in the way she effortlessly throws off billions and billions of seeds in order constantly to reproduce herself. Awareness of that playful intensity can supply us with tremendous energy for creating our own life story.

## What Makes a Play

Just as our lives begin with the combining of our parents' DNA, all plays begin with elements coming together. This joining is the essential force that brings a play to life. It may take the form of a collision or a merging, a wild welcoming or a deflection, an evasion or a confrontation; but, in any case, an event occurs and an action, or a reaction, follows. And each action/reaction impels another. Eventually, a desire emerges for the forces to come together in a new way.

Into the settled household of a wealthy gentleman, for instance, comes a prince and his retinue of friends and enemies (Shakespeare's *Much Ado about Nothing*). Onto the dark battlements of an uneasy citadel strides a ghost with terrifying demands (Shakespeare's *Hamlet*). Into the midst of a happy marriage, a child is born. Or a mother-in-law arrives. Or an old lover suddenly appears. In each case, these new elements instantly bring about new partnerships and invite a new story.

## Structuring Your Play

One way of becoming aware of the desire for new union in the play of life is to study the bare-bones scaffolding called "the plot." A plot describes the means by which a variety of forces seek to merge—for good or for ill; that is, the plot gives us a way to tell the story. Scholars play a game arguing about how any good plot can be told in a single sentence and discussing how many basic plots there are.[3] Denis Johnston, Irish playwright and theatre scholar, describes seven plotlines (and his son Rory added an eighth).[4]

These familiar plots provide mirrors that help us gain clarity about the basic beliefs and actions of our own lives. Noticing when and how we have engaged them provides information about how we might want to change the story we are living to regain creativity and purpose. Rich theatrical plays such as Shakespeare's may have one primary plot, but several other subplots will reflect and/or emphasize the main one. Through our lifetimes, as well, we will utilize other plotlines to augment the way we play the essential one. We want our life play to be as rich and complex as possible, so that when it closes, we have a fulfilling sense of pleasure explored, creativity expressed, and wisdom gained.

Let us look at the Johnstons' eight plotlines, remembering that the purpose is to notice how each describes elementary structures of our life thus far. Most of our life plays move from plot to plot, and it is possible to be living within several at the same time. Unlike a theatrical play, our actual lives are so complex that it's not easy to identify their plotlines, but the effort offers us a fresh way to look at our experiences.

## Looking for the Story

Here are the eight plots that impel the telling of most stories and plays:

1. *The Unpaid Debt*, or *The Pursued and the Pursuer*. An agreement is made and a debt incurred, perhaps unconsciously. If payment is not made, pursuit follows until the debt is cleared or forgiven.

2. *The Fatal Flaw*. A curse, or terrible defect, drives the central character to do everything possible to alleviate that flaw or contain its consequences. Often the hero is unaware of the flaw; nevertheless, he struggles, perhaps blindly, to become free of it.

3. *The Triangle*. A pair is engaged in their ordinary quest for union, and their life is settled in a comfortable way. Enter a third person or force, and the couple must come to terms with the third. In a tragedy, the third person is fatal to the relationship and perhaps to the couple. In a comedy, relationships are questioned, yes, and changed, but they are strengthened in the end. Shakespeare does an elegant job with the Triangle and in several comedies adds his own favorite device: disguise and/or mistaken identity.

4. *Lovers Meet, Lovers Part, Lovers Meet Again*, perhaps the best known and most often used story line. It is the theme for all romances. Comedy and tragedy rest on the final outcome: Do the lovers meet again and live? That's a comedy. Do they part forever, as in death? That's a tragedy.

5. *Virtue Unrecognized.* In some ways, this plot is an inversion of the Fatal Flaw. Rather than a defect, there is a gift, and the action of the play rides on opposing attempts to keep the gift hidden and to bring it to recognition and honor.

6. *The Seductive Enchantment,* also known as *The Spider and the Fly.* In order to accomplish a usually nefarious end, someone lures an unsuspecting innocent into a psychological or physical trap and closes it tight. Working out the details either of the spider's seduction or of the fly's attempt to get free is what creates the primary action of the play.

7. *The Indomitable Hero.* No matter how difficult the circumstance, the hero (male or female) continues relentlessly, triumphing over all odds until the mission is accomplished.

0. *The Lost Gift.* Some precious treasure has been lost. If found by the right person, often this treasure will benefit the world. If found by the wrong person, dreadful evils will follow.

## PLAYING WITH PLOTS

Each of the eight plotlines can be turned inside out or upside down. The inversion determines whether the play is a comedy or a mystery, a farce or a tragedy. Many good plays and almost all stories can shift plotlines back and forth. A play that begins as Lovers Meet can morph into the Triangle, then awaken the sense of The Fatal Flaw and require the courage of an Indomitable Hero to accomplish its purpose of Lovers Meet Again. A clever playwright can employ elements of these plotlines, but they are usually set within one overall framework.

An individual life story has more turns and twists than even a Shakespeare can command. Moreover, it includes so many characters that it seems like many stories woven into a whole tapestry of Story. Nevertheless, it is useful to search for our own underlying plot; this will help clarify the dynamics in our nature and offer guidance to change or move the story forward. Let us look now at the eight plots in detail. Then we'll see how some, or perhaps all, of them have moved through our own lives.

## The Unpaid Debt

Denis Johnston ruefully notes that the plot of the Unpaid Debt catches up with all of us, sooner or later. Early in life we get the idea that it's all about who owes what to whom: we "call in favors," or we "owe you one." Obviously, the debt need not be monetary; it might instead be psychological or moral. Christopher Marlowe's *The Tragical History of Doctor Faustus* is a famous example.

Dr. Faustus is a learned philosopher who gives himself over to an ancient book of magic in order to acquire knowledge—experiential knowledge, gnosis. But there is a catch. To achieve this power, he requires diabolical help. Satan's own personal assistant, Mephistopheles, creates an agreement, which Faustus must sign in blood, saying that when Faustus's soul is required of him he will surrender it to hell. In return, he can enjoy knowledge and enormous power while he is alive.

Faustus willingly signs the devil's pact, vowing that if he can just know and do all he wants in this lifetime, he will happily spend eternity damned to hell. Throughout the play, Mephistopheles aids Faustus in all his exploits but reminds him always of the debt that must be paid.

Marlowe demonstrates Faustus's power through highly dramatic means, but when the last day dawns, the doctor is frantic with despair—nothing is worth the torment of an eternity in the regions of hell. But to hell he must descend, after frenzied bargaining and fruitless attempts at repentance, including a piteous appeal to the Horses of the Night: *Lenti, lenti!* ("Slow down, slow down!"). Lucifer himself appears to send Faustus below, pursued ruthlessly by Mephistopheles and all his minions. The debt that must be paid is paid, indeed.

This theme has captured the interest of many writers, including Johann Wolfgang von Goethe and composer Charles Gounod. Its element of relentless pursuit also inspired Victor Hugo. In his grand novel

*Les Miserables*, Jean Valjean, the one who owes the debt (having stolen a candlestick in a time of dire need), is relentlessly hounded through the years by the man whose very name has become synonymous with the all-powerful Pursuer, Inspector Javert. Movie and television mavens used this plot in the series aptly called *The Fugitive*.

Many people live a psychological version of this plot. Think of the woman who devotes her life to a parent, not out of love but out of a sense of obligation. There are parents, and bosses, too, who operate from a "you owe me" attitude and thus become the Pursuer. We are always in their debt, and no amount of work can get us out from under.

Some of us live out this plot by going into monetary debt. Then we try to stay afloat while literally owing everything we make to someone else.

The doctrine of Original Sin plagues some Christians with the sense that we owe a debt simply by having been born human. Some trace the debt to what is called the sin of our primal parents, Adam and Eve; we women have been accused of carrying Eve's "wickedness" in our very souls. Christian doctrine prescribes a number of ways to pay that debt. The basic one requires us to accept that Jesus's crucifixion was designed to free us of that soul-level obligation. Many Christian faiths have adopted the notion that God, or Jesus, is the Pursuer, chasing us relentlessly until we submit to the truth of his protection and salvation.

Cultural and national obligations are another kind of debt that must be paid. This country owes gigantic monetary, psychological, and moral debts to the many native tribes whose ways of life were destroyed and to the African Americans who were brought here as slaves. Our failure to acknowledge these debts authentically and engage in a process of accounting simply mires us into a deeper and deeper spiritual morass, and our children's children will be paying for it in all the generations to come.

Worldwide there is a vast indebtedness to women at every level. But rather than acknowledge that debt in its full complexity, the miniscule response has been only, "equal rights, equal pay, equal opportunity."

Even that concession has stirred up denial, rage, and accusations of unfairness from men who feel their opportunities are lessened by female competition. The moral debt to women, and the failure of societies to acknowledge it meaningfully, have created havoc in the world. Disrespect for the Feminine has surely contributed to the devastation of what we traditionally call Mother Nature. We now face the destruction of life as we know it simply because we the human race cannot tolerate the upheaval of acknowledging what we owe to womankind and to the earth.

## *Pause, Please*

Consider the Unpaid Debt in your own life. To gain clarity, draw three columns headed 1) Monetary Debts, 2) Emotional and Psychological Debts, and 3) Moral and Spiritual Debts. Make lists of each kind of debt you have and notice if there is an overlap.

For example, do you owe money to a friend, so that the debt is emotional as well as monetary? Notice when the situation feels fuzzy. Where is the line between money and favors? Are they confused in your mind?

Do you owe a friend a psychological debt—perhaps a simple thank you—but have a greater sense of it, at almost a moral level, because she came through for you at a time when you grievously needed someone? Do you confuse the ordinary give-and-take of friendship with a sense of moral indebtedness that may translate into a monetary one—so that, for example, you usually feel obligated to pay for lunch? In other words, do you interact from a feeling of duty rather than of enjoyment?

How does being in debt make you feel: Resistant? Unhappy? Overwhelmed? Do you have debts that you resolutely deny owing? Notice how pretending that there is no debt inflames the situation. By keeping the debt unnamed, it becomes amorphous yet all-pervasive, and therefore more threatening.

One culture has taken a creative approach to redress such a situation: In Australia, where the unpaid debt is very like our country's debt to the American indigenous tribes, the people have instituted National Sorry Day, May 26. It began as a way to apologize for the program of taking aboriginal children from their families and putting them into institutions where they were trained as servants (or worse). The movie *Rabbit Proof Fence* shows the damage done. National Sorry Day gives Australians a way to apologize publicly for this and many other inhuman actions against the aboriginals. Bringing this huge, previously unnamed debt to attention has gone some way to relieving it.

Returning to a personal sense of this plotline, write a scene in which all of the levels of indebtedness—monetary, emotional, and moral—are assailing you in the form of angry creditors. What creative ways can you find to confront, acknowledge, and clear the debts? How many are real; how many come from a deeper, more subjective place? Most importantly, have you lived your life following this plot?

Next, consider the possibility of yourself as the Pursuer. Make another list for those debts that you believe are owed to you: monetary, emotional/psychological, and moral/spiritual.

Sometimes it is absolutely necessary to ask for an accounting. How would it feel to do so? Can you see how failing to hold a friend responsible for betraying you creates a wall of upsetting emotions around the friendship?

Sometimes, on the other hand, the best thing we can do is to forgive the debt, especially when it is a deep and psychological one, such as the failure of our parents to love us as children sufficiently or appropriately. It's important to notice that such a failure can turn us into a lifelong Pursuer of what we feel we were owed but didn't get. Forgiveness is the only way out of this dilemma, not because it lets the debtors off the hook, but because it frees us to new life. We don't want to be entrapped by our need for repayment and punishment, as is Inspector Javert in *Les Miserables*; he has no life except for pursuit.

One way to begin the process of forgiveness is to create an imaginary scene in which you present a comprehensive accounting. Speak clearly about what was done to you and by whom, stating that you hold the "debtor" responsible for the effects in your life, but you wish now for your own sake to release them. Again, by so forgiving, you do not minimize the wrong done to you; you simply free yourself from the burden of carrying it any longer.

## The Fatal Flaw

Sometimes the confusion we feel between owing an actual debt and enjoying the flow of ordinary friendly give-and-take may be due to our identifying with the plotline of the Fatal Flaw.

This is another plot that strikes close to home. It is a relative of the doctrine of Original Sin, that pernicious idea that humans are inherently evil. This feeling of innate unworthiness often persists no matter what we may believe about its being eradicated by a savior's action. The sense of the fatal flaw is ancient; it resides at the heart of one of the most famous tragedies ever written, some twenty-four hundred years ago: Sophocles' *Oedipus the King*.

Before Oedipus was born, his parents, who were the king and queen of Thebes, were warned by the oracle at Delphi that their son would grow up to kill his father and marry his mother. They therefore exposed him on a hillside, with chains on his feet, expecting him to die. But a kindly shepherd freed him and took him to another royal family, the king and queen of Corinth, who reared him as their son.

As a young adult, Oedipus was also told by the oracle at Delphi that his destiny was to kill his father and marry his mother. Believing the king of Corinth to be his father, Oedipus tried to avoid the prophecy by fleeing that country. On the road to Thebes, he met an arrogant older man with armed followers who confronted him and demanded he get out of the way (an early example of road rage). Refusing to do so, the hotheaded young Oedipus killed them all.

Then Oedipus made his way to Thebes, which was being threatened by a Sphinx. No one could pass through the city gates without answering her riddle. Failure had already meant death to many. Oedipus answered the riddle correctly, killed the Sphinx, and was hailed as a savior by the people. The recently widowed queen took him as her husband and made him king. They had children and all was well.

Eventually, though, a plague struck the city. The people begged their beloved king to discover the cause. Seers revealed that the plague existed because the murder of their former king had not been avenged. Oedipus was determined to find the murderer, who turned out to be none other than himself. To his horror, he learned that the man he had killed on the road was his father, the previous king. He, Oedipus, had married and fathered children by his own mother. He himself was the reason for the plague. *He* carried the fatal flaw.

Oedipus mirrors our human dread of having just such a fatal flaw at the level of our very souls. As king, he is proud of his capacity to pursue and destroy the criminal, never suspecting that he himself is the one he seeks. To watch Oedipus fulfill his tragic destiny is to watch a nightmare come to life. And, contrary to what Freud would have us understand, the nature of the nightmare is not only in Oedipus's dire deed of killing his father and marrying his mother. What is worse, it is in exposing the face of the fatal flaw—and that secret, agonizing fear we have that, because of an inner curse, we may unwittingly and through no "fault" of our conscious selves commit some disastrous, even murderous, action.

Poor Oedipus has at least three different manifestations of such a flaw: First the gods, through the oracle at Delphi, reveal his terrible destiny, attesting to the inscrutable force of fate. Next, his temper in claiming the right of way on the road leads him to commit murder, which proves to be patricide. Finally, his hubris, his overweening pride in declaring that he will bring the culprit to justice, leads Oedipus to ignore those who beg him to desist.

A great gift of the theatre is its willingness to set before us our own fears writ large. According to Aristotle, that wise observer of theatre's right role in life, watching Oedipus's tragedy unfold fills us with pity and terror, creating a catharsis of such emotions. The wide, open-air theatres of Sophocles' day called for superhuman characters to take the stage, characters big enough to stand forth and contend with the gods. Thankfully, few of us carry a fatal flaw as enormous as Oedipus's. Hence our way of working with such a flaw can be simply to acknowledge it, notice where it has led us, and observe whether it runs the story of our life.

## *Pause, Please*

Review your thoughts about the Unpaid Debt. Does any of your sense of indebtedness spring from a feeling that something is inherently wrong with you? How might you describe that flaw, and what feeling do you associate with it?

Now review your life for a sense of when your actions, or your refusals to take action, have come from this feeling of unworthiness. Oedipus and his parents were not able or willing to take appropriate action in time to change the outcome of that play, but we can change the outcome of ours.

Begin by returning to the prologue, where you dedicated your life play or the work you are doing with this book. Remember to whom or to what you offered your dedication. Ask that principle or being to stand witness to what you are about to reveal. Then recall the gift and the high purpose that you looked for in the chapter on Incarnation. With those ideas in mind, draw a tragic mask demonstrating your fatal flaw. Now write a monologue to the one to whom you dedicated your play, beginning "Dear _____ (i.e., the principle of Beauty, Divine Wisdom, or Beloved God), I stand here to acknowledge this flaw." Continue with, "I believe it came from _____ (my parents, my circumstance, or even a curse by the gods). It has caused me to _____ (deny, sometimes even hate, myself) and led me to refuse to _____ (dare to love, engage life fully). This fatal flaw has damaged my life, and the lives of those close to me, in many ways. Today, however, I stand willing to claim it and acknowledge its power by looking at it face to face."

By so bringing the flaw into awareness, you may be able to accept and perhaps even honor it. I believe that the act of looking closely at what we may call our fatal flaw provides a core of necessary heat that allows our lives to move and shift, even in the midst of tragedy. It could also be that without such flaws, we would have a different and perhaps less interesting play. A friend carries the fatal flaw of fearing that she is lazy, and this fear drives her to innumerable actions of profound service. I have heard another say, "If you really knew me, you couldn't love me; I'm unlovable." Yet he proves the opposite by always being the one others can count on for kindness and deep listening.

## The Triangle

We are acculturated to the strength and simplicity of pair bonding—the famous two-by-two understanding of the way the world works—and when any third element appears, the consequences surprise and disconcert us. But the third element always leads to an intriguing new story! One classic example, of course, is in the complication that arises when two men fall in love with one woman, or vice versa.

A tragic depiction is Edmund Rostand's classic *Cyrano de Bergerac*. Cyrano longs for the love of the beautiful Roxane, whom he thinks he could never attract because of his ugly, enormous nose. He is, however, a fearsome warrior, a deeply loved friend and leader, and the lady's confidant. He is also a poet, with the gift for spinning words into ecstasy. When he learns that Roxane is in love with a gorgeous young man, Christian, who is about to join his company of cadets, Cyrano agrees to befriend and protect him.

Christian, it turns out, is also desperately in love with Roxane. His fatal flaw is that he is tongue-tied; he cannot speak the words of love that Roxane demands. So Cyrano speaks for him, bedazzling the lady so thoroughly that she agrees to an immediate marriage to Christian, believing that it is he who has wooed her with such exquisite words.

The men go off to war. Cyrano writes to Roxane in Christian's name with such passion that she takes food and wine for the hungry soldiers to the front lines in order to embrace Christian again. When she tells him that his many letters have brought her to his arms, he realizes that the man she really loves is the one who wrote to her.

Just as Christian is about to say so and unite Roxane and Cyrano, he, Christian, is shot and killed. The heroic Cyrano never tells Roxane the truth. She takes refuge in a convent, mourning her beloved, and carrying his last letter always near her heart. For fifteen years, Cyrano visits her weekly. In the last scene, he arrives dying, wounded by his corrupt enemies. Roxane is not aware of his injury. He asks her to let him read the last letter supposedly from Christian. When he surprises her by reading it aloud, she realizes that he has been the letters' true author all along. "Yours! Yours! They were your words," she cries. He responds, "The blood was his," and shortly after dies. Her most poignant words come next: "I have loved but one man all my life, and I have lost him twice."

From that heartbreaking close, we make an immediate about-face to Shakespeare's *Comedy of Errors*, which dizzyingly illustrates the Triangle in its comic mode: Twin brothers, both named Antipholus, with their twin servants, both named Dromio, are separated as babies by a misadventure at sea. In adulthood, one twin, traveling with his servant, begins a search for his brother. He happens to land in Ephesus, where the other twin lives with his own servant—and with his wife and his wife's sister.

So into a settled world of marriage comes a third force, the missing twins (both master and servant). Everyone mistakes everyone for everyone else, and comic mayhem ensues, until the third force is incorporated into the scene when the twins finally come face to face and are reunited. In this case, and in other Shakespearean comedies, the Triangle adjusts to accommodate a fourth, becoming a much more settled square, or two pairs of two. Both twins are together; man and wife are reunited; the other twin and the wife's sister fall in love to become a new pair. Even their parents, also long separated, are reunited at the end.

Many situation comedies utilize the dynamics of the Triangle. Movies use it too, for both comedy and tragedy: remember *Fatal Attraction*? Two classic films come to mind, *Casablanca* and *The Philadelphia Story*. In *Casablanca*, Rick (Humphrey Bogart) is settled comfortably around his bar until one evening "she" (Ilsa, played by Ingrid Bergman) appears, with her husband in tow. Both men love her; she loves both of them and must choose. *The Philadelphia Story* tells of a young divorcee (Katherine Hepburn) who is about to marry again; everything seems settled. Her former husband shows up, upsetting the couple. Then a charming newspaperman arrives and falls for her. So three men are focused on a single lady, creating comic mayhem. A more recent film is *Moonstruck*, with the leading character (played by Cher) about to be married to one man until she falls in love with his younger brother (played by Nicolas Cage.)

## Pause, Please

When a new (or old) person, idea, or relationship arrives on the scene, it can significantly change us, as well as how we enact the story. How often in your own life, when you begin to feel relatively settled, does a third element appear?

Notice what happens when that "third actor" enters. Does the third person support or upset you?

Perhaps the third person is present only as an invisible force. In many marriages, for example, an in-law or a former spouse can be the third person; he or she may be physically absent and yet wield great power.

Conversely, have you yourself ever been the third element, upsetting a relatively calm situation? A friend reports that her parents were securely in love until she was born. Afterward, they tried to maintain their former state of bliss, yet could not do so because of her needs as a baby. She grew up feeling that they blamed her for destroying their happiness.

When the third force enters, we want to ask ourselves: "What is the third force telling me about the current situation of my life? How is it demanding my attention?" The situation can be simple—a friend calls when you have just settled in for the afternoon with a project you've been longing to finish. The friend is in need of your time and sympathy. How do you respond?

When you, on the other hand, are yourself the third force, the questions to ask become: "Is what I am doing congruent with my gift and my mission? Or am I simply making mischief?" Perhaps you have been tempted to flirt outrageously with a friend's lover or husband, or to gossip about someone who is not present but is close to the one with whom you're sharing the juicy story. On a kinder note, perhaps you bring just the right element of surprise and freshness to a pair of settled friends who have allowed their relationship to grow stale.

## Lovers Meet, Lovers Part, Lovers Meet Again

The plot of Lovers Meet, Lovers Part, Lovers Meet Again—also known as Boy Meets Girl, Boy Loses Girl, Boy Gets Girl—is the most familiar in the world.

# THE POWER OF STORY

In a comedy, the lovers meet, part, and meet again in ecstasy or laughter and usually with a firm vow to ride off into the sunset together. The Prince in the story of Cinderella is in the throes of this plotline. Popular movies include *When Harry Met Sally*, *Bridget Jones's Diary*, and *Pretty Woman*. My favorite novel, Jane Austen's *Persuasion*, demonstrates the theme as Girl Meets Boy, Girl Loses Boy, Girl Gets Boy.

In a tragic love story, on the other hand, the lovers meet again, but too late, or only in death. A famous example is Shakespeare's *Romeo and Juliet*. One of its delightful moments is when Boy Meets Girl for the first time. Most of Shakespeare's young lovers give us this marvelous experience that can only be described as a shock of recognition, otherwise fondly called "love at first sight." For Romeo and Juliet, the experience is particularly exquisite.

We know the plot well: even though their families are enemies, Romeo crashes Juliet's family festival, hoping to see another woman with whom he is besotted. Ever since the first production of this magnificent story, audiences have eagerly awaited the moment when Romeo first sees Juliet and suffers instantaneous combustion of the heart. Consumed with love for her essence that shines through her luminous beauty, he exclaims,

> Oh, she doth teach the torches to burn bright!
> (1.5.43)

Once Juliet sees Romeo, she also experiences an immediate birth of love, though hers grows more sedately until the balcony scene, when she virtually incandesces before our eyes in expressing her passion:

> My bounty is as boundless as the sea,
> My love as deep. The more I give to thee
> The more I have, for both are infinite.
> (2.1.175-177)

The two marry secretly, but then Romeo is caught in a duel between Juliet's cousin and his dearest friend (the Triangle at work). The cousin kills his friend; Romeo kills the cousin and is banished from Verona and thus from his beloved (Lovers Part). Juliet mourns; her father determines that she must marry a rich nobleman (another Triangle).

To avert the marriage, the friar who married her to Romeo gives her an herbal potion that makes her seem dead. She is buried in the family tomb, while the friar sends word to Romeo to come wake her up and take her away. The message miscarries; Romeo believes she is really dead, buys poison, returns to Verona, and kills himself by her side. Juliet wakes just as he dies and then kills herself with his dagger (Lovers Meet Again, but only in death). This terrible loss of the two families' only children finally forces them to make peace.

Plays, movies, operas, and musical comedies all use endless variations of this delicious plot. Almost anything that can be designated as a "chick flick" enjoys this basic structure, although, unlike *Romeo and Juliet*, the story usually ends happily in the pair's reunion.

## *Pause, Please*

Write a letter to your first love. (You need not intend to send it unless he or she is still in your life as lover.) Remember (or create) the moment when the two of you first met. Recount the moment when you realized it was love. Read the letter aloud. Notice how it makes you feel.

Did you and your first love part? How? Why? Did you meet again? Under what circumstances? And then what happened?

Reflect on how this first relationship has influenced any later loves of yours. We can sometimes move forward simply by recognizing the insights that arise. Becoming aware of patterns is the first step in altering them. Moreover, just to be in the state of love again by remembering past or present loves in juicy detail generates health and well-being, as long as we do not waste our lives pining away for an irretrievable past.

## Unrecognized Virtue

The plotline of Unrecognized Virtue is an old favorite, especially in folk and fairy tales, and opposite to the Fatal Flaw. Instead of Original Sin, here is "Original Blessing," in Matthew Fox's beautiful phrase; it is a gift of grace, talent, skill, and excellence that nevertheless goes unrecognized for most of the tale. In Hans Christian Andersen's "The Ugly Duckling," the hero's gift of being a swan is not known until the end. Many well-known stories use this plotline to keep us waiting for the moment when the virtue, or the gift, is finally acknowledged. Think of the triumphant moment when the shoe fits Cinderella.

Another charming story is the one about a baby tiger that lost his mother. He was adopted by a herd of goats and always thought he was a goat, too, until another tiger came along and revealed his true face and nature.

Another example is the parable of the Prodigal Son in the Christian Gospel, where the protagonist forgets his true nature until he returns home and his original blessing is remembered and celebrated by a loving father. This story is one of a series of remarkable teachings by Jesus about the nature of the Kingdom of Heaven. While the gift is unrecognized in earthly circumstances, and forgotten or unnoticed by the one who carries it, yet in the Kingdom of Heaven it is seen and honored.

A Sufi teaching story, "The King's Son," relates a similar tale. A noble prince is sent out from his homeland with a mission; along the way he forgets everything—his gift, his mission, his family—until a letter arrives from his father, the king. *Then* he remembers both his incarnational gift and his incarnational task. As I understand it, we are all like the king's son; we have forgotten where we came from, who we are, and what we are here to do. If we are lucky, a "letter" arrives from home to remind us.

Shakespeare's *The Winter's Tale* is a favorite example of the plot of Virtue Unrecognized. Leontes, King of Sicily, his pregnant wife Hermione, and their young son are happy together. Then Leontes (whose fatal flaw is jealousy) suddenly decides that Hermione has been unfaithful to him with his best friend (the Triangle) and that the child she is carrying belongs to the friend. Leontes sends to the oracle at Delphi for the truth, tries to kill his best friend (who narrowly escapes), puts his wife on trial for treason, and has the newborn baby daughter abandoned in the wilds of a foreign land. The messengers return from the oracle at Delphi with the pronouncement that Leontes is a jealous tyrant and will live miserably without an heir until the lost one is found. He denies the oracle until word comes that his living son has died; this news slays Hermione. Leontes, stricken to his knees, begs pardon of the gods and vows to do penance.

Time passes. Perdita, the lost child, grows up beautiful and beloved in a shepherd's family, and in a series of miracles is finally reunited with her father. Then, wonder of wonders, the magnificent Hermione is revealed as not dead but mysteriously waiting until her daughter and husband can be restored to her. Both Hermione and Perdita possess sterling virtues of grace and goodness that go unrecognized, in fact spurned, until the crowning moments of the play.

## *Pause, Please*

Remember the gift you brought from the stars that we talked about in the chapter on Incarnation. Have you yourself adequately honored and recognized this gift in your life? Have you hidden it, or have you allowed others to see and honor it? Have others been frightened or jealous of it? Have they pretended not to recognize it?

Many people carry virtues that lie dormant until needed. A friend's son suffered a terrible head wound in Iraq. Previously, my friend had been a fine mother and a deeply caring teacher. But after the wounding, with the intensity of the fight she and her husband had to wage in order to bring her boy back to life and back to himself and then back home, she became a giant of strength, truth, energy, and power. The whole family is now ablaze with courage. Every day new virtues are demanded to meet the challenges; every day the family members respond from the depths of their souls.

Consider the adventures that your gift has given you, as well as the ordeals that have perhaps called them into being. Write a scene in which an angel commands you to recognize your deepest gifts and strengths. Make an accounting of the ways you have used them and will continue to use them in the days to come.

## The Seductive Enchantment

Another plot structure, one that can entrap the soul for what may seem to be ages, is the Seductive Enchantment, commonly known as the Spider and the Fly. This one occurs in many genres, from comedy to melodrama to romance to tragedy.

At the hard-knocks level of life, this plot might appear as a sting operation—the subject of popular cops-and-robbers films—or one of a variety of confidence tricks played on vulnerable or gullible people. The spider, usually a very attractive person, entices another with a captivating promise. He spins a web of alluring lies and snares the victim (the fly) within it until the fly parts with a valuable treasure or succumbs totally. The Spider-and-the-Fly stories form the basis for many thrillers: The *Bourne* and *Matrix* trilogies demonstrate the ways a character caught in a trap struggles not only to get free but also to take revenge on the person or forces trapping him.

This plot can be seen as a companion of the Fatal Flaw. Often in Greek tragedies, the playwrights make us feel that the gods are using the hero's fatal flaw to entrap him or her in order to expose the flaw publicly—or, even more outrageously, to ridicule the hero in a cruel way. One of the tragic figures in Shakespeare's *King Lear* remarks,

> As flies to wanton boys are we to th' gods;
> They kill us for their sport.
>
> (4.2.37–38)

In the world's literature, tellers of tales use the plot of the Spider and the Fly often. Young Scheherazade is lured into the Arabian king's harem. In the morning after their night of love, the king intends to have her killed, believing all women are faithless and deserve to die. She survives by weaving a web of enchantment through story that will keep the king fascinated and her alive for *A Thousand and One Nights*.

Early Celtic bards and storytellers could spin a web of wonder that held their hearers enthralled to their sound, their rhythm, and the tale itself. They lived in a magical in-between world of forest and mist, caves and seashores. They peopled that world with magical beings and captured the mystery of that world in their songs. There are tales of heroes who stroll into magic mountains, led by lights or music or a sense of presence, and are never seen again. They emerge after what to them seems a day and discover that a hundred years have gone by. Or the hero encounters a fairy being and is changed into a frog or a horse or a spider.

One version of the Seductive Enchantment tells of the powerful wizard Merlin in the Arthurian saga. He falls in love with a young student/ enchantress named Nimuë (or Niniane or Vivien). She captures him through her seductive wiles and keeps him caught in a web in a magic cave (or a mighty oak tree), along with the Thirteen Treasures of Britain, symbols of the island's mythic power.[5] Merlin guards them perpetually, even as he sleeps. The list of treasures appears most simply (without all the confusing—to me—Welsh names) in Charles Squire's *Celtic Myth and Legend*. They include "a sword, a basket, a drinking-horn, a chariot, a halter, a knife, a cauldron, a whetstone, a garment, a pan, a platter, a chessboard, and a mantle."[6] Each object belonged to gods or heroes, and each is capable of fulfilling a wish or need instantaneously, be it a wish for bounteous food, or victory, or horses, or travel, or invisibility. Several objects were capable of discerning between a brave person and a coward and would perform their magic deeds only for the courageous. The legend tells us that Merlin will be free from his enchantment only when another Arthur is born who needs a mentor and wise friend. Or simply when the world needs him—and the Thirteen Treasures—again.

Euripides' classical drama of *Iphigenia in Aulis* also follows the plot of the Seductive Enchantment. The Greek fleet, under King Agamemnon's command, sets out to fight the Trojans in order to bring the beautiful Helen home from Troy. (She of enchanting beauty has been seduced by the Trojan prince, Paris.) While the fleet is becalmed, the king's men go hunting in a sacred grove, killing a deer. The goddess Artemis, whose holy beast they have killed, demands a sacrifice of Agamemnon: his precious daughter, Iphigenia.

Agamemnon lures Iphigenia and her mother, Queen Clytemnestra, to his army camp at Aulis, swearing that he wants to wed Iphigenia to the hero, Achilles. When the women arrive, they learn the truth, but Agamemnon seduces his daughter into believing that her sacrifice will bring her great honor with the gods. She is brought to the sacrificial place, and Agamemnon prepares the blade, but at the last moment a stag appears on the altar and is sacrificed instead. Iphigenia is taken into some enchanted space; we know not where. (This last action is not part of Euripides' story.) The whole play is based on a series of enchantments and seductions, with bloody intent and bloody outcomes.

# *Pause, Please*

The Spider-and-Fly motif is a popular plot device, yet for the sacred player it requires difficult work at the soul-level of belief. Is it part of your life story that you believe yourself to have been lured, captivated, enchanted, or tricked? How would you write about that belief? How have you fought to free yourself?

Conversely, have you lured another into a trap for your own pleasure or cruelty? Have you seduced another just because you could? What can you do today to absolve yourself or the other? Write a monologue from the point of view of the spider and another from the point of view of the fly.

## The Indomitable Hero and the Lost Treasure

The one who won't be beaten—how we love stories of the Indomitable Hero! This plotline is so universal it hardly needs an introduction. Joseph Campbell brought it to new consciousness with his classic *The Hero with a Thousand Faces*. Basically, the hero, often of lowly birth and/or scorned as an outsider, is compelled to undertake a journey during which he or she descends to the Underworld (or the forest, or the desert, or dangerous, unknown territory, or the unconscious). There he overcomes various trials and returns triumphant bearing a gift (of treasure, sustenance, knowledge, or insight) that will benefit the whole society. We recognize this pattern in countless stories ranging from that of Isis in Egypt, Perseus and Odysseus in Greece, Muhammad in Mecca, and Jesus of Nazareth. We can trace the pattern, too, in popular heroes ranging from Robin Hood and Queen Elizabeth I to *Star Wars'* Han Solo, Erin Brockovich, and the astronauts in *Apollo 13*.

On a smaller scale, our entire lives can be seen as a hero's quest for meaning, with us in the leading role.

More particularly, however, the plot demands that the hero have a powerful goal that pulls her relentlessly forward, and it becomes more poignant if the goal is a lost treasure. Thus I have combined the two plots, since it is in seeking that goal that the true hero is revealed. If we wanted higher consciousness, or a world free of hunger and pain, with half the fervor that the hero wants to reach his version of the Holy Grail, the world would be Paradise.

A fascinating example can be found in Shakespeare's *All's Well That Ends Well*, often called one of his "problem plays." In the latter stages of Shakespeare's career, he dramatized some stories that audiences find troubling, partly because they present characters with more obvious frailty and ambivalence than those in the earlier plays. Several such characters appear in *All's Well That Ends Well*. But for our purposes, we will focus on the heroine, Helena.

Helena is the daughter of a poor but renowned physician who served in the household of the Countess of Roussillon. This doctor has recently died, leaving Helena bereft of everything except his medical secrets, including one of such potency that it contains a hint of heavenly magic. Helena is passionately in love with the young count, Bertram. (He is her treasure.) But despite her many virtues, she knows Bertram would not marry her because she is not his social equal— a matter of great importance in Shakespeare's time. So she pines hopelessly:

> 'Twere all one
> That I should love a bright particular star
> And think to love it, he is so above me.
> (1.1.84–86)

Bertram journeys to Paris to serve as courtier to the king. But the king is sick unto death with a fistula, and the country is in despair.

Back home in Roussillon, Helena is in such pain at Bertram's absence that his mother, the countess, questions her until she confesses her great love, adding:

> Be not offended . . . I follow him not
> By any token of presumptuous suit,
> Nor would I have him till I do deserve him . . .
>
> (1.3.202–205)

But the countess, much wiser than her vain son, loves Helena for her true worth. Fully approving the match, she gives her blessing for a deed of great daring: Helena believes that the special cure her father left as her only inheritance can cure the king, and she is willing to hazard her reputation, even her life, in the attempt to save him. (Of course, she also hopes that if she is successful the king will reward her suitably. Remember, the play takes place at a time when women had little or no power, except what they could manage through a powerful man.)

Heroically, Helena makes the arduous journey to the king's court in Paris. She succeeds first in seeing and then in healing him through her persuasive powers and her faith, both in the medicine and in her magical nature. In gratitude, the king agrees to reward her by bestowing her hand in marriage to any courtier she should choose. Naturally, Helena chooses Bertram, but the nobleman's pride is deeply offended:

> A poor physician's daughter my wife! Disdain
> Rather corrupt me ever!
>
> (2.3.122–123)

Nevertheless, they are wed, following which Bertram runs away to war, leaving Helena a letter declaring that he will never consider her his wife until she wears his family ring and carries his baby—which, as far as he's concerned, means never. (The treasure is lost.) But in another heroic act, Helena follows Bertram to the battlefield, empowered by the deep conviction of her love.

In the village near the war, Bertram flirts with another woman, Diana. Helena persuades Diana to submit to Bertram but to allow her, Helena, to take Diana's place in bed in the dark (Shakespeare's famous bed trick!). Further, Diana is to exchange rings with Bertram, giving him the one the king gave Helena and taking his own family ring. Thus, Helena is able to become pregnant by Bertram and also to carry his ring.

At the war's end, Bertram goes home. There he meets the king, who has come in response to a false announcement that Helena is dead, grieving that "we lost a jewel of her" and lamenting Bertram's folly in lacking the "sense to know her estimation" (5.3.1, 3–4). Bertram, believing her dead as well, now regrets her loss and his cruel treatment of her. Belatedly, he realizes he loves Helena(!), confessing his sorrow

> That she whom all men praised and whom myself,
> Since I have lost, have loved, was in mine eye
> The dust that did offend it.
>
> (5.3.54-56)

But unbeknownst to them all, the pregnant Helena, very much alive, has also journeyed the long miles home, arriving with Diana in secret. Meanwhile, when the king sees the ring he had given Helena on Bertram's finger, Bertram is at a loss to explain, reluctant to mention his night with the woman he thought was Diana. Finally Helena appears, confronting Bertram with the truth. In showing him his family ring and her pregnant body, she has clearly met the two conditions he had thought impossible for sealing their marriage. He declares that he will "love her dearly, ever, ever dearly" (5.3.354). The treasure is found.

Some see Helena's behavior as manipulative, as on one level it is. But in terms of the hero's story, she merely overcomes a series of impossible obstacles to achieve the best outcome for all concerned. Her triumphant return from supposed death serves to heal Bertram's misguided emphasis on social status over intrinsic worth, even as she had healed the king of his fistula. We might say that Helena's undaunted love finally brings Bertram to his senses, so that he can rejoice in recovering the lost treasure that she is, too. In doing so, she also restores a moral balance to the whole society, represented by the happy king in his self-description at the end:

> The king's a beggar, now the play is done:
> All is well ended, if this suit be won . . . (epilogue.1–2)

In many stories, the great treasure may be lost or stolen. Think of Wagner's Ring Cycle in opera or of Tolkien's *Lord of the Rings*. This dilemma can be comical or tragic, depending on the treatment. Farces make us laugh at misers who run berserk when they lose a coin. Stories, movies, and plays make us weep when we see a precious child or friend lost or stolen, or when someone with few belongings is robbed of what little she has. We feel deep fascination when the survivor strives poignantly to carry on. While writing this chapter I have been reading John le Carré's *The Constant Gardener*, a book and movie utilizing both plots. The hero's beloved wife is murdered, and the way she is murdered robs her of her reputation. This incredibly painful loss spurs the hero to discover what really happened. In a frenzy to tell the truth about his wife's beauty and constancy, the constant gardener refuses to allow inhuman forces of greed and power to keep him from fulfilling his love for his lady.

Stories about the Lost Treasure and the Indomitable Hero can feature the equally difficult quest to keep the treasure from falling into the hands of evil ones who will use its power for wicked ends. All the Grail Quest stories engage these plot elements. And in modern days, who illustrates the pattern better than Indiana Jones?

## *Pause, Please*

We've looked at the Power of Story, and we've thought about creation stories as informing our individual ways of creating our lives as participants in the greater Life-on-Earth story. We've also studied various plotlines and reflected on how our life plays have moved within them. Considering it all, what kind of story do you now believe you are here to enact? Can you give it a title? What is the next step you need to take to move the story forward?

## THE PLOT THICKENS

As a sacred actor, you may be aware of the story you are enacting and feel you are doing so with style and grace, only to bump up against your partners, colleagues, friends, and neighbors, each of whom is enacting another play entirely. Remember, for the human story alone, more than six billion plays are running simultaneously, bombarding, intersecting, participating, and blending together. This doesn't even take into account the billions of animal and plant stories also going on.

When stories collide, they are seeking a sublime merger, and you are being invited to remember that you are at a vital choice point. No matter what play you are playing, at that moment you are being asked to take a new element into account. An action has occurred that awaits your response.

Let's say, for example, that you are serenely enacting a play whose underlying plot is the Indomitable Hero Seeking a Lost Treasure. You are a sculptor resolutely engaged with a block of marble, demanding that it reveal its inmost secret, but you fear that you have lost your touch. Along comes someone busily enacting the plot of the Unpaid Debt who declares that you must relinquish the marble since you have not yet paid him for it. Further, he has brought helpers to pick it up.

What to do? Kick the pursuer and his helpers down the stairs? Try to negotiate? Quit the project, give up, sell your body, call for assistance? Whatever you do, you notice that you have been ruthlessly deflected and at least temporarily lost the story you were playing. This happens all the time in life.

In a traditional drama, you could turn to the director or the playwright and ask, "What do I do now?" It is, after all, their job to help a stymied actor make the appropriate choice that will take her to the next part of the story. Of course, any scripted play has lines that indicate your response and take you to the next place. All you as an actor need do is bring a fresh interpretation in the way you express yourself with your voice, face, and body.

Life, on the other hand, is a vast improvisation, with unlikely, even impossible, events happening at every turn. Like crazy cars, we bump and careen into others' stories, are suddenly shunted off in a completely new direction, and the story changes. Here's a hint: The one "rule" in improvisational theatre is to say "Yes!" enthusiastically to everything that comes, no matter what. The sculptor says, "Yes! I do owe you money for this marble. Look at what I'm doing with it! What do you think?" And just maybe your Pursuer will cheerfully respond, "Yes! I see that your work is magnificent. You are a genius, and I would like to help you. Let's explore how that might work."

Sometimes huge events occur—falling in love, having an accident, falling ill—that change the story immediately and irrefutably. The same can be true about the occurrence of what seem to be tiny events. We need only to imagine the chain of small decisions that led to the meeting of our biological parents in order for us to realize the subtle play of life that goes on beneath the surface, perhaps just as insouciantly and playfully as it seems. Change one element, even a tiny one, and pouf! a whole lineage appears or disappears.

My own parents were missionaries to Korea who met on an excursion to the Diamond Mountains in what is now North Korea and were later married in Seoul. What if one of them had chosen not to go on the excursion that day? Perhaps because they were part of a small community in a foreign land, they might have become acquainted anyway. But not necessarily, and not in the intoxicating, magical air of the mountains.

Biologist Stephen Jay Gould demonstrates the extreme tenuousness of existence as we know it in his book *Wonderful Life*. He takes us far back in time to the emergence of vertebrates, showing that if one delicate, little life form had not survived millions of years ago, the entire family of beings with backbones would never have evolved.

So chance and choice can make huge differences. Contemporary Chaos Theory emphasizes how ultimate outcomes are dependent on initial conditions. Our encounters may have special meaning, or a chance encounter might throw us off the predictable course and bring us to an aspect of our play we really need to explore. We may never know, but it makes sense to become aware that tiny happenings and tiny choices can enhance life or leave it high and dry for years.

So the sacred actor, unable to appeal to any director or playwright but herself, needs to be so prepared inwardly that she is open and willing to engage, in a free and intuitive way, all the elements that come spilling at her. She needs to be able to initiate and respond to action wholeheartedly, in whatever piece of the story she has taken on at the moment. And if she's that Indomitable Sculptor working to find the Lost Treasure in a precious piece of marble, she needs to find her way through the other stories that affect hers and may even change it. She can do so by responding to those other stories wholeheartedly and acknowledging them with grace, but then by making her way back to her own search, courage intact and wisdom gained. In a comedy, she might fall in love with or work an enchantment on the pursuer, or he would finally recognize her great gift. Let's allow this story a happy ending. And let's enact our stories to the fullest, so that the Life-on-Earth story has a greater chance for a happy ending as well.

*Do any human beings ever realize life while they live it*
*—every, every moment?*
—Emily, in Thornton Wilder's *Our Town*

# Three

# The Power of *Now!*

The facing page features Emily, the young heroine in Thornton Wilder's play *Our Town*, expressing a poignant truth about the Power of *Now!* It is difficult to pin down, it cannot be held, and only rarely is it realized. This power answers the question, "*When* do I enact the story using the gifts I bring in order to fulfill this incarnation?" All theatre resounds with just one possible answer: *Now!*

## HERE'S THE STORY

You are a gifted playwright intent upon capturing onstage a truth about the Power of *Now!* You do so by isolating successive moments in time within the confines of a small town, Grover's Corners, New Hampshire, in the not-too-far-distant past, the turn of the twentieth century. You are a playful dramatist, so your characters reveal these glimmers of time, in time, from their own points of view, and you manipulate time's passage with grace and humor: Now it is dawn; now it's late morning; now it's evening; now it's night; now it's three years later. Now nine years have gone by, and now we are in eternity. Knowing the potency of reflective devices, you provide a tiny speech about place to provide a mirror for your truth about time and the Power of *Now!* A young character, Rebecca Gibbs, speaks these words to her brother George:

I never told you about that letter Jane Crofut got from her minister when she was sick. He wrote Jane a letter and on the envelope the address was like this: It said "Jane Crofut; The Crofut Farm; Grover's Corners; Sutton County; New Hampshire; United States of America." . . . But listen, it's not finished—the United States of America; Continent of North America; Western Hemisphere; the Earth; the Solar System; the Universe; the Mind of God—that's what it said on the envelope. . . . And the postman brought it just the same.[1]

As this speech plays with place, so throughout the play you the playwright reveal time, taking it, step by step, through the perpetual present moment into cosmic dimensions. This is precisely the Power of *Now!* The theatre always thrusts us immediately into the eternal present, that cosmic dimension where all that has ever happened or will ever happen is happening in this very instant. As Thornton Wilder says, the action of the theatre always "takes place in a perpetual present time. . . . On the stage it is always now."[2]

Remember that theatre began in ritual. Both the ritual circle and the theatrical stage comprise a *temenos*—a sacred space—that takes us from linear time to the archetypal realm of the gods, where we can participate in and be reinvigorated by their energies. In the theatre, we find ourselves in time out of time, and it is precisely this pause that affords us the opportunity to take stock of our lives and accelerate our expansion into who and what we truly are. In Sacred Theatre, the aim is to become aware of the power encapsulated in the eternal present and practice living exuberantly within that power in our daily lives.

Just as a young girl living on Crofut Farm is also a resident of Grover's Corners, Sutton County, New Hampshire, the United States of America, continent of North America, Western Hemisphere, the earth, the solar system, the universe, and the Mind of God, so our lives can open to successive sheathings of time until we find within each moment the unfathomable presence of eternity. That is the Power of *Now!*

Few people can experience that power in the way that the character Emily begs, "Do any human beings ever realize life while they live it—every, every moment?" Ah, but if we could, as Emily asks, stop for just a moment in the busyness of doing, of being filled with thoughts of time past and time future imploding on the present until we lose it; if we could just stop and look at each other with total awareness of the precious gift of this moment and then this one, then we would truly *experience* our lives instead of simply pass through them.

The sacred player who employs the Power of *Now!* realizes that there is no need to stop time, though, for the joys of this present instant are absolutely alive in each succeeding one. Every passing moment of your life—good, beautiful, wretched, dreadful—is gathered together, as T. S. Eliot so elegantly states, in time present. So all of the things that you have thought, observed, learned, and done are here right now and have in fact gathered together to make you who you are today.

## *Pause, Please*

Practice noticing whatever is present now: Where am I? How am I sitting? What is around me? The five senses help: What do I see? What do I hear? How does it feel? What does it smell like? Can I taste anything?

In this moment, is there a truth about time that I can perceive? For example, I look out my June window and see a burst of roses, some in bud, some full blown, some fading away. They seem to image time's mystery: all time in this very moment. What is precious for you in this moment? What is eternal?

See if you can sit for five minutes observing the way the present shifts into the past, holding on as securely as you can to the awareness of *Now!* Such an endeavor slows things down, allows a moment of rest, and provides renewed energy when time picks up again at its ordinary pace.

## The Perpetual *Now!* of the Theatre

The Power of *Now!* is the most intangible power of Sacred Theatre. It is not simply about time; it transcends our notions of time. It comes closest to the Tao in Chinese philosophy, in which, the masters tell us, the Tao that can be spoken of is not the real Tao. Likewise, the real moment of *Now!* cannot be caught or even described adequately; it can only be experienced as part of a mysterious, sweeping river flowing within and around us. Yet, as we are the skillful playwrights of our lives, we can choose to travel backward and forward on the banks of the great river, seeking moments to re-imagine and mine for hidden gold, thus adding them to the treasure trove of life.

Although the Power of *Now!* that we can speak of is not the real power, we can gain a sense of it by studying its qualities. Remember that we are speaking of a power—not just a concept or even a principle—but a dynamic, flowing, energetic entity. Entire books, such as Eckhart Tolle's best-selling one, have been written about the Power of *Now!* from the psychospiritual perspective of living a decent, healthy life. Spiritual practices challenge us to be in the moment without confusing it with thoughts or emotions of past or future and without wishing it were yesterday or next month. In Sacred Theatre, we understand that both the past and the future are dynamically contained in this very moment. Our challenge, therefore, is twofold: to be aware that all of our past thoughts and actions are what has brought us to this moment and, even more mind-boggling, to be aware that everything we ever *will* do is also encoded in this moment. It is as if, as the acorn, we already contain the genetic wisdom we need to become the oak, and in every moment of our lives we are engaged in this process of unfolding. It takes place whether or not we are aware of it. But opening to the Power of *Now!* brings the process to consciousness and so accelerates and enlightens it.

It's relatively easy to understand the first quality of *Now!*, that of the living presence of the past. As a theatrical example, the historical events portrayed in *Hamlet* took place, if they ever did, perhaps nine hundred years ago and were legendary even in Shakespeare's time. Yet when you sit in a theatre watching the play begin, you recognize that what is happening on the stage is unflinchingly present. Right now, before you, two sentries move cautiously toward each other. One speaks, "Who's there?" and you dive into the dark and dangerous world of the Prince of Denmark with fresh immediacy. You may have seen *Hamlet* a dozen times, yet it is absolutely new each time.

Even as Hamlet lives again before us, we as sacred actors realize that all of the past moments that reside within us are not dead and done; they are alive and dynamic and ever capable of new gifts, new understanding. In this way the Power of *Now!* gathers, and, as we play with it, increases our awareness and general joy.

## WORKING WITH THE DYNAMIC PRESENCE OF THE PAST

Contemporary brain research helps us learn how to mine the past for its riches. Some scholars, perhaps beginning with Sigmund Freud (who gave us the idea of the unconscious), believe that certain levels of the mind, deeper than consciousness, encode all our life experiences; and these levels (or *modules*, in modern brain language) stand ready and willing to offer aid in time of need. Steven Johnson, in his recent book *Mind Wide Open*, compares the Freudian sense of the unconscious with the "modern portrait of the brain's inner life: a host of distinct modules competing for control of the organism, each driven by its own priorities."[3] Further, "You are the sum of your modules, but your conscious sense of self is only a part of that system. Beneath the brain's executive branch, matters are more unruly: a host of subsystems [is] dedicated to registering incoming stimuli, interpreting that data, and making emotional value judgments about its nature, connecting these new developments with past memories, maintaining your body's homeostatic systems."[4]

Noted cellular biologist Bruce Lipton tells us that the amount of data reaching us every second is the equivalent of twenty million bits of information. Almost all of it is shuttled into those parts of the

brain below consciousness. Of those twenty million bits, a grand total of about forty make it into the conscious mind. So you begin to
understand how vast the subconscious mind is and yet how little is
required for the conscious mind to do its work.[5] Lipton further tells
us that while the conscious mind can move around in time, like a play
that can be set in the past or the future or the present, the subconscious mind lives only in the dynamic *Now!* He describes it this way:
"When the conscious mind is busy daydreaming, creating future plans
or reviewing past life experiences, the subconscious mind is always
on duty, efficiently managing the behaviors required at the moment,
without the need of conscious supervision."[6]

Thus the parts of our brain below consciousness can utilize millions of bits of incoming information each second and perform thousands of tasks simultaneously and, it seems, effortlessly. The conscious
mind, though, manages to be aware of only a tiny percentage of that
information, and it performs most effectively when it does things one
at a time. Poignantly, the conscious mind believes it is performing a
One-Person Show, when in reality the stored, seemingly inaccessible,
information held below consciousness is actually influencing many
of our outer actions and reactions. Lipton says, "In humans . . . the
fundamental behaviors, beliefs and attitudes we observe in our parents become 'hard-wired,' as synaptic pathways in our subconscious
minds. Once programmed into the subconscious mind, they control
our biology for the rest of our lives . . . unless we can figure out a way
to reprogram them."[7]

Our work as sacred players is to lure that stored information out of
the depths and into our conscious awareness, so that we learn more
about who we are and perform our incarnational assignments with
more grace and accuracy. This is a formidable task, but, like all soul-
level work, worth pursuing. It helps to realize that the information
from these deeper parts of the mind, as we tease it forward, will come
in wayward images and dreams. It may not be "factual" in the sense
that the world deems facts. But images are healing, and this is the theatre. It is absolutely fine to "make things up," because you will choose

to make up only what holds something useful for you to work with, however "factual" it may or may not be.

Jung once said that the way to enlightenment is not to light a candle against the darkness but to make the darkness visible. Accepting that we cannot possibly gain more than a small amount of understanding from the fathomless place beyond consciousness, we nevertheless may find that whatever we do gain allows us to live more effectively. Just as the Cretan princess Ariadne gave the Greek hero Theseus a holy thread so that he could safely make his way into the labyrinth and confront the monster, we can grab hold of a nebulous image from the past and then begin to move along that thread into the darkness below the conscious level. Then we can discover the treasure or tame the monster that sits there and make our way out again with new awareness of how to live more beautifully in the moment.

## THE THEATRE OF THE MIND

We begin our exploration of the subconscious mind by taking three actions. The first provides an opportunity to thank all the supporting systems of the mind and body, the second is some work with what I call erroneous conditioning, and the third is an exercise to gain information about your life today from some image of the past.

### Action One

Picture the mind as a perfect, and perfectly run, theatre. The conscious mind is that part of the theatre the audience sees, the stage itself. But such a theatre has much space for activity behind the scenes: there is a basement for wires and pulleys and mechanisms to control the scenery and provide room for dramatic descents and entrances; there is space overhead for storage of sets and other equipment; and above the audience area there is room for lighting instruments and even a crawl space for technicians.

All this backstage space and equipment can be likened to the myriad unconscious functions of the brain, working tirelessly to support and illumine the onstage action so that the story being enacted—your story, *Now!*—can find perfect expression. The work of invisible stagehands is like that of the various brain modules, all there to make sure that the conscious mind does what it needs to do and has adequate information, handsome costumes, great lighting, and good music and sound effects. It would be wonderful if we could also count on the entire brain being overseen by a single, capable stage manager, as in Wilder's play, *Our Town*, one who could understand everything, see the big picture, and perform heroic acts if necessary should the performance falter. According to the neuroscience of today, however, the conscious "onstage" mind with which we identify as "I" is only a part of the whole system and subject at all times to input and influence from the other parts.[8]

The conscious mind can ask for help in any area. But, like any good actor, it can also simply accept that a great deal of running the theatre is done elegantly and without need for conscious thought. And like any aware actor, the conscious mind would do well to thank often all those unconscious activities and energies that support its onstage action.

Thus it is appropriate to voice frequent appreciation to the autonomic nervous system that keeps our lungs breathing, our hearts beating, our temperature fairly constant, our digestion stirring, and all the other actions and organs of the body running well and without need of our conscious participation. We also need to thank that part of the conditioned mind that allows us to perform actions pretty much without conscious thought once they have been well learned, such as riding a bicycle, or skiing, or driving a car.

## *Pause, Please*

Imagine the vast workings of your mind as a theatre, with all the activity, equipment, and people working behind the scenes to support the onstage conscious part in its revelation of the great play your life is meant to express. Write or speak aloud a simple statement of gratitude to the immeasurable capacities of your other-than-conscious mind.

Now become more specific in your thanks: for instance, to your eyes for the ability to discern and respond to light and dark; to your liver for its exquisite, life-supporting processes; or to your skin for its skill in giving and receiving the subtlest information.

Next, consider one of the skills you have learned to do so well that you no longer even think about how to do it—walking, typing, reading; this attention provides a chance to thank the conditioned mind for its enormous contribution to your well-being.

Expressing such gratitude can prepare the conscious mind for a journey into more troubling parts of the unconscious.

## Action Two

Now it is time to ask for help in dealing with some of aspects of the nonconscious mind that may not always be so supportive. This work entails coming to grips with the inescapable influence of the past in our lives now. One form of help we could use is in uncovering those usually unquestioned assumptions that result from what I call erroneous conditioning. That is, we need help in identifying those energy-destroying ideas with which we sometimes feel we have been born but which, in fact, are rooted in past negative treatment. One common self-view is that "I'm not worthy." Variations include "I don't deserve," "I'm not good enough," "I've have no right to be here, "or even, "Something in me was born sinful."

These negative self-concepts deplete us and can serve as excuses for not doing the true work of life. No matter how clear we may be consciously about the authentic play we are here to enact, our erroneous conditioning may leave us stumbling in the dark. The backstage activity in our minds, instead of serving to support and illumine our onstage action, may be busily at work on an entirely different script. Consciously, for instance, we may think we are acting the elegant, incarnational role of the Healer, but if we have not brought certain aspects of erroneous conditioning to awareness, we will consistently encounter inner sabotaging voices that harp, "Who do you think you are?" "What do you think you're doing?" And often those old voices will begin to grate at the most awkward moment, just when we're about to engage in an important act of healing. When that happens, we can quickly become incapacitated.

We can work on this erroneous conditioning by asking: "What are my negative thoughts about myself that seem to have been with me a long time? Where did they come from? Is there some underlying message that is deeper even than these painful ideas?" For example, perhaps our parents were habitually concerned with protecting us from perceived risks and so frequently inculcated us with, "No no no! You must not do that!" Over time, we interpreted their strictures instead as meaning that something was wrong with us—we were physically incapable, or morally ineligible, or stupid. Remember that for most of us, such conditioning occurred when we were tiny beings, long before we had the power of speech or rational thought. Hence it was easy to misunderstand then and is difficult to address today, residing as it does in the memory banks deep within the nonconscious mind. Such messages may have been influenced by our culture, as could be true if we were born into a religious sensibility of Original Sin, for example, or if our ethnicity differed from that of the dominant society. In such cases, we simply absorbed the negative messages as truths before having any cognitive ability to keep them out.

When we examine such past statements of our unworthiness and seek to discern their origin, we realize that they make no rational sense. Nevertheless, they exert a terrible power and often prevent us from embracing the fullness of the present moment.

What to do? Just bringing the negative statements to awareness helps lessen their ferocity. Then, simply realizing that in most cases they assaulted us when we were unable to defend ourselves releases some of their heaviness. We also find help in seeking an answer to the question, "Have these elements of negative conditioning done anything to assist me? Have they, for example, kept me safe; or did the people who 'gave' them to me have the good intention of keeping me safe?" If so, the conditioning may in fact have served a positive purpose; there may have been times when feeling you didn't know enough kept you from exposing yourself to harm in potentially dangerous situations. In such a case, it is worthwhile to say thank you for the protection. Then it is important to detach yourself from the conditioning by addressing the issue from your present perspective: that was then; this is *Now!* In your being, you are more than the sum of your experiences; with the measured, conscious reason of an adult, you have the freedom to choose what kind of risks to take and when. The sacred actor thus engages the erroneous conditioning lying deep in the theatre of the mind in order to transform its energy from debilitation to affirmation.

## Pause, Please

Relax into the fullness of this present moment. Gently invite the theatre of your mind to provide an example of negative conditioning for today's attention. Remember that just bringing it to awareness helps relieve its damaging aspects. Then work with these steps:

1. Acknowledge the conditioned thought by naming it.

2. Ponder (briefly) where and when this belief may have originated. A common response I have heard from sacred actors is that it arrived when they were in the womb or so tiny as to be incapable of such a thought.

3. Check the belief for its accuracy today.

4. Now ask for an image dynamic enough to counteract the conditioning. The image may be that of a sublimely innocent baby, resting in

rose petals and light. Awaken all five senses so that the image is rich with beauty. Describe it in writing.

5. Make a vow to summon this image whenever the conditioned thought arises. Be aware that the image may evolve over time.

6. If you can, allow for some possibility to forgive those who infected you with this conditioning—your culture, your lineage, your religion, your teachers. One way that may lead to such forgiveness is to consider anything positive you have gained from the conditioning, such as proper caution in dangerous situations, and say thank you.

## Action Three

The third action in our work with the past is to acknowledge the strands from that past that seem clearly to have encoded the present. Often theatrical actors will achieve this understanding by writing a biography of their characters to explore those formative experiences that "made her what she is" when she walks onstage today. The times when they share their characters' biographies with one another are often the most enjoyable of the whole process. For the sacred actor, this work can be equally pleasurable as you ask the theatre of your mind to provide a scene from your past that may offer insights into who you are *Now!*

When I first asked for such a scene, what came is one of my earliest "memories." I believe it is reasonably factual, but the important truth is that it contains strands spun like sugar from a long-ago, distant moment to sweeten my life now. Every detail carries energy, resonance, and information about the way I am today:

The scene is a farmhouse in south Texas. It has a large, long kitchen with a big workspace in the middle. There's an old, white, enamel-top table that to me, the child who sits writing at it, seems huge. My mother, preoccupied with many secrets and distresses, is making her traditional Christmas cake—six slender layers of three colors, gold and red and green. It is my privilege to stir the food coloring into the batter for each layer and watch a miracle occur: a few vibrant drops change the pale cake dough to brightness. I am wise enough to know that in the oven the color will fade, but enough of it will remain to be a wonder when, after Christmas dinner, Mother cuts into the dessert and places a piece on each plate. (Today I believe the cake was a creation to remind us of the gifts the Magi gave to the baby Jesus—gold and frankincense and myrrh.)

The baking is done; the layers are cooling. I wait in some concern for the process of urging them out of the pans. We are both impatient, my mother and I, and sometimes the cakes stick because we try to release them too early. Mother busies herself making the thin, sweet, generic berry paste that goes between the layers. I hold tight to my pencil and writing pad, adjust myself on the high stool, and wait some more. Soon she begins to dictate. She is writing a little scene for my siblings and me to enact for our family and neighbors on Christmas Eve. It is a play—my introduction to the theatre.

The year is 1941 or 1942. The United States is new in the war, but local men and boys are signing up for the army and the navy. Even before this time the grown-ups have spent years listening avidly to news broadcasts about the war in Europe, but now the concerns are almost visible, even to small children. The adults talk in hushed tones; nothing takes precedence over the radio news. Real fear is in the air, along with defiance and naive belief in our country's unconquerability. My father is a veteran of World War I, so his worry includes love for Europe. My parents met and married as missionaries in Korea, so there is also deep fear and concern for friends in the Far East.

All of this tension swirling around is mostly above my head. At that time I live mostly in a world of daydreams and seem to enter into consensual reality only once in a while. But today I'm focused fully on the task at hand. Christmas planning has been underway since Thanksgiving. Having saved her rationed sugar coupons for just such use, Mother has already baked fruitcakes and cookies and mailed them off to her mother, sisters, and brother in Virginia and Pennsylvania. She lives her life in Texas as someone a long way from home.

The play she devises is about a mother alone on Christmas Eve. She describes the mother's eager impatience to see her children, who are both on their way home to celebrate with her. The day has been busy, what with cooking and cleaning. She finally sits down to read the mail that has just arrived: two letters—one from her son in the army, the other from her daughter working in the big city of Houston.

The letters announce that circumstances make it impossible for them to come home for the holiday. The son has suddenly pulled extra duty that he must fulfill. The daughter reports that while she was at the Houston Zoo, her purse, with her ticket home and all her money, slipped from under her arm and fell in with the elephants, who immediately tromped it to bits. (Mother likes a bit of absurdity in her playwriting.) That is the heartbreaking set-up; after reading both letters, in loneliness and sorrow the mother falls asleep in the rocker by the Christmas tree.

But while she sleeps, her children *do* come home—or perhaps she merely dreams they do. They quietly decorate the tree and place presents around it while waiting for the curiously deep sleeper to wake up. When she finally does, it is with amazed delight. The son and daughter explain the miracle of their presence (the details of which I can't remember) and life continues happily ever after.

At the kitchen table, I listen while Mother dictates the two letters to me, and I make props out of them so that I won't have to rely on memory when I read them as the mother during the performance. My older brother and sister will enact the roles of her children. Our neighbors, the Powells, come for the big event. My dad, my grandfather, and my little brother are other members of the audience. Mother is, too, although as playwright she has opening night jitters. The play takes place in the living room, by the unadorned Christmas tree, which in our family tradition is decorated on this night.

*Scene One.* As the mother, I bustle around with tasks and talk to myself about how wonderful it will be to see my children. They've been away so long, doing vital things for the nation's good, and I'm proud of them. And tonight they come home. Hooray!

*Scene Two.* I open the fateful letters and begin to read. But suddenly I the actress am so overwhelmed by the mother's sorrow as she learns she is to be alone that I myself begin to cry, so hard I can barely get my lines out. As the mother, I sob myself to sleep, and the children come in and begin to decorate the tree. When I wake up and see them I fear it is a dream. But no! It's real! Much rejoicing. Merry Christmas!

That was my first play. I tell about it to emphasize that, in the sacred play of our lives, every event that has ever happened is still happening. No matter how far in the past events occurred, in the theatre they are happening right *Now!* with all their poignancy and effectiveness undiminished. In a profound way, my mother and I are still preparing the Christmas cake, she is still writing that little play, and I am still playing the mother in it. I am still overpowered by the imaginary mother's pain—and by that of my own mother, who rarely speaks of her pain—alive only in a tiny piece of drama performed for maybe ten people during World War II in a farmhouse in Texas. All of it, including my experience of World War II aside from that night, is informing my life *Now!*

As I mine that memory for how it defined my future, I remember my mother's compassion for everyone except herself and how deeply I felt her sense of mission unfulfilled during her time on earth. I am reminded of how every part of my experience of her little play touches my days now, including the sense of taking dictation, of playing mother roles (even though I've never been a mother except onstage), of being overtaken by the power of a role, and of delighting in imagining and performing someone else.

In this process, I rediscover a sense of rightness and destiny playing its way in me. I recover something of the child's wonder and sense of miracle, and, in fact, touch into one of the primary patterns of my life.

∽

## *Pause, Please*

Ask the other-than-conscious levels of your mind to provide an image of an important memory from a pivotal moment in your past. You are inviting awareness of some event that gave you a clue about who and what you would be later and that touched your life with special significance, so much so that elements of the scene provide energy, wisdom, and a sense of destiny about your path today.

Now write about the scene. Start with sensory details: what you were doing, what you were wearing, the furnishings, and the nature of the world around you. Then develop these elements into a narrative of what happened. Our purpose is to give you a nugget from the past that is a touchstone for your becoming.

∽

## Working with the Dynamic Presence of the Future

Just as our work encourages greater awareness of the past's influence on the present, so, too, the Power of *Now!* demands awareness of how the choices we make in the present encode our future. Let us invite the tradition of theatre to help us understand. Actors on stage enact their roles in a state of innocence, acceptance, and lightheartedness. They know, of course, the outcome of the story; yet they play each moment as if it were happening for the first time.

In *Our Town*, the young hero George tells his neighbor Emily that he can see the top of her head as she sits at her desk doing homework.

She is so good at math; would she be willing to help him with math problems? Not to give the answers, he assures her, but perhaps a hint?

A hint? Yes, she's willing to provide that. All he needs to do is whistle at his window and she will look out of hers to give him some hints. From that moment on, and in spite of changes as they grow into adulthood, the outcome of their relationship is never really in question. The moment he works up the courage to ask her for help and she says yes encodes their blissful future together absolutely.

It is possible with hindsight to discern future outcomes that were imbedded in those big life moments when we, like Emily, said yes or when, like George, we made a request that turned into a commitment. At subtle levels, I believe that most moments of our lives lead us forward in certain directions, not necessarily in all details, but essentially. It is a truism that the decisions we make now affect the quality of our future. But as the playwright of our lives, we can train ourselves to become more conscious of that truth. One of the pleasures of engaging the Power of *Now!* is in gaining the skill to *choose* our actions knowing that they will imbed strands of our future into each successive moment. We can construct the essence of the future simply by being aware of possibilities and selecting what qualities we wish to carry forward.

## *Pause, Please*

What moments of saying yes can you remember? Which ones profoundly seeded your future? Did you say yes with a full heart, somehow knowing that the future was reaching into your life at that time? Or did you unknowingly make a future commitment, like George did, that was hidden within a simple request?

Review these moments and notice the quality of vibrancy they contained. Trace how your future was irrevocably coded in them.

Recall the recent exercise in which I invited you to write a narrative about a scene from your past. Now create a scene that you deliberately seed with aspects you wish for the future. A good way to do so is to imagine a perfect day as if you were living it now. Spend a few minutes considering those actions that make you happy and feel most alive. Here are clues: people seem to feel happiest when they are engaged with others, helping or serving others, working or creating with their hands, and have beauty around them.

Write about your perfect day in detail: What are you doing? How are you doing it? What important elements does it include? It can go on and on and on; there is no twenty-four-hour limit. Then, once you have written it, study this "script" for themes that you wish to carry forward into your future. Which ones can you follow from the seed of this perfect time that will lure you into the future being you wish to be?

Next, write this heading: "I am now and I will forever be one who loves and is inspired by these things: _____." Use your imagining of your perfect day to list the qualities that you will intend to produce in each moment in order to open that moment to the truth and actuality of your future.

## Encoding the Ultimate Future

Even though every actor in a theatrical play knows its outcome, he must paradoxically act as if he *doesn't* know; nothing is deadlier than "telegraphing" the ending. Nevertheless, at the same time and at every point along the way, the stage actor tempers his voice, his responses, and his body language in accord with what he knows will happen.

As sacred actors, though, we don't know the details of the outcome of our lives in advance. We *do*, however, have a sense of our incarnational gift, which gives us essential clues about who we are meant to become. On the basis of that insight, we can shift our actions and responses here and now, just as a stage actor would do, to be in accordance with our ultimate state of being. Our work is not to know how or when but to cast the gleanings of each moment forward in such a way that when the end arrives, it arrives with the gift fulfilled. As Bernard Shaw put it, "I want to be all used up when I die."

Recently, a friend's mother was ill and came close to dying. In the time they thought they had left, they spoke all the words that needed to be said, bringing resolution and forgiveness, laughter and release to what they feared were the final moments of their relationship. The mother, happily, did not die. But the friend made a decision from the richness of that experience. She determined that every conversation she held in the future would express the love and truth she would want if it were the last conversation she would ever have with that person. Now she gives to each friend and relative all the awareness she gleaned from those conversations with her mother.

## Pause, Please

Death, of course, is the ultimate outcome for us all. As sacred actors, we can even influence who we are at that moment, too. To gain clues about how we might want to shift our actions in order to affect that ultimate state, we will envision the person you will be in the hours before your death. For the sake of this exercise, it will be a time in the distant future. Design the scene just as you would like it to be. Imagine it fully, and write your "Letter to the World," as the poet Emily Dickinson called hers. Say all the things you would want to say; express all the emotions you can imagine having.

Then read your letter aloud. Does it include everything you want the world to hear? Now reflect backward from this imaginary moment of your death. Do you need to send some quality of wisdom back to the person you are today? Do you have a message for *this* moment from the person you will be at the end? Do you need more joy? Do you sense a new quality that you can now begin to develop more fully? Have you lived to your true purpose and offered your incarnational gift richly?

Being aware that the final moments of life will indeed come, begin to orchestrate ideas about the person you would like to be at that time. One suggestion would be to imitate Mahatma Gandhi, who was so deeply in the habit of reciting the name of God that, when facing an assassin's gun, he kept reciting. Perhaps it was his good Hindu understanding that his killer was acting as a god in taking his life and therefore could be saluted with the name of God. Or perhaps he was acting out of another Hindu belief that dying with the name of God on one's lips brings one to a higher incarnation in the next lifetime. Whatever his reasons, Gandhi's practice was so intense that he died saluting God: "Hey Ram, Ram." For Gandhi, it was the name of one of the incarnations of Vishnu, the great one who maintains and sustains the world.

Whose holy name or what prayer can you call on now to help you imbed each moment with seeds of the best possible outcome for this lifetime?

Performing these actions and keeping them fresh in your mind will allow the potencies of the Power of *Now!* to stabilize the actions of the present while attracting the wonder of the future.

One footnote: the truth that each moment of your life is capable of opening to the realms of the sacred. As Jane Crofut in *Our Town* dwells simultaneously in a home, near a town, in a county, in a state, in a country, on a continent, and so on until she is encompassed in the Mind of God, so do you dwell in all those places. And in a parallel way, you dwell simultaneously in eons of past time and unfathomable ages of the future, and you are exquisitely poised in the present and open to the wisdom streaming forth from the Mind of God. That is the mystery of the Power of *Now!*

*What country, friends, is this?*
—Viola, in Shakespeare's *Twelfth Night* (1.2.1)

# Four

# The Power of Place

The question is: *Where* do I enact the story that only I can enact in the play of Life on Earth in order to fulfill the purpose of this incarnation? The answer is: on the sacred stage that you become aware of, create, and grow as you engage the Power of Place. This stage forms the ground of your being. It is composed of scenic pieces, real and imaginary, that give you a sense of security within a space to breathe and live freely. When I urge you to "take the stage of your life," this is the stage I mean. In the traditional theatre, "taking the stage" implies boldness, command, and commitment. First, we become aware of the energy inherent in the Power of Place, seeking to experience four elements:

1. The ground you stand upon

2. The physical body you inhabit and its abilities to create a rich inner life

3. The field of energy that immediately surrounds you, that you personally mediate and control

4. The people and things that make up the world around you at any given moment

These four elements embody the Power of Place as it informs your life. Enacting your great play grows easier when you can draw strength from the earth you stand upon; when you respect your body and remember its innate understanding of place and space; when you engage your energy field, creating with it and drawing energy from it; and when you can sense the rich presence—human, animal, plant, and mineral—in your surroundings. This chapter guides you in becoming aware of the power in these four elements so that you can design the perfect stage for your life—a place you can visit anytime in your imagination in order to feel strong, supported, and at home.

## HERE'S THE STORY

Imagine that you have been shipwrecked in a terrible storm. Through enormous will and strength, and the care of people around you, you have somehow struggled to shore. Exhausted, you are carried the last steps onto the land by the sailors who are your companions. Suddenly, something magical touches you. You are alive, rescued, safe—miraculously so. That's part of the thrill that runs through you, your life force returning in a rush; but, as your feet touch ground and you take your first, tentative steps, something potent in the land itself reaches out to claim you. This is a place of mystery, of possibility, and you feel it throughout your whole being. What is it? You turn in wonder to ask your rescuers, "What country, friends, is this?"

As Viola, the young heroine in Shakespeare's *Twelfth Night*, you have been gripped by the Power of Place. You sense that this strange country, Illyria, is filled with potential. Illusion, elusiveness, hilarity, longing, music, folly, mistaken identities, sorrow, and love all dwell here, and you (as Viola) can perceive ever so subtly, like some faint piece of music, the power of what is to come just by standing quietly and letting your body touch into the energy of this land.

I believe Shakespeare understood the Power of Place and could evoke it so richly that we can still feel it in his plays today. I also believe he gave Viola this immense gift. She carries a personal sense of place both within her body and through the energy field around her. She melds her own Power of Place into the sacred stage of Illyria and its wild, wily, unforgettable people with such grace and authority that everyone is blessed by her presence. She uses her own sacred stage so elegantly that others feel more alive, more loving, more themselves when she is around.

The goal now is to make it possible for you to imitate Shakespeare and Viola and begin to create, both in imagination and in reality, a vibrant sense of your own "stage setting."

## THE GROUND YOU STAND UPON

Illyria was a real country in antiquity; it was where Albania is now. But just as Shakespeare filled it with magic, you can experience places that have the same charm and mystery. *Magical* is a word used to describe many powerful places on earth. Such places carry potent qualities of remembrance and renewal, holiness and history. Some have been so celebrated that people throughout the ages have created temples and monuments to mark them. Stonehenge in England, the Taj Mahal in India, the Western Wall in Jerusalem, and the Greek Parthenon are examples. While the intention of the ancestors who built in such spots may have been to acknowledge a power they felt in the land, for visitors today part of the wonder is in the design of the monuments as well as the stones and marble used to create them.

In some countries, the tradition is to set up prayer wheels or flags or build a small shrine to honor a particular place that holds power. Some quality in the land itself reminds visitors of their connection to a power outside themselves in such a way that they feel strengthened. Alfonso Ortiz, the well-known anthropologist born in the San Juan Pueblo of New Mexico reminds us of this gift in the traditional Tewa prayer:

> Within and around the earth, within and around the hills,
> within and around the mountains,
> your authority returns to you.[1]

What is the source of such power, and how does it support life and the play of life? Dylan Thomas describes it as a force that connects, causes to grow, and changes all things, in a poem the title of which is also the first line:

> The force that through the green fuse drives the flower
> Drives my green age . . .
> The force that drives the water through the rocks
> Drives my red blood . . .[2]

If you believe Thomas—and I do—the energy of life is a driving force that we all share, along with the growing flowers and everything else that lives on earth.

❧

## *Pause, Please*

Consider how you have discovered your own power places in the natural world. Have you climbed mountains, trekked deserts, shot river rapids, or felt connected to a particular tree in the local park? Have you marked a special spot with a stone or some other signal that invites people to pause and acknowledge the gifts nature offers to that place?

Reflect on those places where, as in the Tewa prayer, you feel "your authority return to you," where you regain your sense of wonder in being alive and being who you are. Is it an untamed place in nature, or a building created by others to honor the place?

Note the characteristics of your special place: valley, river, desert, creek, lake, trees, rocks, mountain, plains, rich fields, plants, buildings, jungle. Is it vast or small? What happens when you visit there? Can you feel the "green fuse" force? Does the experience grow each time you return? What occurs when you go to that place in your imagination?

Now on paper sketch in the features of the landscape. Make a note of how you respond to it. These jottings can become foundation elements for the sacred stage you will want to design for the play of your life.

(Note: In our work with this chapter, I urge you to draw as well as write. Even if, like me, you "can't draw," the effort to do so uses a different part of the brain, and attempting to draw a leaf or a mountain calls attention to the miracle that they are, which is a great part of the joy of engaging the Power of Place.)

## THE PHYSICAL BODY YOU INHABIT

The second element for establishing the Power of Place is your physical body. Any work in theatre demands a vigorous understanding of the body and its relationship to other bodies. As you again imagine yourself as Shakespeare's Viola, you observe, from the inside, how the Power of Place affects the body.

*Twelfth Night* begins with a young nobleman, Orsino, the Duke of Illyria, meditating aloud on the relationship between music and love:

> If music be the food of love, play on,
> Give me excess of it . . . (1.1.1–2)

It seems that the Countess Olivia, with whom Orsino is madly in love, does not love him. He pines and languishes and sends an endless stream of ineffective messengers to court the lady for him.

Now enter a body alive with the Power of Place—Viola, after having been shipwrecked and cast ashore. She fears that her twin brother, Sebastian, has drowned. But even while she grieves, she feels herself joyously alive. Because Viola is a heroine in this play, as you are in yours, she opens herself to the Power of Place. The land she now stands on in the magical country of Illyria gives her the strength to acknowledge that everything has changed. She has lost all: her family, her belongings, and even her identity. She has not, however, lost her sense of physical self; her body is still intact and capable of embarking on a daring adventure.

The world is too rough for a young, single woman, so she cannot continue safely in her own person. Embracing her body's physical power and its emerging partnership with her new country, she devises a plan to protect herself, explore the land, learn from it, and make the best of everything. When she learns from her captain that Orsino is the duke of this country, she says,

> Conceal me what I am, and be my aid
> For such disguise as haply shall become
> The form of my intent. I'll serve this Duke. (1.2.49–51)

Pretending to be her brother, Viola seeks to serve the only person worthy of her station, that same nobleman who pines for love. Though aware of her vulnerability, the mode she chooses for survival is to assume a playful, seductive disguise. The charm of her physical presence changes everyone she meets. Ultimately, she finds and wins her beloved (none other than Count Orsino), is restored to her twin, and, with the count, rules the land that rescued her from the sea.

Although Viola never states so directly, I believe that some sense of Dylan Thomas's "force that through the green fuse drives the flower" is what she recognizes in Illyria and what gives her strength. Remember that she was shipwrecked and fully expected to drown; her survival constitutes a rebirth, and her body opens in gratitude to receive the primal energy from the earth on which she now stands.

You, too, can ask your body to open reverently to the "force that through the green fuse drives the flower." You might feel the force as an energy wave, surging up from the ground through your body and then reaching out to embrace the same power coming from the sky above and from other beings: people, rocks, trees, animals, even so-called inanimate objects—telephone poles, tin warehouses, homes, offices. Immersed in such waves of potency, you murmur with Viola, "What country, friends, is this?"

This "country," your physical body, is itself a field of wonder and your authentic homeland. Perhaps, like Viola, you have struggled to be here. The journey of being born, growing up, and making your way through the world is not unlike being shipwrecked (again and again) and having to battle to reach the shore. By now, you have endured many of life's catastrophes—disappointments, failures, betrayals, losses—and perhaps you lie on the sand exhausted.

Living life as Sacred Theatre asks that you imitate Viola by honoring your body's life force and its capacity to pull you up and help you begin anew—over and over again. So respect the body, first for its endurance and then as a vital piece of your sacred stage. The body is the core place where the immense play of your life reveals itself. No matter where you find yourself, in what strange country, your body's wisdom contains the capacity to encounter and happily share the sacred Power of Place.

## Pause, Please

Your physical body is innately able to renew itself and maintain its well-being. But when you *intentionally* ask it to engage the Power of Place, you increase that ability exponentially in creating a partnership with the most potent life force of all, that of the earth. This partnership can sustain and even augment the body's strength. For example, if you are scheduled to meet with people who make you feel vulnerable, you might imagine that you stand protected within the sheltering arms of an ancient oak tree.

More playfully, go outside to the nearest expression of nature around you. Notice what you observe the natural world doing: emerging, climbing, attaching, insisting, flourishing, drooping, creeping, rippling, waving at the sun. Then focus on one thing: a tree, a blade of grass, a flower. Notice everything you can about it: its shape, its color(s), its way of expressing that "green fuse." Touch it and let it touch you. I believe your attention strengthens its energy, and I believe its energy can strengthen you. Allow that exchange to expand, so that you consciously open your body to embrace more and more of the natural world around you. And allow your body to feel embraced by the green, the gold, the flowering, the sturdiness, the gallantry of growing things.

Look at your earlier notes and sketches of your personal power place. Now sketch or imagine your body in the scene, and begin to feel the connections between you and the earth. The goal is to restore these sacred connections. Your notes and sketches will become your "home stage," the base that supports you, alive in your imagination no matter where you are.

## Your Energy Field

Immediately surrounding your physical body is space utterly sacred to you, unique to you, and, to some extent, within your conscious control. It is your energy field, the third element of the Power of Place. The forces of your physical cells and atoms, and the organs they comprise, interact to give off compelling waves and frequencies. These move out, forming beautiful, colorful patterns around the physical body. This space can be felt as the province of divinity, a holy of holies. Your mindfulness strengthens and protects it and, in turn, it sustains your physical body in profound ways.

In world esoteric and energy-healing traditions, this energy body is known by several names, including the aura, the rainbow body, and the subtle body. Hindus describe it in terms of wheels of energy called *chakras*. Many wise people see it as layered. The well-known healer Barbara Brennan teaches that the various layers within the energy body contain different colors, experiences, and information: mental, emotional, etheric, and so on. Rosalyn Bruyere, another famous healer, works with the energy body to relieve conditions on the physical plane.

The remarkable teacher Donna Eden describes a healthy energy field as one that looks and feels like a luminous, buoyant Celtic weaving. I conceive of it as living in a vital continuum with your physical body, though it has a broader range of awareness. This field is totally aware of itself as containing a great portion of your own Power of Place, while interfacing in turn with the power that exists in everything around you. Filling this energy field with intention and beauty adds to your ability to play the great play of your life.

## *Pause, Please*

Now experiment with sensing your personal energy field. By rubbing your hands together and then pulling them apart and bringing them slowly back together, it is possible first to charge that space and then to feel it. How far out does the field of energy seem to go? Does it have a strong boundary, or does it waft off? Some people who work with this field describe it as extending above your head by twelve to fourteen inches, around your body to the width of your outstretched arms, and then below your feet by twelve to fourteen inches. Energy healers can "see" its layers, sense gaps or holes in it, and find ways of working that strengthen it.

One way to engage the Power of Place through our personal energy field is to imagine that powerful, living earth symbols are stored within it. These symbols can change according to need. For example, if you need to feel more flexible, invite a willow tree to inhabit your energy body along your spine; if you wish to feel more compassion for a hurting friend, fill the energy space at your heart with blooming, red roses. Or if you are off-center, feel your energy body firmly planted on a living rock.

# CHAPTER FOUR

## ENERGIES IN THE WORLD AROUND YOU

The fourth element in experiencing the Power of Place is the people and things, including their energy fields, in the environment surrounding you at any given moment. These people, things, and fields interact with us through a complex tangle of needs, emotions, and physical and psychological states. Someone consciously attuned to the plant world can sense a tree's need for water. Most of us can enter a room and find ourselves responding, perhaps below the level of awareness, to the unseen currents that are present: a recent quarrel, a moment of tenderness, a mood of hilarity, and so on.

As you learn to engage these energies, you may find yourself living within several strands of what is called reality. Let's return to *Twelfth Night* to gain a glimpse of those many strands.

When Viola struggles to shore early in the play, the audience is invited to imagine that they, too, have just experienced the overwhelming waters of a huge storm at sea. (The movie *Shakespeare in Love* ends with such a scene, when the heroine, also named Viola, is shipwrecked and struggles to reach a sandy, palm-treed shore). As a worthy, imaginative audience member, you will see before you and almost feel under your feet the reality of land, a beautiful, succoring, welcoming land, with sheltering rocks, perhaps, and friendly trees, all with an energetic force that reaches out to bring the actor safely home.

In actuality, though, all most audiences will see is a constructed stage, probably open and bare, because the scene will quickly shift to another part of the country. But concurrent with your awareness of being in a theatre, you as audience member may enjoy feeling that you have landed on the enchanted shores of Illyria, where magic, madness, mistaken identities, and dizzy romance are about to overtake you. You may sense these things, even if unconsciously, just as the actors do, although it is true that each actor's sense of Illyria will be different, as will that of each audience member, guided by the imagination of the actors, who are themselves guided by each other, the designers, the director, and the playwright. Seeing the charmed world of Illyria this way, within the trappings of a stage and the minds of many artists, gives us practice in experiencing a multitude of realities at one and the same time.

As you again imagine yourself as Viola, you can see that you and your fellow actors must rigorously evoke the precise feeling of the sand and rocks and beautiful shore that now greets you joyously: you are safe instead of drowned! At the same time, as an actor you must be constantly aware that you are standing on a physical stage. Where is your light? You must consider your capacity to be heard when you speak your lines, not to mention the intense emotional content that your body and your voice must express.

Compounding these multiple realities, you must acknowledge that the whole thing is imaginary; you are performing in a play before an audience, and your job is to enact this particular story with grace and truth and skill. In a word, as an actor onstage, you need to have established a powerful sense of place within your body and within your energy field (which is no longer yours alone but also Viola's). What's more, you must relate moment by moment to everything around you so vividly that the air crackles and scintillates. The stage, the other actors, and the scenery itself all shine with aliveness when you thus invoke the Power of Place.

Those are some of the issues that exist for an actor in the theatre. Are they similar for you as an actor on the stage of life? I believe that they are, and that, in life, the challenge is even more spectacular.

In a stage production, the designer arranges every element in order to provide the ground of being for the life onstage. In exactly the same way, our challenge is to engage all elements around us as a way of creating a ground of being to support the play of life. The great stage we live on pleads with us to stay aware of the Power of Place with the goal of cherishing all life as sacred. An important verb in this process is *to honor*. If we simply honor that rose bush, this tree, this friend, it is often enough.

## CHAPTER FOUR

## A Walk through Dreamtime

Nowhere have I witnessed such honoring of the environment as in Australia. Traditional Aboriginal understanding explains the origin of all things in a space/time commonly called Dreamtime. Dreamtime is a mythic concept in that it is conceived of being still alive and generating creative power as long as the people honor it, sing it, dance it, and participate in it.

Aboriginals embody their sense of Dreamtime by living in the dynamic continuum of the physical body, the energy body, and the earth body. In this way they consummately illustrate the interplay of elements in what I call the personal sacred stage. These are people who for perhaps sixty thousand years have known themselves as essential to the sacred space that is their land and who live in union with the earth and all its creatures.

Each feature in the Aboriginal Australian landscape emits the Power of Place so strongly that ignoring it can be perilous to one's emotional health. For example, on the paths around the huge monolith that is Uluru (Ayers Rock) are caves for women's spiritual work and other areas that "belong" to tribal men. Trespassing into such places has been known to make people physically sick as well as emotionally uneasy, until an Aboriginal elder accomplishes a "cleansing" of the energy field. I experienced this phenomenon firsthand when I was with a group of women who ventured into another area not far from Sydney to see the rock paintings. It was a place of astounding beauty, with red ochre hand prints on the walls of ancient caves. The European-derived Australians with us, who had been initiated into Aboriginal teachings, turned pale at the very idea of visiting the site, because it was a place of "men's business." Several of us felt shaken, partly because of the profound spiritual power of the place and partly because we could feel the sense of trespass. When we left the area, Aboriginal and initiated Caucasian women met us and resolutely brushed our energy fields with branches of eucalyptus to make sure nothing unhealthy had followed us out.

Correctly acknowledging the sacred Power of Place, on the other hand, can palpably enhance one's well-being, even for people who don't share the history of the Aboriginal. One of my most strengthening experiences was in walking mindfully around Uluru, the mythic center of the continent—all eleven kilometers—and remembering the sacred stories told about it; seeing the rock formations, the colors, the water holes, the tender green shrubs and bushes; and standing still enough to honor the fenced-off areas of tribal initiation grounds. Perhaps it is the red earth and red rock, with all that iron in it, that makes one feel stronger, but I believe that the power is in the land itself, a land whose native peoples have honored it as a living being since time out of mind. One senses more keenly there than anywhere else I know that the earth is alive and emits a potent field that can sustain all who live within it.

How did this life force grow so strong there?

Aboriginal creation stories tell of ancestral beings who came out of the dreaming nothingness and began to move, creating the land as they traveled and sang. Each action they took, each need for food or water or sex or a fight with an invader, molded the landscape. Everywhere these beings sang the land into being, so that the land holds astonishing storied power. The people remember. They remember the songs and the stories and believe that if they fail to tell them and sing them, the land will cease to exist. And the land remembers.

Every one of the storied places where something happened—a birth, a quarrel, a delicious meal—can be experienced for the Power of Place. One can stand, as I was allowed to do, in Arnhem Land in the Northern Territories, at the very spot where according to myth two of the Dreaming ancestors, King Brown Snake and Pelican, met on their journeys and sang songs to each other. You can hear their voices— I swear it—even European-derived people can hear their voices. And the land sings with them.[3]

Humans have the deep privilege of being the keepers of these stories, ensuring that everything stays alive. They also have the power to become one with their mythic ancestors as they reenact those ancestors' adventures. A friend in Australia told me of a wise old Aboriginal man who said that anyone born on the continent, no matter of what lineage, is now a descendant of the Dreaming. I have seen groups of young Australian-born, European-derived "Aboriginals" drop into tribal-deep enactment of serpent, kangaroo, wallaby, and crocodile at the sound of the didgeridoo. Such reenactment is entertaining, yes, and when appropriately offered as sacred it helps to keep the land flourishing for all people, Aboriginals and non-Aboriginals. Creation and destruction happen every moment, and the land retains its power only as the people sing it and give it life by enacting, painting, and remembering it. Belonging to the tribe of Pelican or Crocodile, or any of the ancestral beings, means that you have a totem who is also a relative, a friend, and a protector.[4] But that connection goes both ways, as the acclaimed Aboriginal writer, Oodgeroo Noonuccal (formerly Kath Walker), explains:

> According to Aboriginal totemic belief each member of the clan automatically inherited at birth a totemic relationship with a particular plant or animal of the region. They thereby became responsible for the general welfare of that species. The word *Oodgeroo*, for example, means "paperbark tree." The bearer of the totem would count these elegant saplings as part of their family. While individual plants or animals might be used to serve tribal needs, a decline of the species reflected badly on its human relatives. It was this deep, familial interdependence, universally practiced throughout Aboriginal Australia, that held the key to their remarkably low impact on regional ecologies that were, in some cases, exceptionally fragile.[5]

Thus a descendant of the mythical Dingo is responsible for the well-being of all dingoes today; a descendant of the Willie Wagtail feels responsible for ensuring the health and survival of all these charming and gregarious birds.

I once watched a wise Aboriginal woman, whom I'll call Mary, demonstrate the dance/story of her ancestral being, the Emu—that huge, mystical-seeming bird (related to the ostrich) with a feathered head, lovely eyes, long and swiftly moving legs, and stately, majestic walk.

The only way I can describe what happened is this: Emu, the woman's ancestor, simply reached out, embraced her, and entered.

In theatrical terms, it seemed a modest action. On a very warm day in Southeastern Australia, a group of us were resting in the shade of a stand of trees near the beach. Our teacher, Jean Houston, was talking about how humans seem to recapitulate the entire process of evolution as they form in the womb and then live as babies and young children. Comparing that story to the Aboriginal traditions, she asked Mary, one of the participants, to share what it was like to be a member of the Emu family.

Mary's response was unaffected, yet profound. Without any "art" or guile, she became Emu, showing us its life purpose, which is to dance, to move ever forward, and to honor the world with its beautiful feathers. Mary and Emu share other private knowings, no doubt, but those were the ones I had eyes to see. Emu was both at home in its sacred landscape and at every moment *creating* that landscape. We in the audience quaked into new aliveness as we witnessed the personal energy field of the woman change shape until she became the bird. And because she did it with honor, with cherishing and belief, she touched into all those humans of her bloodline who share Emu as a mythic ancestor. She also touched into Emu as a living species today and all its forebears (in fact, as a true Aboriginal she feels herself responsible for their well-being), and she touched into the entire landscape that the mythic Emu helped create in the days of the Dreamtime.

In some magical way, Mary's knowledge of her Power of Place, given to her as a birthright and maintained despite painful and disrespectful treatment in many circumstances, generously provided an exquisite understanding of that power for all of us. Moreover, we who witnessed her expression felt our own energy fields grow stronger.

That was the beginning of my belief that if we engage the Power of Place honorably and use it artfully, we can strengthen ourselves, our ancestors, our neighbors, and our world. This is the challenge and delight of being sacred actors occupying sacred space. We charge our bodies with awareness of space; we fill the energy field around us with light and color, making a connection to some vital force—divine or ancestral, animal or tree, or some other version of the high self. Then, in that authority, we acknowledge that the air around us and the earth beneath us are alive and shimmering in response to our desire to give homage.

Hence one of our purposes in life—to create and recreate the spaces around us in ways that support us, thus making it possible to tell our great story more beautifully. And it is good to realize that by relating eloquently to the sacred landscape around us, we enliven and renew the earth itself in a mutually restoring dance.

I cannot close this discussion without referring to the mind-boggling work of scientists experimenting on what award-winning investigative journalist Lynne McTaggart calls the "The Field." This is the Zero Point Field, where the tiny energy quanta of the universe interact together, joining, forming, reforming, and disappearing in a sea of unimaginable intensity. Each interaction is infinitesimal. "But," as McTaggart says, "if you add up all the particles of all varieties in the universe constantly popping in and out of being, you come up with a vast, inexhaustible energy source . . . all sitting there unobtrusively in the background of the empty space around us, like one all-pervasive, supercharged backdrop."[6] She goes on to cite physicist Richard Feynman in saying that "the energy in a single cubic meter of space is enough to boil all the oceans of the world."[7]

What is useful for us to understand is that we are a part of this incomprehensible energy field: it acts on us, and we act on it. As it affects us, so we may affect it, with intention, awareness, and honor.

## *Pause, Please*

Add to your notes and sketches any realizations you may have gained about the importance of other people and things, and especially their energies, in the world around you. What elements feel most essential? What relationship(s) most sacred? What most powerful? Notice how your own energy has interacted with that of other people and places. How have they changed you? How may you have changed them?

Now imagine the dense reality of "The Field," that fierce activity of quantum relationships that occupies every corner of existence. Sense its potency in the space between you and this book, or you and your journal. Picture the way your energy field mingles with the Zero Point Field, and vice versa. Consider your capacity to "sweeten" The Field with loving kindness or with exquisite images of beauty. Try that for a few minutes, and then notice how you feel.

## CREATING YOUR STAGE

Now the fun starts! It is now possible to begin creating your personal sacred stage. Though it is an imaginary construct, this stage will serve to ground you, enhance your creativity, and deepen your relationship to everything and everyone in your environment. Again, the four elements of the Power of Place that make up your stage are the ground you stand on, your physical body, your energy field, and the world around you. Recognizing that you have the whole world to choose from, you can select and design those scenic elements that support your needs and provide meaningful surroundings to help you live accurately and richly.

The Power of Place is a communal, organic creation between you and your environment, drawing upon that primal energy that infuses all things. The impulse to play with that energy is the same impulse that allowed the first musician, listening to the air moving through leaves and grasses, to imagine an instrument that could make music with the sounds of the wind. For sacred players, the initial creative act is one of acknowledgment: Basic life energy is holy. Playful. Wild. Engaging. Worthy of respect and responding only to respect. And with respect—with full awareness that the action is holy—the sacred player studies that energy and imaginatively constructs a stage on which to celebrate the great play of life.

Even though it is only available to your inner senses, the Power of Place is so strong that others can feel it; it can help keep you safe yet appropriately vulnerable, not fortressed. And while all the powers of Sacred Theatre require imagination, none does so more than this one, in part because you can keep changing its elements. The personal stage is imaginary, therefore totally flexible. You, as the ultimate scenic designer, utilize whatever exists around you and then add pleasing features to help you perform with ease, strength, and joy. You are the one who controls and guides your individual Power of Place. You are the one who will play with it to discover its uses for your life experience. It is time to begin creating.

## IMITATE THE PROFESSIONALS

In the traditional theatre, gifted designers create a setting in which the story can be told to greatest effect and in which the actors feel absolutely supported. A memorable production of *King Lear*, for example, featured moveable set pieces that looked like the huge stones at Stonehenge. The different ways they were arranged—overwhelmingly close or wide apart and lonely—heightened our awareness of how monumental the play is and how awesome the great battle that takes place in Lear's soul.

The stage setting also often provides indications of mood and emotional atmosphere. In a recent production of *Twelfth Night*, the designer placed Duke Orsino in a luxurious Turkish palace, with giant cushions and divans strewn around on rich carpets and with flowing draperies to catch the breezes. This setting vividly communicated Orsino's wealth and power, the languor of his court, and his utter enchantment by an unrequited love. It not only assisted him in portraying his love sickness, it also became part of the seductive energy that so captivated Viola when she entered with all her brash, young "male" energy.

THE POWER OF PLACE

The most talented designers supply features that not only help tell a story but also subtly return everyone, consciously or unconsciously, player and audience alike, to the great stream of being from which theatre springs. These features are:

1. *The "dancing ground"*—the platform or floor—on which the action of your life takes place and which contains a potent sense of both your personal and your cultural homeland. This area should include space for an altar.

2. *The backdrop* which frames the area. This feature is the most flexible and one that you may change daily, or moment by moment, according to need.

3. *The World Tree*, a symbol of the connection between the world above and the world below.

As you fashion your personal stage, you will want to become aware of what comprises your own dancing ground. You will become conscious of the scenery you choose and aware of the particular "World Tree" that for you connects the realms of heaven and earth and the inner earth. You can create your stage in such a way that it serves to make you more comfortable, to remind you of beauty and your essential purpose, and to strengthen your sense of inner space for the work of participating fully in the story of Life on Earth.

## THE DANCING GROUND

The platform on which the play takes place represents the earth. Even if it depicts a palace floor, it always symbolizes the ground that supports us. I call it the dancing ground because, even though it may resemble a boxing ring or a jousting field, it originates in the circle around the campfire where our ancestors enacted the stories of their tribes.

## The Four Elements

It helps in constructing your dancing ground to include some illustration of the basic elements of earth, water, fire, and air. Our ancestors believed these four elements to be present in all things. Even though stage designers today may not be conscious of the importance of representing them, gifted ones will nevertheless provide some hint of them, if only subtly and subliminally. For example, a light bulb shining from a tenement window can hold the fire element; a curtain at that window reminds us of air; a table with flowers in the center provides earth; and a pitcher nearby, water.

Shakespeare provides the four elements in his plays' characters and action, perhaps in part because the theatres of his time boasted little scenery. His characters tell us where we are. In *Twelfth Night*, the captain says, "This is Illyria, lady." This beautifully balanced play has characters who sing, bringing in air; characters who burn with the fires of passionate love; and characters who supply the element of water by weeping, not to mention those who arrive from the sea—Viola and Sebastian. And some characters are so earthy (like Sir Toby Belch) that they seem to exude that element.

If any of the four elements is noticeably absent, it may be because it needs to be called forth in order to bring the characters into balance. In *Twelfth Night*, Olivia's refusal to return Orsino's love fills him with too much earth/water melancholy. Likewise Olivia, overcome with sorrow at her brother's death, keeps herself and her household shrouded in black (water), refusing the comforts of laughter, song, or love. Then enter Viola, fresh from the wild ocean but now restored and ready to bring real fire and real air to the scene. She and her miraculously rescued brother, with their fine balance of life elements, transform the society in which they find themselves and infuse it with true joy.

This matter of balance among the elements could be seen in part as what distinguishes a comedy from a tragedy, the latter ending with no restoration of equilibrium. I think of the Euripides' tragedy *The Trojan Women*. There exists no growing thing onstage, no life in the earth of the destroyed city. The only water is the tears the women shed as they say goodbye to their homeland, and the play ends with a huge fire burning what is left of Troy. One leaves the theatre believing that there is no air left to breathe, no water, and precious little earth.

In Shakespeare's *Antony and Cleopatra*, Cleopatra speaks of herself as comprising the elements: "I am fire and air; my other elements I give to baser life" (5.2.290). The charming and ironic truth is that, throughout the play, this dear, errant queen displays a dizzying capacity to shift from earthiness to fluidity and back again, with flashes of passionate fire and occasional exploits into the quick and infinitely various realms of her mind (air). After her and Antony's suicides, what remains is only the cool, Roman intelligence of Octavius Caesar, who shows none of the elements of authentic life. With his grim force of arms he conquers over the sumptuous, so-seductive land of earth and water that is Egypt and leaves us in a world more unbalanced and less colorful than before.

## A Sense of Home

To balance your "dancing ground," then, you would do well to pay attention to the elements, both in your self and in your environment. More importantly, this ground should include a deep sense of home. Even if the role you are playing now is that of a poor wayfaring stranger, something on your sacred stage should contain a whisper of home— your soul's home, your spiritual home, perhaps, but home.

The word *home* itself evokes a profound sense of the Power of Place, especially the childhood home, with its memories of seasons and holidays and playgrounds. Even should you be a nomad, no longer feeling connected to that place of origins, you remember it. Even if, more painfully, what you remember is what "should have been" but never was, there is still nostalgia in the very word *home*. The "home" element of the Power of Place springs primarily from memory, memory tied to landscape, to latitude and longitude, and to the senses: the smell of honeysuckle and the taste of homemade cinnamon rolls, the creak of the glider on the front porch and the chirp of crickets singing, the sight of flocks of birds changing course over cotton fields, learning to swim in lazy lake water, standing under a pelting rainstorm and shouting back at the thunder.

My own dancing ground consists of a layer of black dirt from my childhood home in Texas; near the center is the jasmine bush my grandfather planted when he married my grandmother and brought her to live on his piece of rich, black soil. Zinnias, the indestructible flowers I once planted along the path leading to the front door, line the whole space. The element of earth is strong here; water also—this is humid, rain-rich southeast Texas!—and the grass grows green. The element of air is present in the waving of the flowers in the breeze and in the birds that flock overhead. Fire is present in the vivid colors of the zinnias and in the passionate love my grandparents shared.

If I need to go to a quiet place in my mind, this is the first place I visit. If I am mentally rehearsing a conversation or presentation, this is the first stage on which I practice. In my experience, this imaginary dancing ground will give me the first hint of something I need to do. I may not know that I feel stuck, but suddenly there will appear a fountain of clear, gushing water. Or I may not be aware that things are dull, but suddenly fireworks begin exploding. These are definite cues for rethinking and redoing.

## *Pause, Please*

Make some notes about your sense of home in order to choose its essential physical elements. As a child, what space allowed you to feel free and strong, playful and creative? Focus on the places that gave you extra fortitude or a sense of sweet refuge. Which elements fed you with power—a garden, a lilac tree, an imaginary cave under the bed, a tree house, or porch steps where you could see the stars? Remembering that you are a gifted scenic designer, how might you include some power elements from your sense of home in the imaginary, but very real, dancing ground of your stage today?

## A Sense of History

The sense of belonging evoked by the idea of home can include historic places important to our many tribes. At some such sites we celebrate; at others we mourn and pray. This, Americans say in wonder, is where our ancestors signed the Declaration of Independence! This bustling marketplace was once a slave auction. On this peaceful, green hillside our great-grandfathers fought a dreadful battle.

The United States still bleeds from the unacknowledged wounds of those fatal hills and marketplaces. Though perhaps invisible, those wounds are all too present on the stage we occupy as a nation. Because we as a people do not collectively mourn for them (perhaps since opening the door to such grief would overwhelm us), we must learn to do so as individuals. The air around such places—Gettysburg, for example—holds a trembling frequency that allows us, for a moment, to touch the past and the lives of those who died there. Standing in such a place is like standing at a potent, fragile crossroads of time; if the tiniest detail had changed, everything in our present lives might be different. As we construct our personal stages, we need to tune into those places that are part of our history, for good and for ill. We will be more capable sacred actors if we consciously include some symbol of the wounded places in our dancing ground, not to weaken us or make us feel guilty, but to remind us that we are part of the human family and that it is not a perfect one. These symbols of the pain inflicted on others remind us that all actions have consequences far beyond the present; they inspire us to be more mindful of what we say and do in every moment.

I include such a symbol as part of the altar I place in the center of my own imaginary dancing ground. It began as a cotton cloth embroidered with the names of places—fields, states, territories—where my ancestors fought with one another or with others they saw as less than human. Recently, I have placed over the cloth an eternal flame honoring the places where people, animals, and plants have died from war or hunger or injustice or human cruelty, places where the spirit of the land is damaged because of human action. Rather than making me sad, this altar asks me to remember and to be ever more aware of my words and deeds, even my thoughts. It asks me to be more willing to take responsibility quickly when I hurt others and to be alert and politically responsive when the sacred Power of Place in and around other people is being damaged.

## *Pause, Please*

As you move outward from your individual sense of home to include potent places of ancestral memory on your imaginary personal stage, what do you find? The birthplace of your grandmother in a tiny village on the coast of Norway? The sacred sites among the Black Hills where your ancestors went for ceremony and to pray? Perhaps you feel the urge to travel way back to a place of origins, like the Olduvai Gorge in Africa where the Leakey family and their colleagues have discovered footprints and bones of our earliest parents. Or do you feel called to a place of incredible accomplishment by our forebears: the Great Wall of China, the Parthenon in Athens, the magnificent Mexican city of Teotihuacan, the tantalizing mystery cities in Zimbabwe?

The essential thing is to "remember" those sites where your ancestors survived long enough to have children who survived. Notice the primary physical elements as you know or imagine them to be.

Again, picture yourself as a gifted set designer, at work on a scenery project that will win an award for its beauty and creativity. What features from the world of your ancestors would you include on your dancing ground?

# THE BACKDROP

In the traditional theatre, the backdrop frames the scene and gives focus to the action in front of it. Perhaps it shows a pastoral landscape or a cityscape with buildings or a wall. It can be an exterior or an interior. It can depict the gray starkness of army barracks or a lush palace with flowing, colorful silks. In any case, the backdrop informs the audience about the world in which the play takes place. It also provides doors, windows, and other forms of entrances and exits, as well as escape hatches and places to hide.

Whatever the setting for your personal story, it needs to be one that supports your intention as a sacred player. In my own experience, I notice that, while my sense of my dancing ground remains the same, the surrounding scenery shifts according to my circumstance, mood, and need. Of the three features that comprise your personal stage, this one of background scenery is the most flexible and can grow richer with experience. A recent visit to the Maldives, for instance, adds the presence of a tranquil, turquoise sea to my personal scenic surround.

It is possible to "create" this backdrop as a meditation. It is also possible to call up the needed scenic elements while busily engaged in the work of the moment. When I want total exhilaration, I create for my personal scenery my memory of the northern tip of the northern island of New Zealand, a place high above the meeting of three seas, tumultuous and windswept. It's where Maori people begin the journey back to their spiritual homeland after they die. At other times, when I want more endurance, I "paint" in beautiful rocks and sturdy trees and feel myself firmly situated in the circle they create. Or perhaps I'm asking for greater vision, in which case my background scenery will be a high mountain lookout, with farseeing eagles soaring by.

# *Pause, Please*

Begin to construct your inner ideal stage from experience or from the notes and sketches you made earlier. The delightful thing about building sets in your imagination is that you can change them easily and frugally. As you consider the scenic background for your primary action, you may decide you want it to represent a place of awesome beauty. Or perhaps it is the place to include your ancestral monuments. Often the ancients built on high places; even in a flat landscape they worked to erect tall stones or pyramids, creations that invite one to climb up or to look over. These are places that multitudes of others have felt as powerful and where the builders' achievements fill us with awe even today. Would any portion of them serve you well as the backdrop of your play? Would a touch of Stonehenge or the Great Pyramid give you a sense of strength and protection?

Other things to consider: Where do you feel peaceful? Where exhilarated? What features, if any, do your favorite places share? What occurs when you stop whatever you are doing and go to that place in your imagination? Do you breathe better? Do you find yourself expanding? Do you feel at home?

Now imagine that you, as a brilliant scenic designer, are creating a setting for a very important person in your life. What would you include? A glimpse of the Pacific Ocean? A sentinel redwood tree? A basket of golden prairie grasses? All of the above? Notice that you don't need the whole ocean or an entire range of mountains; you need only a vibrant representative of the whole—like a single, glowing, California poppy.

## The World Tree

The third essential feature of your personal stage is a representation of the World Tree, some kind of pole or pillar that links the three realms of heaven, earth, and the underworld. An actor can use this simulation as a ladder to ascend or descend at need in order to support the emotions that fit each realm within her character.

You may already have put a tree on your personal stage, either in your background scenery or in the central area—offering shade or an invitation to climb or a swing to enjoy. It need not be an actual tree; a telephone pole or an iron scaffold will fulfill the same purpose if it seems rooted in the earth while reaching toward the sky.

For me, the most important and permanent part of my inner sacred stage is not one, but three, pear trees. They symbolize the three trees that still stand in a line between the cotton field and the hay field on the farm in Texas where I was reared. My mother, when she was learning to work with oils, painted those trees during their three seasons. So the most potent symbols of my sacred stage have a physical correlate. Through them I am connected not only to the three trees on the family farm, but also, somehow, to *all* pear trees. Thousands of miles away from those trees in Texas, I live in a valley famous for its pear orchards. Because those three trees have been with me all my life, and because they form the heart of my sacred stage, I've written these words in their honor:

**Pear Trees in Winter**

Three brides, remember;
Three mothers, remember;
Three ancient dancers,
hold up your barren arms to beseech the winter sky;
have you lived long enough to trust the earth?
Will it grow warm again?
Even now in this dark sky,

some loving breeze is waiting
to shake out your wedding veils
and begin again the beauty work
that spins a spell so strong
the bees coming flying to the source.
Listen, you can hear them in the wind:
Enchantment, Enchantment.

## *Pause, Please*

Create a poem about your own World Tree. Or draw it. Writing or sketching helps stabilize the work you do in the imagination. As you invoke the natural world on the playing ground of daily life, you gain in strength, and so, I believe, does the natural world. Writing about those pear trees, I become more energized; and I imagine that those pear trees across the miles in Texas open to new life, while the pear trees in this valley also catch the drift and respond. But I'm not trying to persuade you of that phenomenon. It is important only to believe that you are expanding your imagination in ways that add to your sum total of awareness and joy.

## TAKING YOUR STAGE ON THE ROAD

As you have experienced, creating your personal stage is the work of the imagination, augmented with notes, poems, sketches, photographs, or whatever your chosen medium. Now we begin the process of making the features of your stage available at all times to your body and of consciously bringing that stage into your body's energy field. Finally, we will pay attention to our outer stages—where we live and where we work—and align them with the beauty and power of the inner stage.

## The Signature Piece

You are invited to select at least one aspect of your stage as your "signature piece." This feature may be part of your physical body or a permanent part of the field around it. It is a single, meaningful thing to you (tree, mountain, lake, flower) that reminds you of your true home. Like other features of your inner stage, the signature piece can shift and change, but it provides an ever-renewing touch of grace that can connect you kindly to a sense of place. Happily, we have the entire world for inspiration.

One quick way to bring your inner and outer stages into alignment is to have an illustration of your signature piece physically present at home or on your desk. But for now, let's discuss the nature and further uses of a scenic signature piece.

A friend recently endured a difficult operation in a hospital a long way from home. We talked about the stage elements she wanted to take with her to clear and enliven the hospital space. She spoke of coming upon a leafy bush during a recent walk on a mountainside. As she approached the bush, clouds of turquoise butterflies rose from it, hovered for an enchanted moment in the air, and then settled back. She decided to invite that bush and those butterflies to be around her during her time in the hospital; when a nurse or doctor entered her room, in her imagination she saw the butterflies fly up and settle around each person's head and body. Throughout her stay, she remarked about how unusually caring and kind the hospital staff people seemed. They probably are caring and kind under any circumstances, but I believe her turquoise butterflies helped everyone have an easier time.

Of all the stages you can devise, you will soon find several that feel exactly right for making each day more vibrant. Eventually, you will find yourself selecting a feature of your sacred stage that you wish to keep with you at all times. This becomes your signature piece, as mine is the three pear trees. Those trees walk with me everywhere; their presence is vivid even in the dankest street. For me, they occupy that part of my sacred stage that is my physical body. We grew together, sharing nutriments from the same soil. Breathing different components of the same air, those trees are an indissoluble part of me. If I'm unhappy and want to feel less so, I sense them in riotous bloom and feel bathed in their fragrant white blossoms. Soon, I'm much more cheerful.

If I'm walking down the street feeling lonely, I invite those trees to bear exquisite ripe, luscious pears. Then I make a conscious choice, extending the trees beyond my physical body and asking them to move out into my immediate energy field. In my imagination, I offer a delicious pear to every person I meet. Soon I'm not feeling so lonely and am encountering lots of smiling people. Those pears are "real" and can be sensed by others, including animals, not necessarily as pears but as something warm and sweet with summertime. (Notice I said that others can sense them; they aren't forced to take them. These imaginary gifts are never intended to be invasive.)

## Focusing on Energy Fields

This thought brings us to the interaction of our own sacred stage with that of others—how you and I meet and affect one another in healthful, pleasant ways. Here it is important to focus on the energy field, that part of your sacred stage you carry everywhere with the physical body moving at its core. This field is always working as a primary container of your personal Power of Place and as mediator and bridge to all other forms of matter. As such, it deserves the same respect that an Aboriginal in Australia gives the earth.

This field can also bring us great enjoyment. As you and I walk toward each other on the street, the energy field of each of us is busy, paying attention to the sidewalk and to the energy from the buildings and other people. Every breath brings into the physical body millions of atoms and molecules from everything surrounding us, and information is being exchanged even more intensely between and among the energy fields. Long before we decide to smile at each other (if we do) we have shared huge amounts of data. And if you don't remind me, even subliminally, of somebody I fear or dislike (which would activate an incalculable train of psychological as well as physical responses and make easy exchange between us impossible), then we might enjoy lifetimes together in the space of one smile.

## EXPLORING THE BOUNDARIES OF YOUR STAGE

Because our energy field interrelates so constantly with those of others—animate and inanimate, human, animal, insect, and divine—we need guidelines about how to maintain it with integrity.

A story I love about the ancient Greek goddesses (especially Hera, Queen of Heaven and Earth, and Aphrodite, Goddess of Love and Beauty) tells of their need now and again to visit their favorite bathing places—their spas—in order to restore their virginity. The scholars of such Mysteries infer that the goddesses have poured out all their energy to their loved ones, their friends, and those in need. Now they need to reclaim their energy for themselves. This they do by traveling over land and sea to the holy bath and then soaking in it for a long time. That done, perhaps with other Mysteries unknown to us, the Lady is fully recuperated and ready to be a goddess again. (It is possible to visit the watery cave on the Island of Cyprus where Aphrodite is said to have gone to bathe and restore her virginity; one can also drink of the waters of Hera's bath near the town of Nauplion in the Peloponnesian Peninsula of southern Greece.)

It seems even more necessary for a mere human, who may not have a goddess's resources, to find ways to restore her energy field when it feels depleted. That is, in fact, a major purpose for our work with the sacred stage. Bringing to awareness the Power of Place inherent in the settings we love can restore the energy field to its pristine vigor. So can your work with your signature piece, that element of your sacred landscape that you choose to have with you at all times.

When you really begin to have fun with this work, that central element will tell you when you need to imitate the goddess and head for the spa. Sometimes, for example, when my awareness opens to my pear trees, I sense how thirsty or droopy they are. This image signals that I need to get into some water right away—the best thing for me is to stand under a pelting rainstorm, but any water will do. Or it's time to pull out a blanket, spread it under the trees, and rest for a while.

To revitalize your energy field, it's helpful to bring in color and fragrance and to use all the senses: hear the birds talking, children laughing, wind stirring the leaves. Touch the earth, caress the grass, smell the breeze, chew on a honeysuckle. Such restoration can be done in seconds. As you gain practice, you can ask your sacred stage to do what needs to be done to refresh your energy and know that it will simply be so.

My experience is that this personal stage changes shape and attitude according to need and desire. Walking through a forest on a summer day, we can expand that personal space to include all the woods and all the animals and birds within it in a tender embrace. Likewise, in an intimate evening mood with a beloved friend or lover, we can gently open the energy gates to allow the most profound intermingling of exchanges, knowing that the other person can be trusted with this precious space, knowing that we are safe, as he or she is safe with us.

Conversely, if we are walking down a dark street in an unknown town, we activate the energy field with acute sensing but keep it close at hand and very strong. We may send a ninja aspect of the field ahead on lookout duty; or we may decide to let it melt into invisibility, into the shadow and light in such a way that we are almost indecipherable. In such a situation it is vital not to send out vibrations of challenge.

All of these conditions require practice and willingness to experiment with the field around you until you recognize and come to respect its full power.

It is possible to be invasive with your field; it is also possible to be invaded by another's. This is where boundaries become particularly important. Sometimes our field becomes depleted because we (like the goddess) have given our energy away, and sometimes it becomes depleted because we have no clear understanding of its limits. This lack is most often, in my experience, the result of a wounding in our sense of the sacrality of the body's space and its field, which is common in the case of physical or verbal abuse. In this condition, it is as if the energy field is running up and down the street trying to find a safe haven for the body. Instead of walking serenely toward others, the field frantically sniffs the air and checks others out in ways that may not be appropriate, trying to determine whether it dares to trust in a modicum of safety. Or the field may shrink to accommodate the size we were when the wounding occurred. Sometimes the shock of that wounding is so great that the field itself disappears. (A friend who teaches energy medicine reports that when she worked on a Chernobyl survivor, she experienced the energy field as totally burned away. It took many hours to restore it.)

Working to heal the shockingly wounded sense of place requires a whole village of wise men and women and is outside the province of this chapter. One can begin, however, by paying scrupulous attention to the Power of Place felt in nature and inviting that power to invest the body and its field with beauty and healing. In addition, focusing on the presence of a signature piece for an imaginary sacred stage helps prepare the body and psyche for the possibility of buoyant health. This piece can change with time (or with the seasons, as my pear trees do) or evolve into something else as healing occurs.

For people whose sense of the Power of Place is not overwhelmingly damaged, the signature piece offers solace as needed. It will remind you of when to call your energy back home and when and how to set up flexible, permeable, clear boundaries. If I imagine the pear tree in my body, then my energy field grows above me and below me and around me at a distance that feels right. The blossoms, leaves, and branches create a gentle boundary as well as a beautiful surround. If I need to feel more protected, it's amazing how quickly the branches can become a martial artist's weapons or how suddenly a swarm of bees can appear to warn me of some perceived threat.

# CHAPTER FOUR

## CELEBRATING UNION

This chapter has been about a kind of marriage, a melding of space, place, and imagination. It begins with your physical body, which includes the vast areas of pure space within you. Just becoming aware of the incredible energy in your cells, each of which is invisibly charged with vast whirling forces of movement and attraction, can restore a sense of lightness and spaciousness to life.

To feel also within that physical body the particulars of your life and lineage—to imagine that each cell holds "memory" extending back to before time as we know it—can give you a sense of ever-renewing strength. Made specific, these scenes and imaginings can emanate from your physical body to enliven your energy field.

So this is the first union: those spaces and places of your present and ancestral life that you invite into awareness come together to create the two primary aspects of your personal sacred stage: your body and its energy field.

Another union occurs when your body and its field open out to interact with others, giving and receiving the blessings of place. This union enhances our capacity to love and care for others; the most exquisite experience of the Power of Place is to share it with someone else's.

I enjoy remembering my own marriage as a sacred space where my warrior husband came for a while to rest among my pear trees and where those trees drank his stories and his heritage with fascination and gratitude. I envision his long line of forebears, many of them Hasidic rabbis, dancing their ecstatic love of God with my own Protestant missionary ancestors, who gaze openmouthed and in wonder at such love for the Divine.

When we love another, we give generously and totally; the gift we make is the gift of who we truly are, and the Power of Place provides a significant part of that gift. As we offer friendship and love to one another throughout our lifetime, we share information about, recipes from, and photographs of that power. As we welcome beloved friends, each with her or his own sacred stage, onto our own, we learn to blend energies so dynamically that each of us is richer than we were before.

It is our task as sacred players to be aware of each individual's personal sense of space, to recognize, honor, and connect with it gracefully, with clear good will, and in expectation of the same for ourselves. This skillful interplay demands practice. Not only must you be aware of the sacred space of your own body and its field, but you must also attend to the constant movement of others' fields through yours. And this movement changes you, perhaps only slightly, but definitely. You know that from the times when you have caught a bad mood from someone in just passing or picked up laughter when a child looked up and said, "Hi, lady." Sharing the great stage of life entails a willingness to encounter others in ways that allow us to change and grow together.

The third union is created when you acknowledge that you are prepared to grow with the most holy earth itself, in wisdom, in protection, and in dynamic belonging. According to our birth and upbringing, we each experience the Power of Place as individuals. Our work is to enlarge that sense of location ultimately to include the whole world. At all times we seek to open ourselves to the power of each space we touch, so that each becomes *home*. And all space is sacred in the same way that your personal stage is sacred. No matter what scenery may physically be set upon it—be it the jaws of hell itself—the space is sacred. There is enough holiness in the ground beneath our feet to invest our bodies and our lives with its power, the same power that feeds everything that lives and grows. Once we tap into it, we find ourselves, not just at home, but at Home.

*We'll have a speech straight. Come, give us a taste
of your quality. Come, a passionate speech.*
—Hamlet, in Shakespeare's *The Tragedy of Hamlet,
Prince of Denmark* (2.2.432– 434)

# Five

# The Power of
# Expression

Among his manifold qualities, Shakespeare's Hamlet embodies the Power of Expression, that capacity to discover and present the truth of who he is through language, including his body language as well as, most poignantly, his words. One of Hamlet's endearing characteristics is his love for theatre. In the words on the facing page he is greeting a troupe of touring actors who hope he will sponsor a performance. Their presence inspires Hamlet to set a plot in motion that will enable him to be clear about his own appropriate next action. Thus he uses the Power of Expression, as demonstrated by the traveling performers, to move his personal play forward—just as you may do.

The Power of Expression answers the all-important question about the sacred play of your life: *How?* How do you, as a splendidly incarnate individual, enact your great story, in the ever-present moment, on this sacred stage of planet earth?

Three powers help answer that question: those of Expression, Point of View and Conflict. These are the means for fulfilling your incarnational obligation; through them you give thanks for the precious gift of a human lifetime. This chapter on the Power of Expression focuses on inviting full articulation of all that you are here to be and do.

The word *expression* implies something moving outward that can be seen, heard, and perhaps understood. It also implies a choice, as almost everything in the theatre does. At any given moment, the variety of things that we might choose to express—feelings, ideas, thoughts, associations—is so great that the process of selection can often be difficult. Our work with this power demands that we become clearer in deciding what to express and more skillful in how we do it. A theatrical actor's instrument of expression is his body; most tellingly, his face, his hands, and his voice. This is also true of the sacred actor, whose job is to illustrate as fully as possible her incarnational gift and task.

## Here's the Story

Let's return to Shakespeare. Imagine that you stand center stage in darkness. Lights, one by one, pick out first your dark cloak, then your hat with its feather plume, then your hands, your face. We in the audience watch with eagerness the movement of the muscles of your face and your hands, one of which rests on a dagger's hilt. Your eyes stab fire, twin pistols pointing into the darkness. At exactly the right moment, you begin to speak:

> O, that this too too solid flesh could melt,
> Thaw, and resolve itself into a dew!
> Or that the Everlasting had not fix'd
> His canon 'gainst self-slaughter! O God! God!
> How weary, stale, flat and unprofitable
> Seem to me all the uses of this world! (1.2.129–134)

You, of course, are Hamlet, a prince of the Renaissance, epitomizing, as your beloved Ophelia says, "the glass of fashion and the mould of form"(3.1.156). And yet your speech expresses the quagmire of your despair: your father, a good king, suddenly dead; your mother, Queen Gertrude, married even more suddenly to your uncle, Claudius, who has maneuvered himself onto the throne in your place. Having been away at university, you have now returned home to this upheaval and are expected to behave as if nothing were wrong or out of place. These lines speak your desperate truth and reveal both your weariness and your deep desire to be done with it all. There is no decent future that you can imagine. Many of us know by heart the words you speak, yet once again we are mesmerized: How will *you* speak them? What shadings and nuance will *you* bring with your voice, your body, your mind? We in the audience yearn for you to express your full understanding of this favorite character.

In the same way, so also does the audience for the play of your life desire you to speak truly and reveal accurately what your flesh knows and experiences. Playing Hamlet is the life dream of many actors; he is an incomparably rich, vivid creation of the playwright's art. So are you.

I believe that the life you are living is one that you and perhaps others have dreamed of, a life you have longed for in the same way that a good actor longs to play Hamlet. And the reasons for the longing are similar. The good actor wants to play Hamlet because it is a great role; he wants to give it all he has—every bit of his skill, wit, brain power, humor, wisdom, awareness, and brilliance—and then express it fully, with daring, courage, and panache. In just this way, you want to play the great role you have accepted in life, with everything you are and have and know. Just as a theatrical actor uses his body, his face, his voice, and all his inner strength to express the role, so do you use these gifts to express who you are at every moment.

## Pause, Please

Look in a mirror. Ask your face to relax. Soften your eyes so that they are kind. Describe the character you see. What does your face express?

Now think about someone you love; imagine this person standing behind you, visible in the mirror. Let your face, especially your eyes, greet this person, and then look again at your face.

Do you see a difference in your expression? If your face now looks and feels more alive, you have just realized how wonderful it is to share the stage with another actor; and how much easier it is to express character and emotion when someone else is present, even if only in your imagination, to inspire and receive it.

A goal of Sacred Theatre is to align character with the Power of Expression so that the truth can be experienced both by you as the actor in your life and by others as your audience. Consider again your reason for being and allow its power to move in you. Then look at yourself in the mirror again. Has anything changed? If so, what? It is to be hoped that your face came again to new life as you felt the power of purpose infuse your body and mind.

Set the mirror aside for now. Allow the sense of your sacred purpose to fill you once more. Then ask your body to assume a posture and your hands to make a gesture that for you, in this moment, portray your incarnational role. Enjoy expressing that role as a living statue.

The look on your face when you "saw" the loved one's face in the mirror, and the form of the posture into which you have just moved, are reminders of the love and purpose you are in this life to express. You can use them as a gentle template to guide you through the more intense kinds of expression life will call upon you to portray. When you feel confused, return to the facial expression, the posture, and the gesture; they will help you remember your power and provide information about what is best to do next.

## FEELING AND SPEAKING

Many of us have learned that there can be a vast difference between what we feel and what we say. We often try to hide or disguise our feelings and can generate much drama in the dissonance. This kind of tension is fun to see onstage, because we the audience are in on the game. It's delicious to watch a skilled actor playing a character who has just fallen madly in love but feels he must pretend he hasn't—all the while revealing his feelings unmistakably through artful expression so that we know what's going on.

In life, though, when we try to deny our true feelings the one person we must not fool is ourselves. On occasion we may well decide to tell a lie, but we need to be aware that it *is* a lie. We may choose not to express a feeling, but it is important to recognize privately that we have made that choice. It is also important not to express negative feelings that contradict the fulfillment of our primary purpose. For example, if my purpose is to learn to love, then a violent expression of annoyance at a friend would not only damage the friendship but also impede my soul's work. And when it comes to even stronger feelings, such as fierce rage or unreasonable terror, my purpose will be better served by acknowledging them privately instead of expressing them publicly.

Further guidance on expression comes from the great teacher and well-known writer Gay Luce, transpersonal psychologist and author of *Longer Life, More Joy.* Gay describes the Buddhist aspiration of Right Speech as "conscious communication that is both truthful and harmless." She says that, in a conversation, Right Speech entails being clear about four things:

1. What the subject is. "Believe it or not," Gay says, "some people forget the subject because they are so excited about their opinions."

2. Whether we speak from opinion or knowledge. It is important to state when our communication is based on the former and so is not necessarily the truth.

3. How we feel about the subject. Gay remarks that acknowledging feelings is difficult because of our cultural conditioning that expects us to hide our emotions. Often to be taken seriously, we must appear detached and objective.

4. What our reasons for speaking are, which we rarely reveal. Gay says we need to be aware of our motivation for communication in order to be transparent. As she puts it, "I need to state what I would like to

have happen between me and you, the listener, and also what this utterance does for me. For instance, 'I hope you will be impressed with my intelligence, and I will boost my self-esteem.' Or, if I'm being really honest, I might say, 'I am just in need of a little attention and I want a hug or reassurance.' Or, 'I have too much energy, so I'm releasing some by yakking to you.' Often motivations are hard to dig out because we have been conditioned to hide them."

Here is one of Gay's examples of Right Speech: "When you said you'd call me last night and you didn't, I was hurt, thinking you didn't care about my feelings. I am saying this to you because I want clarity between us. And I want to check out your feelings so that I don't create disappointment for myself." [1]

These mindfulness practices provide a powerful tool we can use to strengthen our Power of Expression. In alignment with the principle of Right Speech, as well as within the context of Sacred Theatre, *expression* means to increase one's energy with the goal of communicating not just to the mind but to the heart. The word *communion* more accurately describes the Power of Expression for the highest purpose, which is that of portraying the essence of who we are.

Listen to Shakespeare's Juliet, who in the bright daylight experiences such a flood of ecstasy that she commands the sun to move to the west and "bring in cloudy night immediately" so that her beloved may "leap to these arms, untalked of and unseen." (3.2.4, 7). She goes on to say:

> Come, night, come Romeo; come, thou day in night,
> For thou will lie upon the wings of night
> Whiter than new snow on a raven's back.
> Come, gentle night, come, loving, black-browed night,
> Give me my Romeo, and when I shall die
> Take him and cut him out in little stars,
> And he will make the face of heaven so fine
> That all the world will be in love with night
> And pay no worship to the garish sun. (3.2.17–25)

Alive with just-discovered feeling, Juliet expresses it freely. Her home is in the mind of William Shakespeare, so the words she uses happen to be sublime. Even though we are not so lucky as to have Shakespeare for our wordsmith, we can come closer to the truth of who we are by choosing to express that truth dynamically and fully.

## SPRINGBOARD FOR ACTION

We lay the framework for engaging the Power of Expression through active verbs. The word *act* comes from the Latin verb *agere*, meaning "to do." So to be an actor is to be a doer and thus to work from an inner structure composed of verbs. Verbs underlie all expression of the onstage actor and likewise form the springboard for the sacred actor to express who she is, what she is, and what she is here to do.

### The Primary Verb

Anchoring this springboard is the primary verb that holds our overall life purpose and from which the Power of Expression flows. We first discussed it in chapter 1. It is your means for living the questions: What are you born to do? What unique gift do you bring? The primary verb is like our bone marrow—the essence that keeps us alive—inspiring us to take the actions that keep us on track with our inmost purpose. This gift that we came with, this truth of who we are, deserves to be presented with élan and verve. Expressing our unique purpose for incarnating is not some awful weight imposed on us against our will but a wondrous means of engaging the world with honor, respect, and happiness. It allows us to offer freely something that only we can provide.

As I've said, my primary verb is *to celebrate*. Perhaps yours is *to heal*, or *to dance*, or *to ponder*, or *to initiate*. One way to know if you're working with the right verb for you is to notice how you feel when you are not doing it. When I'm not celebrating life or learning how to celebrate it more effectively, I feel bored, tired, rootless, stupid. When I forget to celebrate, I struggle, I lose myself, I deny myself.

# CHAPTER FIVE

## Supporting Verbs

Once we're clear about the primary verb, we begin to explore all the other active verbs through which we can satisfy it. All other verbs that describe our actions evolve from this primary one. These include the many verbs we use to learn the most accurate means of expressing our life purpose; the verbs we use to experiment, study, and explore it; and the verbs that give us the greatest joy in fulfilling it.

If my primary verb were *to learn*, or, more deeply, *to seek*, then I would notice all the ways I follow the path of learning—taking classes, finding teachers, writing, reflecting. And I would create a feedback system so that I pay careful attention to those ways of learning and seeking that provide me with the most happiness and engagement. Which classes did I love, which subjects challenged me in good ways? Which helped me to offer my incarnational gift most effectively? Our desire here is to achieve mastery at expressing our primary purpose.

## Objects and Adverbs for Focus and Quality

To the springboard of verbs we add other words: nouns as objects that provide focus and precision for our actions and adverbs that describe the quality of those actions. To use myself as an example again, I have a gift for singing praise and believe that part of my purpose is to provide a sense of joy; these converge in my primary verb *to celebrate*. I also know that my way to express that verb most effectively is through the springboard it provides for many other verbs: *to study, to learn, to seek, to share, to travel, to teach, to perform*. These lead me to discovering appropriate objects for celebrating: *life, friendship, music, healing*, other *cultures*, and *words* themselves. When I add adverbs, my Power of Expression becomes stronger: I celebrate life *passionately*. Then, like a magnificent feedback system, all of these verbs, object nouns, and adverbs give me greater clarity about how best to express my primary verb, and I can see a pathway toward *becoming* the gift, *becoming* the purpose. This is my ultimate goal.

As one's life progresses, the primary verb may shift toward a more precise statement of purpose: in my case, the drive *to celebrate* moves toward seeking wisdom in order to celebrate life more effectively; and that in turn moves toward learning to love wisdom more deeply in order to celebrate life more truly.

It is useful to keep your primary verb in the back of your mind at all times. Faced with a daunting, probably boring, series of meetings, if I remember that, "in this lifetime, I am here to celebrate life, and the most natural way I do that is by learning," then the task becomes to seek whatever is available for learning, and celebrating, in that meeting. And there will always be something to find. Holding on to the primary verb keeps me aware, awake, and interested.

If, on the other hand, your primary verb is *to heal*, your task is to find whatever it is in any scene that needs healing; it may not be visible, but it will be present. Then your choice becomes how best to express your verb in this moment: By touching lightly? Praying silently? Speaking softly?

## *Pause, Please*

To stay focused on your primary verb, consider keeping a Purpose Journal. You can use it to record how you lived your purpose each day, how you expressed that purpose, and how you may have neglected or forgotten it temporarily. For example, having just attended a difficult meeting, I can write,

> At this meeting, I learned from Joe that it's possible to keep everyone on task gracefully without getting sidetracked or being a taskmaster; I celebrate that learning and I celebrate Joe. I learned from Linda that writing a song about what's going on is a cheerful way to underscore the important issues we're covering, and I celebrate that. And I learned from myself (again) that nothing is served when I lose my temper and

143

shout out my frustrations. Furthermore, when I start yelling, I forget my purpose for being.

The journal is also a splendid way to record your active verbs. "Established in Being, perform action," says the Bhagavad Gita. Established in your deep purpose, you can enjoy a multitude of verbs that support your expression of it. For instance, a friend whose deep purpose is to nourish souls is also a marvelous cook. She played with the verbs she uses to express that purpose through cooking: *broil, knead, sauté, blend, fold, stir, peel, slice, boil, mince, poach, grind, bake, simmer, fry, sear, dip, mix, grill, marinate, whip, melt, cut, steam, love.* Most of all, *love.*

## How Others May See Our Purpose

It is fascinating to consider that other characters in my play may understand my life purpose as something else entirely from the way I do. And they may also be right. In Sacred Theatre, we all get to be right about deep purpose.

Think of Shakespeare's Juliet. An actor playing the role might decide that the primary purpose of her life is to love. "I *love*" is her bone-marrow truth. But from the point of view of the chorus, who outlines the entire play for us from the beginning, Juliet's life purpose might be instead to heal the feud between her family and Romeo's—which she does, but the *way* she does it is through active, passionate loving. That is, whatever others perceive as our purpose may be, not the purpose itself, but the results of our living *through* that purpose. What they see as the *cause* may in truth be the *effect.* And while, as I say, in Sacred Theatre no one is wrong, ultimately it is only you who can choose your primary verb and your ways of expressing it.

On the bone-marrow verb "I *love,*" Juliet builds a network of other verbs that support her expression of it, such as "I *dream,*" "I *listen,*"

"I *ponder*," "I *question*," "I *bubble*," "I *comply*," "I *tease*," "I *challenge*," "I *watch*," "I *wonder*," "I *hold*," "I *quake*." These verbs form her subtext; although she does not actually speak them in the play, the energy of them is what gives her spoken words their power. Then when she meets Romeo, her inmost purpose of "I *love*" billows to the surface and she unites with it unquestioningly. And, like the heat-seeking missile she embodies as a lover, for her verb she finds an object: "I *love* ROMEO!" Finding a specific object to fulfill the primary verb opens a new gateway to full engagement of the Power of Expression, because it opens and engages the heart.

It is relatively easy to perceive Juliet's life purpose because she is an invention of a brilliant playwright and her life is not very long. Also, working with active verbs is easier for a theatrical actor than in real life because the lines are already written, the progress of the action known, and the end determined. The stage actor knows exactly where she has to be at the end of the play, and she is given a rich palette of verbs to take her there. On the other hand, for those of us who muddle into life and only pick up on the ideas of purpose later—much later—the verbal underpinning of our existence may be less obvious. It may be hidden away beneath the thousand-and-one conflicting and confused ways we have chosen to express ourselves. That is why it is useful to ask the questions about incarnational purpose, choose the primary verb that holds that purpose, and then give it a rich array of supportive verbs that will allow us to fulfill it. If we are immaculately clear about this primary verb, we can also respond to the actions of others in ways that are in consonance with it: "I *listen*," "I *hear*," "I *pay* attention," "I *support*," "I *answer* with a full heart," "I *question* kindly," "I *pause*," "I *breathe*."

## Engaging the Heart's Passion: I *Want*

For an actor entering a play, it's important to begin with the primary verb that provides the through line for all the action. Then there is another verb that must be satisfied: "I *want*." Sometimes the sentence leads to yet another verb, "I *want* to hide what I want," or "I *want* to deny what I want," or "I *want* to kill somebody," or "I *want* to kiss you." Whole scenes are driven by this verb, and the play occurs in the tension between the characters' often opposing desires. In life, as in the theatre, there is always more energy in action than in reaction. We always gain more power in stating a positive desire than a negative one, in saying what we *do* instead of what we *don't* want. For instance, in refusing someone's unwanted advances, instead of saying, "I don't want you to kiss me," it would be stronger to say, "I want you to back off." Practicing this simple principle is an effective way to avoid passivity. Playing the victim does not engage life with enough passion to entertain the gods, which you recall is the primary task of a sacred actor. Instead, one can *deny* passivity and *fight* victimhood; these actions fascinate us and the gods, too.

## *Pause, Please*

As sacred players, we need to define the truth of what we want and make sure that it is in alignment with our purpose. Ask yourself, What do I want? Answer in a playful way, by writing a song of praise to all the things you desire. You might set it to the tune of "These are a few of my favorite things." Sing your list aloud, and commit to it with fervor.

Now, once again, choose the primary verb for your life. This is the theatre, remember, so things can change dynamically from moment to moment; just write the verb that feels accurate right now. Perhaps it is, "My purpose in life is to experiment—with verbs." Which of your statements of "I *want*" feel in sync with your life purpose? Notice them.

Then write a praise song to those things that make you feel alive and joyful. You could set it to the tune of "Oh, What a Beautiful Morning." Sing it aloud with delight. Notice what those things tell you about *how* to express your purpose—and your desires.

## Engaging the Heart's Passion: I *Love*

Whereas in the theatre the underlying verb is "I *want*," I believe that in life the underlying verb for all living things is "I *love*." Sometimes the two come together, especially when we are in a quandary or a fight: "I want to love, but . . ."

In my thirties, I experienced a long time of desperation. I was in mourning for my husband's death and seeking some wisdom through my sorrow. That search led to the insight that everybody needs two things to make life meaningful and rewarding: a cause, something larger than they are; and beauty, a source of joy in beauty. Then a second insight came: Everything I hear is "I love you"; everything I say is "I love you." No matter how desperately opposite to love whatever is said seems to be, under the anger, hatred, disappointment, and unhappiness is the root truth, "I love you." Or, more accurately sometimes, "I *want* to love you but am finding it impossible at the moment."

Romeo is a great teacher about authentic love. In the play's opening scenes, he moons around self-pityingly, believing himself enthralled by the young woman Rosaline, who refuses to acknowledge his existence. He crashes the Capulet party (I like to think it is Juliet's birthday feast) because he hopes to see Rosaline there. But in that first incandescent moment when he sees Juliet instead, all of Romeo's useless moaning for Rosaline falls away, and his inmost verb "I *love*" finds its magnetic true north. It is Juliet that brings Romeo to authentic life: powerful, willing to engage, and daring.

Life is glorified when our inmost verb's highest form moves from having a general object, such as "I study *literature*," to "I study *SHAKESPEARE*." Passionate engagement begins when the primary verb is activated by a specific other, be it an idea, a person, an animal, a tree, a flower, or God.

In this state of full engagement, three central activations take place: that of the heart, the body, and the throat. When all three are working together and focused on the activating object, there is no mistaking it, and the actor playing Romeo, or the sacred actor enacting her life, is capable of free and total expression.

## *Pause, Please*

Reflect on the times when your heart was full, your body glowing, and your throat open to express your total being. Notice if those times are similar to, or the same as, the moments of greatest aliveness that we spoke of in the chapter on Incarnation. Think about the object that your primary verb focused on during those moments.

Now let your awareness move through your immediate environment, seeking an object worthy of your attention, something capable of touching your heart, awakening your body, and inviting your throat to open and speak (or sing). When you find the object, concentrate on it until you feel your heart, body, and throat activated. Pay attention to that feeling and notice how alive you are, how open to delight and awe.

## How Acting Can Help

Once you experience the joy of full expression through the practice of activating the three centers of heart, body, and throat, you can train yourself never to be satisfied with life at half-mast. If you want to confirm your preference for such expression, just remember the times when you allowed yourself to express but without full activation of all three centers. Perhaps your throat was engaged, but your heart and your body/brain were not. What was the result? Yada yada yada, right? Or, like a Don Juan, perhaps your body and throat were engaged, but your heart was not. Or, more poignantly, your body and heart may have been engaged, but your throat was not open; you could not even speak.

The good news is that, once you know about this practice, activating any one center can engage the other two. If you notice something that engages your heart, for instance, focus on it, and soon your body will wake up (if only to stretch toward the heart object) and your throat will open (if only to say "ahhh"). Expression will flow. Even if your body cannot move, it can feel alive and experience a yearning to express. That in itself is a powerful expression. Or if, with your throat wide open, you want to say things that absolutely must not be spoken, it is still better to be aware of the desire than it is not to feel it; that awareness alone is a powerful form of expression.

If your heart feels temporarily closed and you want it to open, allow your throat to hum or speak lovingly, or your hands to tend to something with gentleness, and new brain chemistries will start to flow; your heart will actually begin to feel open.

If your body feels depressed, smile, look up, and move to see and sense. Fall into beautiful details—flowers, leaves, dog's eyes. And you will soon be less depressed, because the body has given the brain a request for pleasure chemistry, and the brain has cheerfully obeyed.

This is one of the reasons why training in acting is useful for all of us. An actor may not "feel" like doing the day's performance. But when she enters the theatre, sees her fellow actors and friends who work behind the scenes, and puts on her costume and makeup, she aligns with her character and steps out on stage totally engaged.

## *Pause, Please*

Notice the verbs that each of your three activation centers provides to support full expression of your purpose:

When the throat engages, we might say that it *warms*, it *opens*, it *yearns*, it *sings* (sometimes silently, yes, but it *sings*).

The body/brain *pulses, throbs, thrills, teases, commits, enjoys, luxuriates, jumps, assesses, measures, clarifies, dances.*

The heart, like the throat, *warms* and *opens*, and it also *recognizes*, *teaches*, *learns*, *absorbs*, *guides*, *reveals*, *knows*.

Find as many verbs as you can for your heart, your body/brain, and your throat to use as examples of full expression. Speak them aloud. Notice that simply naming the verbs can activate aliveness.

## CHOOSING GOD AS YOUR OBJECT

To come into alignment with your life purpose, and to express that purpose with everything you are and know and want, requires a worthy object on which the primary verb of your life can focus its generativity and laser-like intensity.

For the sacred player, I recommend God. Or whatever name you wish to call the Endless One, recognizing that all aspects of the energies we call divine might be inventions of humankind in its yearning. I also recognize that those beings created by the imagination live in a reality beyond our capacity to understand.

If you want totally to engage the Power of Expression, go for God. Write love poems, longing poems, questioning poems, challenging poems, daring poems, believing poems, or disbelieving poems all directed to God, and you will feel alive while you live in ways no other action can offer.

I recommend God.

*I have never believed in a single truth.*
*Neither my own, nor those of others.*
—Peter Brook

# Six

# The Power of Point of View

By statements such as the one on the facing page, Peter Brook, a genius of modern drama, inspires the idea of grappling with point of view as a power in living life as Sacred Theatre. In his book *The Shifting Point*, this legendary theatre and film director demonstrates the importance of this power:

> I believe all schools, all theories can be useful in some place, at some time. But I have discovered that one can only live by a passionate, and absolute, identification with a point of view.
>
> However, as time goes by, as we change, as the world changes, targets alter and the viewpoint shifts. Looking back over many years of essays written, ideas spoken in many places on so many varied occasions, one thing strikes me as being consistent. For a point of view to be of any use at all, one must commit oneself totally to it, one must defend it to the very death. Yet, at the same time, there is an inner voice that murmurs: "Don't take it too seriously. Hold on tightly, let go lightly."[1]

Brook further helps us understand the Power of Point of View in describing a trip to Dublin where he encountered the work of an Irish philosopher (whose name he does not provide): "I remember a phrase of his, quoted by someone in a bar, which struck me at once: it was the theory of the 'shifting viewpoint.' It didn't mean a fickle point of view, but the exploration as made in certain types of X-rays, where changing perspectives give an illusion of density."[2]

Hence Brook gives us three important concepts: 1) that we can only live well by being totally and passionately committed to a particular point of view; 2) that, nevertheless, over time there will come an opportunity, sometimes a demand, to shift that way of seeing; and 3) that, when such a shift occurs, one is not being fickle but rather is becoming capable of perceiving more richness and density.

The Power of Point of View offers us a way to look at our lives through different lenses and from different vantage points. It is the second answer to the question, "*How* do we fulfill our incarnation by enacting our story, in the exquisite and demanding present, on our sacred stage of life on earth?" (The first answer, discussed in chapter 5, is through the Power of Expression.)

The Power of Point of View rests in the uniqueness of the perspective from inside our heads. With it, we develop a clearer understanding of the psychological ground on which we stand. Thus we can know ourselves secure in a worldview unmistakably our own, yet simultaneously find ourselves capable of changing that view when driven by our core purpose.

Seeing is such a vital part of our way of knowing the world. The sense of sight accounts for some 70 percent of our awareness of physical surroundings, and we can assume the same is true in respect to our viewpoint *about* those surroundings and the people in them. Gaining the ability to change perspective strengthens us. Our relationships feel renewed when we see our friends and loved ones with fresh eyes.

## HERE'S THE STORY

You are a famous, highly experienced, noble-hearted general serving the Dukedom of Venice, in the days when it held rule over much of the Mediterranean world. Your name is Othello; you are a Moor. You exist in the mind of William Shakespeare; he is writing at a time when the word *Moor* means "Blackamoor," so you are sublimely Black. This quality makes you fearful in the eyes of most people in Venice (and in England, too); you live in a time when radiant blackness was seen as both mesmerizing and terrifying. However, you know that your wisdom and service to the state make you highly valued. You are also a man whom others like to call friend, so you are fêted and honored by many Venetian notables.

Before the play begins, two important things have happened. The first is that you have fallen in love with Desdemona, a Venetian woman, and she with you, and on this night you and she are running away to be secretly married. The second is that you have chosen for your lieutenant a young soldier named Michael Cassio, who has been helpful in your courtship to Desdemona. This appointment gives Cassio the power to act in your name if necessary. It also enrages your closest friend and ally, Iago, who believes you should have named him your lieutenant instead of merely your primary aide-de-camp.

With these two actions—your elopement and Cassio's appointment—you have unwittingly loosed upon the world a devastation that will destroy your sanity, your career, your life, and the lives of everyone you love. At least some of the disaster might have been averted had you been willing to change your point of view.

In your view, Iago is an honest man, incapable of deceit. Throughout the play, you listen to every venomous thing he says without ever once being able to see him differently. Had you questioned his integrity, he could not have led you to believe that Desdemona was unfaithful and so deserved to die. (Of course, in that case there would be no play. But such is the mesmerizing intensity of *Othello* that its audience members, more than is true about any other play I know, desperately want somebody to shift the leading character's misguided perspective.)

So Point of View is a formidable power, involving a demand that we learn to change. How do we engage this power? As with all the others: practice, practice, practice. It also helps to question the beliefs that restrain us in a rigid and limited viewpoint.

# *Pause, Please*

Let's begin to engage the Power of Point of View by doing some simple eye exercises; they can open the doorway of the mind and strengthen a practice of really looking, really seeing.

First, blink your eyes a few times. Read this exercise one or two sentences at a time, then practice the eye movements they suggest.

Now close your eyes and invite them to rest in soft darkness.

When you open them, pay attention to what you see, lifting your eyes from the page and looking out in all directions: right, left; left, right; up and down; down and up; and then in circles. Move your eyes slowly so that you feed your vision field with all the color in it.

Now widen your gaze by noticing what is at the periphery. Do this without straining and while remembering to breathe.

Then practice the clockwise and counterclockwise circles again. Then rest and close your eyes for a few moments.

This time when you open them, practice shifting your gaze from things that are very close (I see the dust on my glasses, for example), to those in the middle distance, and then to those that are as far out as you can see.

Then slowly bring the gaze back in. And close and rest your eyes for a few moments.

Now begin to notice details. I, for instance, see the precise flow of the wood grain in my desk and the color and faces on my storyteller doll. I notice for the first time that not only is the storyteller's mouth wide open, but all the little ones' mouths are open, too. Why is that? Is it because the story is a miraculous one for all concerned, or because it is not a storytelling doll, but a song-singing doll?

Because my focus on this one little work of art has raised a question, my imagination begins to play. And it can go on and on, until I shift my perspective again and notice further details, as once more I widen my gaze to embrace the whole room and the world through the window.

Notice what happens in your mind as you widen and then narrow your perspective to focus on some object. Do your thoughts change? When I reflect on what I see when I look carefully, I notice that in the moment it takes for a thought to form, a shift occurs: My point of view immediately changes from casual seeing to sharp attention. The perfect orange rose that was in the background moves to the dramatic foreground.

By changing your perspective on objects, you may become aware of changes in mood. And by taking such steps, you can progress to imagining seeing through someone else's eyes, if only for a moment. For instance, a doe and two fawns are in the driveway munching on plants, and I begin to wonder how they see the world. The leaves are falling from the dogwood tree; what does each leaf "see" as it wafts toward the ground?

Notice when an object in the foreground catches your attention and invites your imagination to play. Now widen your gaze again and allow yourself to wonder how the world looks to a particular tree or the grass or the sidewalk.

## Opening the Inner Eyes

Such practice with the eyes and noticing the train of thoughts that ensue provide us with an initial understanding of the Power of Point of View. However, its greatest riches lie deeper in the psyche. The eyes may be windows to the soul, and we sometimes find we can look into a friend's eyes and see the rich depths therein. But our work with Point of View requires that we turn our gaze inward toward our own depths.

When we look inward, we can see that our perspective is a vast field of psychological assumptions, most of them rooted in our upbringing and cultural programming. It can look like a tangled morass of wiring, and it's fun as well as useful to trace some of these wires. At one extreme, they show up in the outer world as our opinions or, more richly, as our sense of values. But where do they come from? And what keeps them valid now? Seeking answers to such questions leads to the treasure house where the glory of this power resides.

## *Pause, Please*

How much of your worldview comes from that of your parents or your geographical homeplace? Or your ancestors? Your parents' friends? Your ethnicity? Your religion?

Explore these questions by writing a description of the way you believe your parents see (or saw) the world. How does your life appear from their perspective? Make this description the first part of a dialogue. How does it differ from the way you yourself see the world? Present your own perspective as the second part of the dialogue. Then write another dialogue, first speaking from your parents' viewpoint about their lives and then responding with how you view them.

In the course of this exercise, are you being asked to change something about your view of your parents' lives, and even about the way you see your own? You may find that your relationship with them deepens in the shift. Even if your parents are no longer in the world, you can still write these dialogues and respond to the questions.

Shifting your point of view about your parents may make it possible to see them with greater kindness, more lightheartedness. It can even change how you feel about actions they took.

You can repeat this process in writing dialogues between your children's and your perspectives.

## GAINING A GLOBAL POINT OF VIEW

As the Power of Place gives us a physical foundation, the Power of Point of View offers a psychological foundation from which we can begin the process of change. This is a time of exponential increase in global awareness, and those personal, familial, and cultural viewpoints into which we were born no longer serve if we are to become planetary citizens—which is the formerly fantastic possibility open to us today. We are not only being asked to widen our point of view to include that of other inhabitants of our planet, we are also being asked to learn how to "think like a planet" and to see as we imagine our earth "sees." The visionary poet James Bertolino says it best:

> To survive
> our minds must taste
> redwood and agate,
> octopi,
> bat, and in the bat's mouth,
> insect.
> It's hard to think like a planet.
> We've got to try.[3]

As Bertolino describes, our work as sacred actors in the early twenty-first century requires us to cultivate a broad variety of differing points of view. Happily, our work in the Power of Incarnation has taught us many ways of embodying the roles we are each invited to play.

The first step in working with Point of View is to acknowledge that you have one. Your way of sensing, considering, and responding to the world is primarily shaped by the environment in which you grew, your experiences in relation to it, and your innate personality. The second step is to acknowledge that you can change. One of the pleasures of the theatre is to witness the moment when the perspective of one character intersects with that of another who has an entirely different sense of reality. From those moments on, the actors' job as characters is to try to maintain, and perhaps defend, their own viewpoint and then challenge, fight, or submit to the opposing one. Above all, the dramatic need is to be changed by the encounter, just as we as audience members feel our viewpoint shift: now we agree with this one, then we are seduced by that one. In any case, we are being asked to enlarge our perspective. That request runs like a river beneath the action of any play, including the sacred play of our lives.

Point of view in its lesser form (called an opinion) often underlies statements of criticism regarding a play or a movie. When we say, "I didn't like it" or even "I hated it," it is often because the story presents a viewpoint we find offensive or unreal or painful, so we become either bored or outraged. We often become bored when we cannot understand the other's perspective and therefore dismiss it, usually as unworthy. And outrage often ensues whenever a situation challenges us more insistently to change our own perspective, as Iago is outraged when Othello gives the job that Iago perceives as rightly his to someone else.

It may be helpful to discuss the subtle differences as I experience them among opinion, point of view, and judgment:

1. *Opinion* is often irrational, based on the flux of emotion and subject to frequent change depending on mood and circumstance.

2. *Point of View* may also be irrational, but it is more engrained, usually since childhood, and so less subject to change. It expresses our core values.

3. *Judgment* can be a curative to either, since it requires somber, rational reflection.

You might consider your point of view a deeply rooted tree, with your core values part of the root system. This gives you your way of standing in the world. Opinions, on the other hand, are like the breezes that blow through the leaves, ephemeral and without substance. Your capacity for deeply considered *judgment* forms the flower-like expressions that bloom when your point of view is challenged and has to adjust.

For instance, it might be my unexamined point of view that democracy commands respect for every voice. At the same time, it might be my opinion that the Republican Party is full of money-grubbing, power-mad, cruel-hearted jerks. And I could go blithely on opinionating, not disturbed in the least by the contradiction between the two. Then, suppose I meet a human being who is none of those objectionable things, and yet he is a Republican. Whoops! This perplexing turn of events demands that I make an important shift. I must alter my opinion to align with my point of view, which also needs adjustment: democracy commands respect for every voice, *including* those of Republicans. Then, after careful thought and observation, I can come to the judgment that my opinion about Republicans is foolish, perhaps fed to me long ago in a narrow world where nobody had ever even seen a Republican. I might thus be led to assess all my unthinking opinions and shift my belief structure and behavior in the realization that, when opinions come up against facts, they need to rearrange themselves or let go and die.

Many of the memorable moments of our lives come about when our cozy reality is exploded by the sudden, often dramatic, appearance of an entirely different mind-set, embodied in a stranger or a new friend or an old lover now changed entirely. The richest vein of conversation between old friends could boil down to the question: "How has your point of view changed since last we met?" Unlikely as that question is as a stated topic, it nevertheless underlies many exchanges. "How have you changed the way you see and what you believe about the world?" is what interests us. "Before, you were someone who thought such-and-such . . . now I sense a sea change. What happened?"

My teacher and friend Jean Houston works with an exercise called "Old Story, New Story." She provides various subjects, such as religion, education, government, gender, and race; then she asks us to consider the old story (what we used to believe about each subject) and the new story (what we understand now). Then she asks us to trace the process of change in our point of view. How did I, for example, change my belief that Protestant Christianity, with Methodist overtones, was the true and only path to God; that such salvation offered the only hope for a sinful world? This conviction came to me early in life, through some undefined process of osmosis. My parents lived their strong Methodist faith as church leaders, and somehow I absorbed the "truth" that it was my holy task to convert as many people to Christianity as I could manage.

## *Pause, Please*

Head a sheet of paper with the words, "What Happened?" Then begin a monologue: "Once I believed that _____." "Now I believe that _____." Fill in the blanks with something important that has really shifted. You might want to create a poem about what happened.

Next, write about fellow players in your life who have held wildly diverse points of view. How have your encounters with them expanded, changed, or even transformed your previous perspective?

Include in your writing the moment when your earlier, firmly held faith began to re-form around a different centerpiece. What brought you to that new center? Was it a step-by-step or an all-at-once event? These memories and thoughts mark the stages on the path to creating a new worldview.

A note to remember: your point of view differs in quality from your opinions. Opinion is often the result of unanalyzed, highly volatile emotions, whereas point of view, while it may also be unanalyzed, is deeply rooted in our beliefs and core values. As such, it is more firm than opinion and does not change as rapidly. That is why a dramatic encounter may be necessary to bring about a significant shift. That is also why working with the Power of Point of View requires such rigorous examination and truth telling.

## WHY CHANGE?

Change can be difficult, so why undertake it? Primarily, it is because life itself is fundamentally about flux and movement. We must adapt and respond appropriately to life's invitation to go with the flow. If we cannot, we die.

Neale Donald Walsch, whose *Conversations with God* and subsequent books have brought him onto the world stage, says that in order for the earth to become more peaceful, human beings must change "at the level of belief."[4] In other words, we must change at the level of point of view. How do we accomplish that kind of shift?

The first step, as we have just practiced, is to notice how our personal beliefs have changed through time. The next step is to ask ourselves what change is being required of our beliefs now in order for our holy purpose to be fulfilled. Noticing how we have changed in the past may offer clues.

Changes in point of view are of many types. Religious conversion is a sudden type. Evolution is a slow type. We can walk the middle path by making small shifts in how we see things over time until doing so becomes a habit. When we recognize that change is necessary for growth, we become open to the delight of welcoming others into our personal world. So many things happen in every encounter with another person that we can be changed by each one, if we allow it.

Ideally, we might view each person or sentient being we meet as a sacred carrier of a precious elixir. This includes old friends and lovers who we believe have nothing new to show us. When our own point of view has matured and grown generous, we acknowledge that our standing within its grace can gently affect the other person, and we sense that he or she also affects us. This can make both of us aware of the quality of exchange of energy, in giving as well as receiving.

The Power of Point of View runs through our whole being at every level, affecting us and others, physically, emotionally, spiritually. In order to move forward in a dynamic and healthful way, we need to keep questioning our beliefs and challenging our prejudices, our automatic assumptions, with every encounter. Each is a tiny step.

I can choose to believe, for example, that all homeless people are slackers, or I can choose to see that they have decided to live off the grid, or I can believe that they need something from me that diminishes me. In each case, my prejudice prevents me from authentically experiencing the human being standing at the storefront before me. I refuse to let his condition affect me in any real way (or so I mistakenly believe). Thus, however I respond to his financial plea—give him money, listen to his story, bring him food, ignore him, snarl at him—is tainted by a soured point of view fed by inherited opinions, many of which can be traced to Puritan ancestors who believed that the only thing worthwhile in life was work—preferably hard work, the harder the better.

If, on the other hand, I imagine how it might feel to be in the homeless man's place, with his viewpoint, I have taken a step that will open my heart a tiny bit more than it was before. To meet eyes and receive his "God bless you" truly is then to become aware of many more possibilities than I previously held. Maybe the man has in fact chosen to live for this lifetime in what Mother Teresa of Calcutta called Jesus's appearance "in the distressing disguise of the poor."[5]

Yet I note remaining within me a Puritanical view that the man should be trying to get work—or that he must have brought this condition on himself. After all, at the moment I am in Canada, where hardworking people can make it. It's important to notice that my point of view still has an edge of criticism, to the effect of, "Everybody needs to work!" That critical attitude can lead me to pretend that I'm not hardhearted by being overly generous with my donation. Or I can simply acknowledge the encounter as one more crack in my consciousness to ponder and work on.

The homeless man matters, yes, just for who he is and by virtue of his existence. Moreover, he matters to me now in part because I can see myself more clearly as a result of our encounter. I can test how our meeting changes me. It brings me up sharp against my old conditioning and allows me to see with eyes of warmer compassion.

Point of View is a vital power because it offers an opportunity to take a stand with courage and vigor. It brings us to the very ground of our being. It's possible to float through life unaware of how it can run us and ruin us. Remember, this is a *power*, not just a concept. It exists to guide us in our work of living fully, gracefully, and generously.

## More about the Story

To increase awareness of the Power of Point of View, we return to Shakespeare's heartbreaking *Othello*. This play may be the most terrifying version of the plot of Seductive Enchantment, or the Spider and the Fly (see chapter 2), in all of literature.

Remember that the task of the Power of Point of View is to bring us to change. Othello illustrates, in the most dramatic way possible, how disastrous it can be to fail in this work. He shows us the danger of not stopping to explore options or ask questions when we find ourselves running amok emotionally, in the midst of a maelstrom of activity brought about by our inability to alter our perspective.

Othello is strong in most of the powers of Sacred Theatre. He has, for one thing, a profound sense of place. He is a Moor, away from his homeland, but he carries the immense dignity and sparse elegance of the desert. Indeed, the word with which other characters most often describe him is *noble*. All of his experiences, and the travels and travails of his life and lineage, surround him as a field of attraction. Moreover, in being a military general charged with protecting the security of the state, he totally embodies his incarnational gift and task. He is also gifted with the Power of Story: having lived through a world of battle, he claims to have won Desdemona with his adventurous tales and enchants his audience with his depth of understanding. His skill with the Power of *Now!* is evident in his immediate departure for Cyprus to defend against a Turkish invasion. And he has so realized his Power of Expression that he is an unforgettable lover and a triumphant leader.

And so on. In terms of all the powers, Othello lacks only in one: Point of View. And love being Shakespeare's favorite teaching device, it is Othello's love for Desdemona that Iago uses to put Othello's soul and sanity at risk. "Love," as the song so truly tells us, "changes everything" and hence is Point of View's most forceful agent.[6] In the desire it evokes to become closer to the beloved, nothing more than love carries such power to transform us; and in that process our way of looking at the world is what changes most. Had Othello not come to love Desdemona, he would not have been willing to suffer all the turmoil that his love for her brings him. As he says,

> But that I love the gentle Desdemona.
> I would not my unhoused free condition
> Put into circumscription and confine
> For the seas' worth.
>
> (1.2.25–28)

For her part, even though Desdemona is the elegant daughter of a crusty old Venetian senator, she is brave enough to recognize the dark, foreign warrior Othello as her beloved, which requires a radical departure from her inherited point of view. And she is brave enough to steal away from her father's house—and his prejudices—to marry the magnificent blackamoor. Here she is:

> That I did love the Moor to live with him,
> My downright violence and storm of fortunes
> May trumpet to the world. My heart's subdued
> Even to the very quality of my lord.
> I saw Othello's visage in his mind,
> And to his honors and his valiant parts
> Did I my soul and fortunes consecrate;
>
> (1.3.248–254)

As a learned young gentleman, Michael Cassio, the lovers' secret helper, has been able to visit Desdemona's home and carry their letters back and forth without raising questions. Perhaps his loyalty in this respect is what prompted Othello to promote this relatively inexperienced soldier to a lieutenant. (It is this kind of seemingly minor misjudgment that the hero of a tragedy always makes.) Othello being weak in the Power of Point of View, promoting Cassio may have been his first mistake; possibly he let his sentiment outrun his judgment. Then again, it is equally possible that he simply preferred the gentleman Cassio over the rough soldier Iago. These are only assumptions; Othello never explicitly tells us why he chose Cassio (he doesn't have to, he's the boss).

In any case, Othello's decision sets a terrible wheel of events in motion, controlled absolutely by Iago, incensed as he is with the belief that he himself should be Othello's second-in-command. Yet virulent though Iago is, Othello's tragedy stems largely from his own incapacity to shift or even question his point of view about his aide-de-camp. And in his delusion he is not alone. "Honest, honest Iago," are the words we hear spoken by person after person onstage. Nobody ever stops to question anything Iago says or does. A good actor playing him is so apparently sincere, plain spoken, and true that we in the audience can absolutely see why everyone onstage believes him honest. He could never trick anyone. He would never lure someone into madness. Never! Yet he takes such advantage of Othello's trusting, loving, noble nature that it steals your breath away to watch him do it. We listen in horror as "honest" Iago persuades Othello that Desdemona has betrayed him with none other than Michael Cassio. Thus does the arch manipulator seek to destroy all three of them. Listen to him begin his connivances:

> . . . yet that I put the Moor
> At least into a jealousy so strong
> That judgment cannot cure . . .
> I'll have our Michael Cassio on the hip,
> Abuse him to the Moor in the rank garb . . .
> Make the Moor thank me, love me, and reward me
> For making him egregiously an ass,
> And practicing upon his peace and quiet
> Even to madness . . . (2.1.299 ff.)

There is a perhaps apocryphal story that attests to the character Iago's almost supernatural believability. During the late nineteenth century, a mining town in the western United States hosted a troupe of traveling Shakespearean actors. At the height of their performance of *Othello*, in a scene showing Iago's diabolical activity, one of the miners pulled a gun and shot the actor playing the role.

Othello's calmness under attack, his assurance, his bearing, his settled power—all great strengths—may be the very traits that prevent him from doubting Iago. His point of view is so strong it is unshakeable. And that rigidity proves to be the fatal character flaw that leads to Desdemona's death and his tragic undoing.

## *Pause, Please*

Ask: What assumptions do *I* live by that cannot be shaken? Where is my point of view so rigid that I would never change it? Create a Credo statement: "This I believe _____."

Then consider whether you are right to hold your beliefs with such fervor. What might you be risking? What other point of view might you need to encounter in order to change your own?

## TRUST LOVE

If Othello's tragedy stems partly from his inability to change his point of view about Iago, it also stems from his equally disastrous inability to trust Desdemona. At the beginning, he does so trust her absolutely: "My life upon her faith" (1.3.294). But when Iago pours his slow, subtle venom into Othello's ear, the Moor ceases to trust his own wisdom, and his faith in himself and in Desdemona's ability to love him becomes cruelly undermined. Just listen to them:

**Iago** [*alone onstage*]: The Moor already changes with my poison.
Dangerous conceits are in their natures poisons,
Which at the first are scarce found to distaste,
But, with a little act upon the blood,
Burn like the mines of sulphur. I did say so.
[*As Othello enters*] Look where he comes.
Not poppy nor mandragora
Nor all the drowsy syrups of the world
Shall ever medicine thee to that sweet sleep
Which thou owedst yesterday . . .

**Othello**: Avaunt, be gone. Thou has set me on the rack. (3.3.325–35)

Unfair as it may be to use a Shakespearean tragedy as a teaching text for life, we audience members sense the lesson here so clearly that it's all we can do not to shout aloud to Othello: "TRUST LOVE, TRUST YOUR LOVE, TRUST HER LOVE FOR YOU! Or, if you can't, at least take some time to ask questions and get a second opinion." Even if, in our own lives, our loves have been founded on folly and cannot withstand the trials of time, we can still trust the truth of love itself, more than we can trust those who would persuade us to love less.

His Holiness the Dalai Lama teaches about point of view in his book, *The Art of Happiness*. He remarks that when problems arise our outlook narrows.[7] Certainly that happens to Othello. He becomes so obsessed with his belief about Desdemona's unfaithfulness that it drives him mad. This insanity leads him inexorably to conclude that Desdemona must be killed, "Else she'll betray more men" (5.2.6.).

The Dalai Lama recommends that in hard times we look at things from a broader point of view. We need to recognize—as Othello cannot—that other people may have it much worse or that other things are more important than our single problem. Another of my teachers playfully recommends that when agonies arise, we expand our point of view until we are looking at the issue from outer space and then notice how small it appears.

## BEWARE OF POISON

Even as Othello can't shift his perspective about Iago, so too the villain's plotting seems to stem in part from a damaged point of view. Iago implies that his not being made lieutenant is a mortal injury to his very selfhood, any revenge he takes being thereby justified (whereas in truth Othello may have simply wanted Iago nearer him than the role of lieutenant would allow). We won't go into a study of why Iago does what he does; we would be here until doomsday. We have focused on his acrimony over the military appointment, but we can never really know what turns him against Othello, beyond that his own foul nature comes up against the innate nobility of the Moor. His expressed motives are never fully convincing—he even claims to hate Othello for seducing his own faithful wife, Emilia—and he seems almost to revel in destruction for its own sake. The point is, though, that once Iago's perspective (whatever it is) drives him to his machinations, he destroys his world so methodically that eventually he himself is destroyed. Thus the danger of acting on the basis of a poisonous point of view.

## *Pause, Please*

Iago's teaching is to notice how, when our feelings are hurt or we've been overlooked or we perceive that others have done us damage, we must question our perceptions to keep the poisons of envy and rage from laying our world to waste.

Consider your incidents of emotional upset and ask, How are these events inviting me to change my point of view? What is being challenged by this perceived insult? Is it my prideful ego? In the worst scenario, could I be driven by an urge for revenge that far outweighs the perceived offense? Or—God forbid—by a delight in malice that feeds upon itself if I remain unconscious of it?

The antidote to such shadow qualities is to ask, Where is the love in this situation? How can I widen my perspective until I comprehend the love and focus on it? How can I realign my perspective so that it serves my fulfillment of the role I have chosen for this life? And may I remember the truth that such a way of seeing also enriches the whole.

*There is a kind of merry war betwixt Signor Benedick and her.*
*They never meet but there's a skirmish of wit between them.*
—Leonato, in Shakespeare's *Much Ado About Nothing*
(1.1.59–60)

# Seven

# The Power of Conflict

We met Beatrice, the other fighter in the "merry war" Leonato describes on the opposite page, in chapter 1. Sharp-witted Beatrice, who delights in laughter, is said to have been "born in a merry hour." "No, sure, my lord," she replies, "My mother cried. But then there was a star danced and under that was I born" (2.1.313–314).

Most human lives are made up of that combination of tears and laughter, of crying out in pain at the same time that stars are dancing. Such a blend of sorrow and joy sets the tone perfectly for this sunny comedy of Shakespeare's and offers a jumping-off point for exploring the Power of Conflict.

Conflict, the seventh power of Sacred Theatre, helps answer the question, "*How* do I fulfill this incarnation?" If a single power can be named as more important than any other to the theatre, it is this one, regardless of whether the play is a comedy, a tragedy, a history, or any combination thereof. In good theatre, the deepest conflict is internal, inside the main character. In great theatre, conflict is visible within and among all the characters; it is the measure of the grandeur of the play. Indeed, conflict is the engine that drives the whole work; there would be no forward movement without it. Think of how boring a story would be without any struggle, as in Boy Meets Girl and Lives Happily Ever After. In such a case, there *is* no story.

The merry war between Shakespeare's Benedick and Beatrice plays out in a delightfully convoluted plot of Boy Meets Girl, Boy Loses Girl, Boy Loses Girl Again and Yet Again, and finally, Boy Gets Girl after All. In these happy skirmishes, Beatrice is often the exultant victor. Of Benedick she boasts, "In our last conflict, four of his five wits went halting off, and now is the whole man governed with one" (1.1.52–54).

The comedy's main action is a scheme by all their friends to achieve the impossible: bring the warring pair "into a mountain of affection, th' one with th' other" (2.1.343–344). After much ado about many things, they accomplish this Herculean labor, and Benedick and Beatrice are joined in happy marriage.

This play gives us a wonderful example of the miracles that can occur when the Power of Conflict is joyfully engaged. And just as there can be no play in the theatre without conflict, so it is in our lives. If we engage this power wisely, conflict can move us forward and result even in self-transformation.

Ironically, though, most of us do our best to avoid conflict at all costs. As a friend remarks, we do everything *but* engage it: "We enable, we capitulate, we dissemble." Women especially in our culture are taught from an early age that to engage in conflict is not polite, not ladylike, not conducive to "feel good" relationships. We see conflict as stressful, and we use charm and manipulation to circumvent it.

But it is important to recognize that conflict is vital for growth. The point is not to *avoid* it, but to embrace it in a meaningful way. Conflict teaches us; it stretches us, tests all our skills, and makes huge demands of us. The better we become at engaging its power well at small and intimate levels, the more capable we will become of facing gigantic, world-shaking levels of conflict more wisely.

Hence I invite you to engage, resolutely and joyfully, the Power of Conflict in the play that is your life. To do so authentically, we take four essential steps, and in the right order:

1. *Acknowledge that conflict arises as an opportunity for growth.* Authentic conflict always signals the soul's movement toward its fulfillment in this lifetime, and we must be brave and wise enough to recognize it as such.

2. *Know that we are on sacred ground.* Authentic conflict is a sacred endeavor. When we are in conflict, it is important to stand aware that we have stepped into a holy place.

3. *Name the loss.* In dealing with conflict, it is essential to acknowledge and name whatever feels lost, broken, violated, or betrayed.

4. *Take appropriate action.* Having named the loss, it is essential that we act with integrity in whatever way is indicated for growth.

## STEP ONE:
## ACKNOWLEDGE THAT CONFLICT IS AN OPPORTUNITY FOR GROWTH

The first step is simply to acknowledge that the great Power of Conflict has arisen. This seems self-evident, but in fact we often refuse to face discord, pretending that it is something else or that it is too hard to confront now. It may become easier to accept that we are in a state of conflict if we can see it as an opportunity for growth—of skill, compassion, wisdom, and courage. Here are some sure-fire signals that conflict has arrived:

### A Sense of Invasion

We know that conflict is present whenever we feel attacked in some way. This sense of invasion may be physical or psychological. A car cuts in front of you; someone breaks into your home; your boss yells at you; your husband tells you he dislikes your cooking; your teenager uses your credit card without permission.

Many such incursions are barely noticeable and hardly seem worthy of the word *invasion*. But they, too, signal that something has arisen requiring response. The sense of invasion creates a wound, slight but real, and deserves to be honored as we would care for a cut or bruise— by paying attention. Attending to even the smallest felt invasion prepares us for when we are required to engage in the epic conflicts of our lives. And, just maybe, by paying attention we can learn how to stop wounding ourselves and others so carelessly.

## A Shift in Energy

Another signal that conflict has arrived is the sudden arousal or depletion of energy, either of which can follow an invasion. In the first instance, even though you may not consciously recognize an invasion as such, your subconscious does, and it responds either with blood rushing to your arms and heart or in readiness to run with energy rushing to your legs and feet. Conversely, in a state of sudden depletion your system shuts down to fainting level in order to survive.

These responses are extreme, appropriate for saving your life. When the invasion is relatively unimportant or subsides quickly, the arousal or depletion of energy may be minor. Nevertheless, any such shift may be a clue that conflict has arisen. (Of course, good news may also bring about a lovely upsurge of energy; and running a marathon may well leave you feeling depleted, neither shift having anything to do with invasion.)

## An Excess of Emotions

You can be sure that an energy shift signals a conflict when you simultaneously experience worry, anxiety, fear, anger, obsessive concern, or unremitting sorrow. Conflict may also be present when you simply feel a tiny flicker of uneasiness. Any of these feelings requires awareness. It helps to calm the emotions if you stop, breathe, and acknowledge that the sacred Power of Conflict has arrived and that something in your life is being asked to grow.

## The Need to Make a Choice

You can also trust that conflict has arisen whenever you have to make a difficult choice that challenges your principles and deeply held values. In my experience, the hard choice is usually the right one. For instance, what do you do when a friend asks you to tell her husband that you went with her to the movies last night, and you know she was seeing someone else? The right choice, I believe, would be to say no, even though you may sympathize more with your friend than with her husband.

I want to pause to talk about the word *grow*. Growth in the life of a sacred actor is a push from the eternal self, or the soul. I believe that the soul asks for, and sometimes demands, growth as a means of fulfilling its journey in this lifetime and that the Power of Conflict is the most potent means for achieving this goal. One part of the soul resides in the physical body; when we feel the soul's push toward growth, we are experiencing its desire to be more fully and gracefully embodied. Growth is the movement of the soul desiring to reveal itself ever more clearly. For one dramatic example of how conflict can lead to growth, we turn to Aeschylus's immortal play, *The Eumenides*:

# HERE'S THE STORY

Imagine that you embody a terrible and terrifying task: you exist to wreak vengeance on any person shedding the blood of anyone related to them by blood. With others of like kind you are called the Furies, and when needed you come raging up from under the ground to pursue the guilty one unto death. Some call you the fearsome Daughters of the Night.

At the moment, you pursue Orestes, who has killed his mother, Clytemnestra. Frantically, he races for sanctuary to the shrine of Apollo at Delphi, the holiest place in your world. The gods decide that Orestes should go safely to Athens, there to stand trial before the citizens, with you Furies demanding your rights and acting as his accusers.

The voting goes against you: the gods pardon Orestes inasmuch as he murdered Clytemnestra because she had killed his father, her husband King Agamemnon. In ancient Greek philosophy, this is the Divine's way of ending generations of family violence and revenge. For you Furies, though, it is a crushing and infuriating blow, and, speaking in chorus as one being, you threaten vengeance on the whole country:

> I, disinherited, suffering, heavy with anger
> shall let loose on the land
> the vindictive poison
> dripping deadly out of my heart upon the ground;
> this from itself shall breed
> cancer, the leafless, the barren
> to strike, for the right, their low lands
> and drag its smear of mortal infection on the ground.
> What shall I do? Afflicted
> I am mocked by these people.
> I have borne what can not
> be borne. Great the sorrows and the dishonor upon
> the sad daughters of night.[1]

Such is the conflict that you Furies face, and all you want is to make the whole world pay for your not being able to destroy Orestes. But the playwright shows that even this dire conflict can be seen as an opportunity for growth. The wise goddess Athena, rising to the occasion with glorious promises of honor and respect that only a goddess could devise, persuades you Furies to change your very nature and become Gentle, Kindly Ones instead. Athena asks:

> Do good, receive good, and be honored as the good
> are honored. Share our country, the beloved of god.[2]

178

Throughout the long interaction with the goddess, you, the Furies, feel a fundamental shift taking place within until you are free to say on behalf of the people of Athens:

> I speak this prayer for them
> that the sun's bright magnificence shall break out wave
> on wave of all the happiness
> life can give, across their land.[3]

Thus Aeschylus orchestrates the transformation of the hideous, raging Furies into Kindly Ones who become guardians of the city. No passage in literature of which I know shows more vividly the promise of growth inherent in even the most painful conflict.

## *Pause, Please*

By now, as a skilled sacred actor, you know that deep work always involves questions. In engaging the Power of Conflict, the questions include: What is this conflict requiring of me? What skill, what understanding, what quality needs to grow?

Survey with kind eyes a recent conflict in your life. Were you merely defensive, or were you willing to open to the conflict and allow the alchemy of it to change you?

Notice whether the conflict involved a choice. What was the nature of that choice? What conflict of principles did it evoke?

For instance, suppose you are leaving a bookstore with a new book, one you can hardly wait to read. You spy a young friend, obviously distraught, who begins to talk haltingly about what's distressing him. It's late; you're tired. He's not easy to understand, and your real friendship is with his mother. What to do? Stay and talk, take him for coffee, or brush him off with an "I'll call you"?

The easy choice—the one I took—was to say good night and leave. The hard choice would have been to give up on the book and listen to his story. I had lots of excuses not to make that choice, but I know it would have been the right one because my heart has been hurting ever since. And I haven't been able to open the book. What was being asked to grow then was my empathy and compassion, and I turned the invitation down. What is being asked to grow now is my self-forgiveness. Further, I can call the young man and make a date with him.

Regarding a similar recent conflict in your own life, is anything left for you to do to bring an affirmative closure to the event?

## STEP TWO:
## KNOW THAT WE ARE ON SACRED GROUND

To repeat, when any sense of invasion occurs, we begin by acknowledging that the Power of Conflict has arrived. The second step is to acknowledge that, when we are in a state of conflict, we are on holy ground.

Conflict transports us back to the origins of Western theatre, when the plays of Aeschylus, Sophocles, and Euripides were enacted in the service of the gods, grappling with the overriding mysteries of life and death. Greek tragedies were a cry about what it means to be human, in which we hold our arms up to the heavens and shout, "Who? What? Why? What is this agony called life about?" Even today, whenever conflict makes itself felt, we can know that we are on sacred ground and in the hands of the gods.

In wrestling with the question, "Why is conflict sacred?" one answer is that the stakes are so high; they often involve life and death, not just of the body, but of values, ideas, hopes, and one's very sense of self-worth. In extreme cases—betrayal, the violation of innocence, the undermining of sanity—even the soul is at risk. Conflict places our entire lives on an altar. Sometimes we are sacrificed to it, and sometimes we rise again reborn, or transformed.

In his book *In Over Our Heads*, Robert Kegan of Harvard University speaks of the psychological work of conflict in our lives and gives me a new way of looking at conflict in drama. He says that the purpose, especially of sustained conflict, is not resolution but transformation. When we become aware that we ourselves are in fact the enemy, then the opportunity for transformation opens. Kegan writes eloquently of this process as "Fifth Level Consciousness," or "Postmodernism":

> In essence, the postmodern view bids disputants to do several things: (1) consider that your protracted conflict is a signal that you and your opponent have probably become identified with the poles of the conflict; (2) consider that the relationship in which you find yourself is not the inconvenient result of the existence of an opposing view but the expression of your own incompleteness taken as completeness; (3) value the relationship, miserable though it might feel, as an opportunity to live out your own multiplicity; and thus, (4) focus on ways to let the conflictual relationship transform the parties rather than on the parties resolving the conflict. Postmodernism suggests a kind of "conflict resolution" in which the Palestinian discovers her own Israeli-ness, the rich man discovers his poverty, the woman discovers the man inside her."[4]

Such a joining of opposites is the supreme, transcendent level of the Power of Conflict, and what a miraculous world we would find ourselves inhabiting were we able to embrace it.

A culture that regularly practices the possibility of transformation through sacred conflict is the Balinese. Their island is so close to the equator that day and night there are almost equal in length all year round. They have no twilight. One minute it is day; the next, night. The seasons are similarly balanced: at the equator, there is no movement of the earth toward or away from the sun to produce longer nights in winter and longer days in summer.

It is a useful oversimplification to claim that this balance in the climate and geographic location of Bali has perhaps contributed to a mind-set and a spirituality unique in the world. The Balinese culture rests on maintaining a sense of balance between the forces experienced as of the earth and those felt in the air above. The Balinese way

181

of maintaining equilibrium is to present daily offerings that honor both light and dark, the above and the below; to keep a ceremonial calendar that balances the seasons of planting and harvest; and to dress in such a way—with a wide sash at the waist—that indicates a clear division between the higher and lower forces and yet respects them both. When a bomb exploded some years ago at a Kuta Beach nightclub, thoughtful Balinese did not blame outsiders; instead, they asked, "What has gone out of balance that such an act could occur?" They then proceeded to hold ceremonies all over the island that would restore balance to their country.

## HERE'S THE STORY

Imagine that you are a Balinese citizen preparing for a ritual enactment of an archetypal conflict. It is a ceremony you know well, consisting of a battle between two massive energies: one in the form of *Rangda*, perceived as the witch of black magic, and the other in the form of the *Barong*, perceived as a mystical deity of protection and beneficence.

Rangda is portrayed with a fearsome mask with dripping fangs and tangled hair. She hisses horribly, screams threats in an eerie, high-pitched voice, and utters terrifying laughs sounding like curses. Able to turn her opponents' knives back on them, she seems to embody all the negative forces in life against which we must do legitimate battle.[5] Barong, on the other hand, is a (two-person) long, lion-masked, godlike creature of pure goodness. Imagine yourself one of the actors whose role is to manipulate the Barong mask from inside the costume and to stand firm when confronted with Rangda's evil intentions against your helpers and allies.

Hours before the battle is actually joined, the ceremony commences with priests performing a sacrifice and blessing the performers and audience with holy water to protect them against the powers about to be unleashed. Then the fight begins! Rangda, driven by pain and malevolence, emerges from the darkness of the woods, uttering a bloodcurdling cry. She is terrifying and very powerful; her movements and vocal incantations can induce trance in bystanders as well as in those on the battlefield.

You as the Barong, in your goodness, purity, and courage, stand calm in the midst of chaos, representing an equal and opposite force to Rangda in a wild and mesmerizing dance accompanied by the music of the gamelan orchestra. As your followers rush forward to destroy her, your holy presence keeps them from physical damage. Caught in Rangda's spell, they turn their knives against themselves. But you move toward them protectively, and then priests pour out holy water to bring them out of trance. Undaunted, you as the Barong continue to challenge Rangda. Finally, you drive her back into the darkness from which she came.

In the end nobody, yet everybody, wins. Rangda retreats; she cannot defeat you as Barong. At the same time, she cannot be defeated. In some accounts, after the confrontation Rangda and Barong overcome their differences and are at peace again.

The audience members as well as the actors know that the battle is fought on behalf of the community and every individual in it, that it represents the forces that contend within every human soul. You know that the Barong wins only for now. Rangda's retreat is only temporary; when she retires from the battle, she is simply leaving the field. After the ritual, her mask and costume are protected with as much care as the Barong's, ready for their next appearance.

Thus do the Balinese honor, even in the handling of ceremonial objects, the dynamic balance that pervades their sense of spiritual and physical reality. Fred Eiseman, an expert on Balinese culture, says that for them, the question of the "good" guys winning is irrelevant. Perhaps rooted in their experience of the balance between day and night, they know that the point is the symbolic struggle "to maintain an equilibrium of opposing powers."[6] The deep truth is in the tension between opposites, in the "ground" that supports figures and contenders of all sorts, including good and evil.[7] This way of knowing is the truth of paradox and metaphor. It involves a perspective that can embrace *both* sides, protagonist and antagonist, as any playwright must do in order to create great villains—and great heroes.

Importantly, though, for the Balinese this ceremony is not a performance but an enactment of mythic truth. They have the courage to engage the metaphysical battle between good and evil (as we would think of it) through ceremonial representation. The Great War is not out there, but right here, and the forces are not just an idea safely contained in the mind. Rangda is an actual spitting, cursing reality, Barong a great lion-hearted being of playful goodness. The actors conceive of themselves not as acting but as believers participating in an eternal battle taking place right now. And because they believe it, the audience does, too. One's skin virtually crawls with being in the presence of someone brave enough to do battle with what we perceive as evil incarnate. Not only are the actors transformed in this embodiment, but the people who watch it are, also. When we see Rangda retreat, if only for a moment, it renews our courage to do battle with the opposing forces that seek to drive us off balance and away from a sense of the sacred in our own lives.

## *Pause, Please*

Just as the Balinese dance is fought on holy ground in a community that knows its world as sacred, we, too, need to recognize our own conflicts as sacred in order to engage them authentically.

Continue imagining that you are the actor playing the Barong and are thus an instrument for good. Look at an issue you have resolutely shoved under the carpet, perhaps a long-standing one you have been unable to resolve. Try calling it forth now and inviting a divine witness—whatever you think of as God.

Doing so carries you and the issue to hallowed ground. Can you see this conflict as a message from your soul calling you to grow? Can you see the growth being asked for as a move toward balance? Might you shift your point of view to see the situation as your opponent does? Can you hold the tension of opposing viewpoints long enough to sense what new thing is wanting to emerge?

# Step Three:
# Name the Loss

Courage is required when authentically engaging the mighty Power of Conflict, courage to look at what the situation has cost and is still costing you. That loss need not necessarily be of anything tangible, such as your home in an acrimonious divorce. It can, and significantly usually does, entail more of a psychological or even spiritual cost, such as betrayal, psychic diminishment, or loss of respect or trust.

Whatever the anguish, in order for conflict to be a catalyst for growth, the loss it involves needs to be named. Storytellers have always known the power of such naming. In Homer's *The Odyssey*, Odysseus's most touching action is to call aloud the names of shipmates he has lost during every struggle, be it with storms, sea creatures, or mythical beings. Such naming is an essential part of grieving. It does not complete the process, but it does close the gaping wounds the loss has opened and make it possible to move forward. In naming his dead companions, I believe Odysseus is also making a promise: he will not forget them.

Note that it is important to name the loss regardless of whether it concerns something inflicted upon you or that you have inflicted upon someone else. In twelve-step programs, the latter is addressed in the suggestion to "take a fearless moral inventory." Just as you, the sacred actor, need to know the great verbs on which the action of your life moves, so too you need to acknowledge the results of that action.

If you have taken the steps 1) to recognize that when you have entered the realm of conflict, you are being asked to grow, and 2) to remember that in conflict you are on holy ground, then, whether the cause for distress is in the past or in the present, you can now take step 3) to name the loss. As long as the pain we suffer from or inflict remains unnamed, we are likely to be unconscious about its effect. The more we become aware of the precise nature of what the conflict costs, the less likely we are to enter a new fray blindly.

Naming the loss also opens the Power of Expression and provides an avenue for experiencing the true feelings sometimes hidden in the losses. We may feel enraged because some friend has betrayed us. We need to notice the rage, yes, and name it, but naming it also opens us to a deeper sense of the real sorrow that may rest within it. This sorrow, too, needs to be named: the betrayal has left you vulnerable and untrusting; it has changed your life; it deserves respect and time.

## Here's the Story

Imagine that you are an aging, powerful queen. Your name is Hecuba. Troy, your city, lies devastated after a ten-year-long war perpetrated by marauding Greeks. Your sons are dead in battle; you are a prisoner about to be enslaved by a Greek general. Only two people remain alive in your lineage. One is your daughter Cassandra, driven mad by grief and her clairvoyant ability to see the horrors that still await her. The other is your beloved six-year-old grandson, Astyanax.

Then the triumphant Greeks decide to throw Astyanax off the walls of Troy to make sure he never grows up to take vengeance on them. You, Hecuba, protest but to no avail. They bring his broken body to you for burial, lying on the shield of his father, Hector, your dead warrior son. You speak your heartbreak over it, naming the many faces of your loss:

> Beloved, what a death has come to you.
> If you had fallen fighting for your city,
> if you had known strong youth and love
> and god-like power, if we could think
> you had known happiness, if there is happiness anywhere . . .
> Poor little one. How savagely our ancient walls,

186

Apollo's towers, have torn away the curls
your mother's fingers wound and where she pressed
her kisses—here where the broken bone grins white—
Oh no—I cannot . . .
False words you spoke to me
when you would jump into my bed, call me sweet names
and tell me, "Grandmother, when you are dead, I'll cut off a
great lock of hair, and lead my soldiers all
to ride out past your tomb."
Not you, but I, old, homeless, childless,
must lay you in your grave, so young,
so miserably dead . . .
Come bring such covering for the pitiful dead body
as we still have. God has not left us much
to make a show with. Everything I have, I give you, child.
[*She begins to wrap his body in a piece of cloth*]
So on your wedding day I would have dressed you,
the highest Princess of the East your bride.
Now on your body I must lay the raiment,
all that is left of the splendor that was Troy.[8]

Hecuba's poignant speech primarily concerns the loss of her grandson's life, but she also identifies the sorrows that lie within that loss. She names her love for the boy, she names the loss of his future and his possibility for happiness as a grown man, she names the truth of his physical wounds, and she names her sorrow at the disruption in the natural course of life (he should have buried her). She names her shame that there is nothing splendid left with which to adorn his body, and she names her sorrow at never seeing this adored child married. At the end of the speech, her sorrow opens to include the loss of all the riches and power her great city of Troy once had.

Such insistent naming is the potent device that allows Hecuba to begin the healing process of grieving. This process is absolutely necessary in order for her to retain her sanity, support the other women who still look to her as their leader, and maintain her dignity. Hecuba's heart and body are broken, but her mind and soul are intact. During the formal dirge that she chants while wrapping her grandson's body, she suddenly pauses and then cries out:

> O Women, I have seen the open hand of God, and in it nothing.
> Only pain for me and pain for Troy, those he hated bitterly . . .
> And yet—had God not brought us down,
> not laid us low as dust,
> None would have heard of us, or told our wrongs,
> In everlasting story and in song, that men will listen to
> Forever.[9]

It is the power of naming her losses that fires Hecuba's revelation that the story of Troy will be told in the ages to come. And it is precisely this revelation that gives her and the other Trojan women the strength to endure when they walk off together into "a new day of slavery" at the play's end.

## Pause, Please

Our work here is to deal gently with an old conflict in which you experienced a loss—of face, trust, truth, or health. The conflict may have been huge, having to do with illness or even the death of a loved one. Or it may have been small, perhaps in some dispute with another person—your boss, your son, your neighbor, your best friend.

Choose one situation and review the first two steps of engaging the Power of Conflict. Look courageously at what occurred—"He said, she said, I said back"—but consider it in terms of what was being invited to grow. Then bring in your divine witness as a way of remembering that conflict is a sacred endeavor.

Now name on paper whatever you feel was lost in this conflict. Don't bother to put your list in any kind of order; just name as many actual losses as you experienced. If emotions arise, as they probably will, name them as well. Treat yourself kindly in this process.

Read your list of losses aloud. If more grieving is needed, acknowledge that truth. Notice what happens when you speak your losses. Do you feel clearer about the situation? Has honoring your losses through naming them given you new insight?

## Step Four:
## Take Appropriate Action

We're here to add to the sum of human goodness,
To prove the thing exists, and however futile each individual act
Of courage or generosity
Self-sacrifice, or grace—it still proves the thing exists.
Each act adds to the fund.

—Josephine Hart[10]

One result of doing the work of the first three steps is to buy time. In any conflict, it behooves us to postpone acting to assure that the action we finally *do* take is life-affirming instead of destructive. If we first simply acknowledge that conflict has arisen, recognize that we are thus on holy ground, and name potential losses, we are more likely to respond to any volatile situation in a fresh and thoughtful way.

### Conflict vs. Violence

Violence is a failure to engage the Power of Conflict in a healthy way. When I speak of taking appropriate action, I am definitely *not* speaking of any form of violence—physical, psychological, or verbal. To the contrary, it is only when we do not deal with conflict authentically that it turns into violence. When that happens, we realize painfully that our skills have been inadequate to the great task. We then have the unlovely job of cleaning up the mess we've made, internally or externally. On the other hand, the more skillful we become at handling conflict well, the more we reap the benefits it affords of leading to positive change.

Further, the Power of Conflict is not—repeat *not*—at play when we are the victim of another's violence. However, it is possible to respond to random or even intentional violence by taking the steps outlined above, especially by acknowledging what you have lost, declaring the wound as sacred, and eventually being able to ask: "What is being tested here? What needs to grow?" Our response may be one of a thousand things, ranging from, "My desire and capacity for vengeance wants to grow," or "I need Justice!" all the way to, "My compassion for myself needs to grow," or, "My capacity for forgiveness is being tested." All such responses are appropriate in Sacred Theatre.

The role that violence plays in news of current events, and in many movie and television presentations, has conditioned us to impulsive, inappropriate, and soul-killing responses to conflict. But beyond this cultural conditioning, we have a deeper, biological formation to be aware of and even grateful for.

## Hijacked by the Amygdala

Our knee-jerk response to aggression is triggered by a spray of chemistry coursing through our bodies called *adrenaline*. We probably owe our existence to it, in that thousands of years ago its capacity to spark a sudden, energetic response saved our ancestors' lives repeatedly in the face of dangers such as a charging saber-toothed tiger.

My favorite term for this instantaneous reaction is "being hijacked by the amygdala." The amygdala are two little, almond-shaped glands, in the left and right hemispheres of our brains, responsible for the biochemicals that surge forth in reaction to real or perceived danger. They help us determine the nature and intent of what we see approaching and prepare us for immediate response. And I mean *immediate*. When we are walking in the woods and happen to see a stick that looks like a snake, our reaction completely bypasses the cognitive brain and its capacity for rationality. No time for that! We are up in the air and six feet down the path in what seems to be a split second. The amygdala's response is not as precise as our ordinary cognitive understanding, but it gets the job done.

The difficulty is that, in bypassing those parts of the brain that make us most aware and judicious, these little glands can have us in a screaming, punching fit within seconds. And even though the amygdala have given us the ability to leap tall buildings, they have also regrettably caused us immediately to label a stranger as benign or dangerous, depending on our cultural conditioning. When this happens, the amygdala have "hijacked" the frontal cortex and can quickly lead to widespread violence.

Our task as sacred actors is to slow this process down. Various spiritual traditions and meditative practices can be useful in enabling us to gain time for the cognitive powers to assess a situation more accurately. Befriending people of diverse cultural backgrounds is a pleasant way to stop the seemingly automatic response our own culture may have engendered in us.

If our lives are to be more enjoyable and less stressful, certainly these issues need to be understood. I believe that the capable little amygdala are at play in most of our cataclysmic wars and hatreds as well as in our more modest personal conflicts. So we need to know about them. We need to notice when they are activated communally, for then it is much harder for our cognitive minds to quiet our collective response. When our automatic response systems overtake us, we can feel righteous about going to war and wreaking vengeance without consideration of consequences.

But here's the good news. True conflict need not descend to violence if the whole brain and body can come to attention and ask what capacity is being invited to grow and what action is really appropriate.

## Questions that Guide Us

At a deep level, even superficial conflicts pose a choice between supporting life or not. Even if the decision is just between taking a walk and watching TV, one choice is healthier for my heart than the other.

More critically, if I hold on to my resentments and hatred, I may be choosing a kind of death of my emotional life. In all situations, our work is to seek the action that leads to greater well-being. Three questions will take us there:

1. *Is my opponent weaker than I am—physically, mentally, emotionally?* If so, often what needs to grow is the realization that to engage in conflict is to diminish life. When children, for example, make us furious, we can rapidly become childish ourselves. I remember driving by a small boy playing in his yard. He pointed his toy gun at me and went "Bang!" I hit the brakes, leaped out of the car, and assaulted the child with words: "Never do that again!" traumatizing him and myself for some time.

   What was I to make of this embarrassing incident? My soul had sent out this small conflict to remind me that there's real inner work I need to do and action I need to take—but it doesn't include terrifying a child. In such uneven conflicts, I must stop, breathe, and become aware of what's been aroused within me, in this case my hair-trigger response to the sight of a gun pointed in my direction. Then I need to make clear decisions about my next steps, which include asking for forgiveness for being a bully.

   It is a truism of war that we choose enemies who are weaker than we are, thus easier to defeat. These uneven violent conflicts, however, cost the soul of a people much more than it can afford. They leave a generational debt that must and will be paid, in ways we cannot begin to calculate.

2. *Is my opponent my equal—in energy, resources, skills?* Engaging in conflict between equals carries enormous challenge and can be lots of fun. Men in our culture often tease and spar with one another as a way of demonstrating affection and of learning more about the other. Playwrights dramatize such equal conflict in the "merry wars" between hero and heroine, a delightful, humorous repartee that is usually a cover for love. Sometimes what's being asked to grow is a

greater sense of joy in the pleasure of the relationship. The action to take is the vital one of asking the next questions, including, "Where do we go from here? What are we accomplishing with this contention? What are we truly expressing?"

If this equal conflict is antagonistic, then we take action to determine what is needed for the conflict to become transformative. "What do I need to embrace about her or him? What shadow piece have I projected, and how can I reclaim it?"

This is the level of the conflict between Rangda and the Barong. The forces are equal over time, and each must acknowledge the power of the other. For the Balinese, these two contenders represent the forces that dwell within each human being. Great theatre puts the inner conflict out in front of us, center stage, so we can see it and feel it and know it to be our own.

When heroes fought with each other in the ancient world, this sense of equality was clear, and they battled to learn more about the other and about themselves. Only chance (or fate) dictated the victory.

3. *Is my opponent greater than I am?* Here we enter the realm of myth, of tragedy, of truly worthwhile conflict. In "The Man Watching," Rainer Maria Rilke speaks the truth that, in such a situation, victory is simply not possible:

> What is extraordinary and eternal
> does not *want* to be bent by us.
> I mean the angel, who appeared
> To the wrestlers of the Old Testament: . . .
> Whoever was beaten by this Angel, . . .
> went away proud and strengthened
> and great from that harsh hand,
> that kneaded him as if to change his shape.
> Winning does not tempt that man.
> This is how he grows: by being defeated, decisively,
> by constantly greater beings.[11]

193

As Rilke perceives so well, at this level of contention, it is never about winning; it is only about growing. But that doesn't mean we shouldn't engage in the battle. One noble action we can choose is to fight what is greater than we are. Here, the contention is with the gods themselves, as it was in the theatre of ancient Greece; indeed, it is a worthy match for the soul. That's why it is inappropriate to cop out of disagreements with an unjust government, for example, by whining that you can't win. The point is not about succeeding; it's about growing into the soul.

## Pause, Please

Now divide a sheet of paper into three columns headed with the words 1) Opponent weaker, 2) Opponent equal, 3) Opponent stronger. List one of your current conflicts in each category. What part of you is being invited to grow in each circumstance? What actions can you take to begin the process? When will you begin?

Let us return to one of the most magnificent plays ever written, Sophocles' *Oedipus the King*. We met Oedipus earlier in chapter 2. In this play, Sophocles shows us a human being who contends against the gods.

### Here's the Story Again

You recall that Oedipus was fated before birth to kill his father, Laius, king of Thebes, and marry his mother, the queen Jocasta. To thwart the prophecy Laius leaves his infant son on a mountaintop to die, but a shepherd finds and gives him to the royal family in Corinth. As an adult, Oedipus hears the dreadful prophecy and to avoid fulfilling it runs away from the people he thinks are his parents. On the road he kills an arrogant old man. The people of Thebes hail him as a hero for conquering the Sphinx, and he marries Queen Jocasta. A plague strikes; a seer declares that it will not lift until King Laius's murderer is found. Oedipus begins a manhunt, only to discover that he himself is the murderer, the man he killed having been Laius, his true father. In spite of Oedipus's best intentions, he has brought about the patricide and the incest he tried so hard to escape.

The moment when Oedipus realizes that he is the dire criminal he seeks is heart-wrenching. We in the audience hang breathless as he responds to the news. In all the productions I've seen, the actors playing Oedipus have worn masks; the naked human face would be hard put to portray the fullness of his reaction. The great Laurence Olivier poured the character's response into sound, uttering a scream that originated in the agony of a small animal cruelly injured and swelling from there.

Action follows hard upon the news. The mother/wife, Jocasta, realizes the truth before Oedipus does. She begs him to seek no further for answers and runs agonized from the stage.

As soon as Oedipus grasps the truth, he pursues Jocasta offstage to do . . . we cannot know what. We imagine a horrible confrontation. She has become the last person outside of himself that he can accuse. She is the last possible external enemy, and she has moved herself beyond the reach of his terror and ferocity. In the royal bedroom they shared, where their children were conceived, she has hanged herself.

We learn all this from a witness, who tells us the last bitter episode as well. Oedipus has ripped the brooches from the shoulders of Jocasta's gown and, using them as daggers, stabbed out his eyes. He is unable to look upon the woman he has loved as a wife, who is now revealed to be his mother, and whose body swings from the rafter of their bedroom. In his deep shame and self-loathing, he cannot bear to look into the eyes of others and see their horror and terrible pity.

Ironically, it is when Oedipus finally sees the truth that he blinds himself, and, in becoming physically sightless, is able to look inward. For he doesn't die. Now his new journey begins. The conflict is acknowledged as internal. Fate has done its worst. All that is left is to choose to allow the alchemical process of true growth and vision to begin. As a blind exile, Oedipus wanders the countryside, enduring all things, slowly becoming what he most deeply is, a holy man burned in the fires of pure wisdom, eventually able to remark that "suffering and vast time have been instructors in contentment."[12] And in this exquisite and hard-won equanimity, he can finally be said to have overcome his fate.

Oedipus has been called the world's first murder mystery, and we watch it with edge-of-our-seats attention. How is it possible that poor Oedipus, who carefully did everything necessary to avoid the fate the oracle decreed, would nevertheless fulfill its dreadful prophecy? The great questions posed by the playwright about the remorseless, fated qualities of human life are far beyond the reach of this book. But when we view the story from the vantage of Sacred Theatre, we see that no matter how good or righteous an individual may be, no matter how determined his efforts to escape his destiny, something much stronger may be in charge. We can call it fate, or we can call it genetics. One's only possible course is to endure all, as Oedipus does, perhaps with the same tragic nobility.

## *Pause, Please*

The Oedipus story holds wise guidance about how to deal with the most overwhelming and tragic conflicts of our lives. The questions it poses are difficult ones. Please be kind to yourself as you try to answer them.

What long-term conflict, involving perhaps much blaming of someone else, may be requiring you to look inward and see the truth with new eyes? If it involves years of dispute with a spouse or a parent, what is your role in the conflict? Have you contributed to its intensity? What healing choice might you make that would allow the energy of the conflict to dissipate, even if only slightly?

Do you sense the presence of fate? If so, what appropriate action can you take to shift that terrible burden?

In this exploration, it is important to investigate our own conundrums with courage equal to that of Oedipus. We don't put out our eyes, certainly, but we do become willing, finally, to confront the truth. Otherwise, we can waste years not facing it and continuing to let our denial do damage. A key is to withdraw our projections and become willing to look at the internal, not just the external, dimensions of the conflict. That's when we gain clarity and begin to grow.

Part of this process is to become willing to shift a rigid point of view, especially one held in self-righteousness. It is to acknowledge that we humans share a fear of discovery equal with the fear of falling. The more sternly we hold the stance of self-righteousness, the more likely we are beneath it to be terrified that our true self is unbearably unworthy and will be revealed as such. And as Oedipus plays out for us, in our most excruciating conflicts we may indeed have to face that we are not the Golden One but the pariah. We ourselves may be the one who has to change (heaven forbid!).

Few of us must endure such absolute heartbreak as Oedipus did. The quintessential sacred actor, he elegantly demonstrates the growth potentiated by such wounding. Our best ultimate response to the deepest conflicts of our lives may be simply to accept with Oedipus that no one is ultimately to blame. Life just is what it is, as is true, say, when you have inherited a troublesome disease that manifests in spite of your best efforts to maintain your health.

If we take on these deepest challenges in life with courage and integrity, and even though we may never win—instead always being, as Rilke says, "defeated, decisively, by constantly greater beings"—we may nevertheless achieve a kind of serenity, even as Oedipus does. Remember, he ended his life with immense dignity, revered far and wide as a wise and holy being. So, by the grace of heaven, may we all.

*Friends, Romans, countrymen, lend me your ears.*
— Mark Antony, Shakespeare's *Julius Caesar* (3.2.74)

# Eight

# The Power of Audience

**M**ark Antony's line on the facing page in Shakespeare's *Julius Caesar* is one of the most famous in the world. Caesar's murdered body lies onstage before us; one of his assassins, the noble-minded Brutus, has just addressed an audience of ordinary Roman citizens, beginning, "Romans, countrymen, and lovers, hear me for my cause, and be silent that you may hear"(3.2.13–14). He has assured them that Caesar was a tyrant in the making, and in order to protect them from his tyranny, he—Brutus—and others have killed him. But when Caesar's particular ally, the young Mark Antony, begins to speak *his* version of Caesar's funeral oration, a different story emerges, to the audience both onstage and in the theatre. By the time Antony has worked his furious magic, his onstage audience transforms into a riotous mob and begins rampaging through the city.

This is one of Shakespeare's many demonstrations of the Power of Audience: a potent actor speaking charged words with great intention can so affect his hearers that they surge into action to do his will. As sacred actors, we, too, need to be aware of this power and to understand its effects on us and others, both as speakers and as listeners. In life, our audience is everyone we know and interact with. It gives us one of the two reasons for doing our play and provides a noble answer to the question, "Why? Why am I going to all this trouble of living as fully and as consciously as possible?" (The other answer, as the next chapter explores, lies in the Power of Celebration: we do all this work in order to be able to say *yes*! to life, no matter what.)

## HELLO IN THERE!

What makes an audience? The word originates in the Latin *audire*, meaning "to hear." Thus an audience comprises those who not only observe the action but are also capable of authentic hearing, of deep listening. Brilliant scientists and practitioners of the importance of music and sound to our lives and bodies differentiate between the act of hearing and the art of listening. One is Dr. Alfred A. Tomatis, Parisian physician of the ear, nose, and throat, best known for his studies and treatment of singers, awarded the Knight of Public Health of France in 1951. He authored fourteen books and inspired whole schools as well as many other books, including some by a good friend, the musician, musicologist, and author, Don Campbell. Dr. Tomatis says in *The Ear and the Voice*, "Hearing is a superficial use of one's ear, while listening implies an act of will to connect with the sonic environment and learn what must be known."[1]

True, the art of seeing sometimes subsumes the art of listening. Molecular biologist John Medina observes that "vision is by far our most dominant sense, taking up half of our brain's resources."[2] But geniuses of the study of sound, including Tomatis and Campbell, say that a much wider spectrum of sound waves is audible to us than the band of electromagnetic waves comprising our visual range. That is, the band of waves we can hear is much wider than the band of waves we can see. More importantly, the art of listening helps to support our awareness of where we are in space and whether we stand balanced; it provides information about things to the side and all around us; and it helps to regulate our voices in singing and in speaking.

Recently Don Campbell spoke to me of the effect of sound waves on eleven of the twelve cranial nerves: they affect how we stand, how we respond, and how the brain functions. About one of those nerves, the vagus nerve, Dr. Tomatis says: "The vagus nerve plays an essential role in the act of singing as well as in speaking. . . . Usually, nerves are either motor with direct command over muscles, or sensory if their task is to refer perceptual information. Some are both somatic motor and sensory. . . . The vagus nerve combines all of these functions. It is somatic, motor, sensory, and parasympathetic, giving it the ability to regulate the abdominal viscera. Moreover, it spreads over an immense area of the human body."[3]

The vagus nerve thus forms the greatest part of the parasympathetic nervous system and balances with the sympathetic nervous system. Here is Tomatis again: "It is this nerve that helps the singer to consciously rediscover the correct respiratory rhythm as well as the cardiac and visceral rhythms so that a synergy is created between this internal network and the larynx, the posture, the attitude, and so forth. . . . It is equally important in mastering a fluid and correct verbal flow in speech. The same synergy must take place if we are to have a coherent and orderly train of thought."[4]

Dr. Tomatis focuses on the need to develop the art of listening in order to be a good singer or speaker and provides evidence that engaging the art of listening affects one's entire internal balance and well-being. Following his lead, our focus is the conscious engagement of the power of listening to others and of increasing our awareness of who it is that listens to us.

## *Pause, Please*

Let us practice the art of listening. Sit quietly for a moment. Relax your body as much as you can. Breathe easily and slowly.

Tense the muscles of your neck, and relax them. Again, tense the muscles of your neck, and relax. Tense the muscles of your face, and then relax. Again, the muscles of your face, tight. And relax.

Breathe easily in and out, perhaps reciting silently one of the mindfulness *gathas* offered by the saintly Vietnamese Buddhist teacher, Thich Nhat Hanh: "When I breathe in, I know that I am breathing in. When I breathe out, I know I am breathing out."[5] Continue that for a few moments and for several breaths.

Now bring attention to your ears. Focus first on the outer ears; they both amplify and filter sounds, selecting particular ones to convey to the inner ear. Let your awareness extend to the middle and inner parts of the ear. Imagine you can sense the nerves that connect the reception of sound waves to the brain and all the organs of the body, every part of it flowing with information coming from sound waves.

Now let your eyes go soft and listen to the sounds around you. Pay attention to them for a few minutes. Notice all the different sounds: the chirping of birds, the swish of traffic, branches moving in the breeze, the hum of an electrical appliance, and so on. Notice, too, if your body responds to any of these sounds in an unexpected way. If a sound startles you, notice that your body usually responds more quickly than does your ability to identify the sound.

## Hello Out There!

All performance artists depend on the Power of Audience for their existence. No piece of theatre is created without the expectation that, somewhere, sometime, an audience will attend it. Further, each time the play is performed it will be different, partly because it and the audience provide a feedback loop: the play sustains and moves the audience, and, by its responses, the audience sustains and enlivens the players. An audience member will cry aloud at something unexpected that occurs on stage; another will laugh at a strange moment; another will make a comment. The audience thus becomes an active participant, affecting—subtly and not so subtly—the play's quality and effectiveness. The theatre becomes an interactive cauldron, where nobody knows for sure exactly what is going to happen next. This unpredictability heightens everyone's awareness, enabling performers and viewers alike to adapt at need. In this way, every work of theatre, including your life play, contains the force not only to change its witnesses utterly but also to be utterly changed by them.

## Here's the Story

Imagine that you have been present at several theatres across time, both as performer and as audience member. We'll begin with a reconstruction of the first play.

It is night. We are in a cave; you can see faces in the flickering firelight and hear the murmur of voices. The clan has been fed (thank all the powers!) and there has been enough for all. Tonight is special, though: something new has been discovered. Honey! All around the circle, voices marvel at this strange sweetness.

You, the heroic provider of this gift, begin telling the story of how you found the honey and brought it home. But suddenly you make a mind leap: instead of simply recounting what happened, you stand up and begin to *enact* it. We in your audience gasp at this electrifying difference. Immediately, we are transported into the magic of *Now!*

We look on avidly as you show us with voice and body how it is to move through the forest and spy a solitary bee sucking at a flower. You decide to trail it back to its hive. You wonder what the hundreds of bees there are humming about. Then you make a marvelous connection: the sweetness of the smell and the nectar taste of the flower are somehow related to what's happening in the hive.

Suddenly you hear a large creature crashing through the woods and recognize the sound and smell of BEAR! To dramatize the moment, you begin mimicking a bear's movements—you *become* the bear. Thus as the first actor in the world you add to your repertoire by portraying another character.

A small boy in the audience, in order not to feel frightened, jumps up and "becomes" your baby bear. You improvise a bear dance with him (notice that this unforeseen eventuality of the boy changes the story; notice also your actor's skill in quickly accepting it). Then you as mother bear show your cub the hive. He wonders and listens. You hide him behind you and carefully approach the hive. The audience murmurs with appreciation and understanding.

Then, returning to your role as storyteller, you show us how you hide behind a tree. You watch as the mother bear swipes at the hive and buries her paws inside, pulling out a dripping substance. The angry bees start to buzz and bite. We in the audience know how fierce these stings are, and we cringe for the bear. Does the bear care? No! Her baby is safe; her fur and hide protect him.

Once more playing the bear, you swat the bees away, focusing only on the substance wrenched from the hive. You share it with the baby bear, who licks his fingers and sucks enthusiastically. (The young actor is really getting into his role!)

You, the watcher, playing yourself again, show us how you smell the honey and the bears together. You see both bears go lumbering off pursued by the bees, who are torn between punishing the robber and bewailing the condition of their home. As you follow cautiously, you notice that the bear drops a piece of the glistening substance. The bees, meanwhile, give up and move back to the ravaged hive. You pick up the broken piece of stuff. It's dripping and sticky. Tentatively, you stick your finger in your mouth, and—for the very first time in the experience of humankind—you taste the sweetness of honey. We in your audience laugh at the delight on your face and the sounds of pleasure you make; we are tasting the miracle again, too.

This is the story you intended simply to *narrate*, and it is a good one. But tonight, you have been moved further to *show* us, your audience, what happened. And notice how our reactions help you shape the play: As we in your audience watch you wander through the forest, we encourage you onward. We see you notice the bee sup. And we see how our response inspires you to enhance the story: you don't just tell us about the bee; you become the bee, buzzing your way back to the hive.

Some of us grab the idea and join in to make the sounds of the hive: an orchestra and a chorus are born!

Notice, too, how this enactment catches fire in the audience's mind; some want to join in the action, some want to observe. I like to think of such an instance also as the first in which theatre became a teaching device. After the excitement has died down, I can imagine the audience discussing how to steal more honey and do it safely.

## A Passion Play:
## How I Fell in Love with Being an Audience

I saw my first professional performance at about ten years old. For weeks my parents had thrilled me with the news that we were going to Houston (the biggest city in my life) to see a Passion Play. Having only a vague notion of what *passion* meant, I tormented myself wondering what a play of passion could mean. The dictionary didn't help, and I was such a secretive child that I didn't have the courage to ask. By then I already knew what a play is: people become other people and act out a story. But a *passion* play?

The long-awaited day finally came. The excitement was palpable as we struggled through the crowds thronging into the huge Houston auditorium, filled with more people than I had ever seen in one place at one time.

I met my first lover that day—Leonard. He sat next to me; I was at the end of my family's seats and he at his. We whispered together, and I fell madly in love. Afterward, and although I didn't know how to spell his name, I wrote it over and over: *Leonhard, Lentard, Lion Heart.* It was a relationship born of the shadows of the auditorium, and there it stayed, an integral part of the passion of that play. In my no-doubt faulty memory, we grip hands in secret, wild possessiveness as we watched the play unfold.

Had my family been Roman Catholic, I would surely have known by the age of ten that *passion* in this context referred to the Passion of Our Lord and Savior Jesus Christ, albeit I might not have comprehended how the story of Easter involved passion as I understood it. But even as a Protestant child I soon recognized the story as one I knew by heart. Then I became obsessed over the crucifixion scene. Dear God! Would the actor have to endure the nails, the sword, the obscene degradation of hanging so long on the cross? One thought particularly alarmed me: would the actor playing Jesus actually die? If so, could we count on his resurrection?

Lion Heart and I surreptitiously clasped hands ever more intensely as the scenes progressed: Jesus's triumphal entry into Jerusalem; the Last Supper, staged as in Leonardo da Vinci's painting; the Agony in the Garden, attended by sleepy disciples; the savior's arrest, trial, and judgment; Pilate washing his guilty hands; the Stations of the Cross; and, finally, the actual death—the *Passion*, as I now know it to be called.

My mind split in several ways, as it does in any audience member. One part followed the story, alert to and critical of any deviation from character or event. Another part was aware of my emotions as I watched the actors work: "Ah! That's what it looks like, feels like, sounds like to be driven to exclaim, 'Let this cup pass from me!'" Another part was vastly relieved that nails weren't actually being driven into the actor's hands and feet and that somehow he was supported on the cross, not hanging from it. Yet another part was asking, "How did they do that?" while another was shushing this curious part, wanting only to give in to the experience. I would later learn that a sophisticated audience willingly suspends disbelief when it enters a theatre.

Thunder in the mind! Passion born! Something happened to me in that auditorium. What was born was a passion for witnessing theatrical performances—wholeheartedly engaged with the unfolding play and with other audience members. Also born was the insight that the drama mirrored the many variations of the story that the audience members were themselves playing out in their own lives.

That insight has evolved as a central life teaching. Each of us lives a Passion Play. Enacting particular aspects of it, or seeing others enact it, profoundly affects the way we live our play, understand it, and learn from it. That awareness has inspired my years of offering workshops in Sacred Theatre, as well as given me the energy to try to capture the essence of the transitory experience of the theatre and translate it into words on a page.

As for being an audience member, even today, many years after that first experience, a passion for the play re-ignites the minute I step into the theatre, any theatre, anywhere in the world.

## HERE'S ANOTHER STORY

It is dawn in Athens, Greece, in the year 406 BCE. You are the actor portraying the god Dionysus in *The Bacchae*, a play by that troublesome genius, Euripides. The lonely, embittered playwright has recently died in exile, and his son has brought his play to be performed as one of several in the annual theatre festival that is also a contest, with entries by all the best playwrights.

Dionysus, also known as Bacchus, is the god of wine and ecstasy. In the Greek pantheon, his status is high, indeed: he is the patron god of theatre, to whom the Athenian festival of drama is dedicated, and he is also revered as the god of prophecy. But Euripides' characterization of Dionysus is fiercely ironic. With his usual irreverence and ambiguity, he presents the god as at once beneficent and ruthlessly vengeful, "most terrible, and yet most gentle, to mankind."[6]

Hence you the actor portraying Dionysus have a controversial and difficult role (and one any actor would sacrifice his eyeteeth to play) for which you have been rehearsing for months. For you, the risk is doubled: portraying a god at any time is perilous—who knows how the god himself might react to the way you present him? But portraying *this* god the way *this* playwright has written him increases the hazard exponentially: You will perform in a festival dedicated to Dionysus, in a theatre named for him, and from a stage where you will see the priests who serve this god sitting in special reserved seats. And you will perform before thousands of people who may love and worship Dionysus.

Yet you will portray this beloved god to them all as utterly merciless and cruel. No wonder you are nervous!

You wonder what might happen if this vast audience becomes displeased or feels incited—nay, *invited*—to riot. Nevertheless, your respect for Euripides, as well as your training in the capacity to enchant and control your audience, sustains you. As the sun's first rays strike the stage, you step into the scene with the grace of Dionysus's animal associate, the panther.

Now shift your attention to become a member of the audience filing into the theatre. You have looked forward to this festival for months: How will the stories of the gods and ancestors be presented this time? What new twists, what fresh and daring interpretations, will the most outstanding playwrights offer?

Your fellow playgoers are murmuring over Euripides' death and whether his new play will stir up controversies. You remember his *Trojan Women*, presented some years ago, and how clear a protest it had voiced against what many perceived as Athenian imperialism. Today, nearing the end of Athens' crushing defeat in the Peloponnesian War, you are aware of how far that "imperialism" has led your city and civilization toward destruction, and you recall Euripides' scathing criticism with some rue. Euripides has always been famous for his outrageous (some say sacrilegious) characterizations of both mythic and human beings.[7] In this new play, *The Bacchae,* will he once again threaten the worldview you hold dear? Even though you are properly reverential on this sacred occasion, you are also the citizen of a proud city, and you don't always take kindly to criticism, either direct or implied, of yourself or your leaders. Nor do your leaders respond graciously to real or perceived attacks from playwrights. Nevertheless, Euripides' work is always as fascinating as it is difficult, and you have anticipated this new work so eagerly in part because you never know what he's going to say next. You only know that, whatever he says, it will shake you to your core.

In this charged atmosphere, the play begins. You in the audience become rapt with attention as you watch the powerful figure of Dionysus assume the stage. Lithe and golden, radiant and stealthy, he pads in like a great cat ready to pounce and eat someone. He has just arrived in the city of Thebes after a long journey from the mountains of what is now Turkey. Thebes is where he was born to a princess, Semele, beloved of the high god Zeus, his father. The Thebans, however, claimed that Semele lied in declaring Zeus his father and that for this lie Zeus had struck her dead. Dionysus has come now to avenge the Thebans' dishonor to both him and his mother. He is especially angry with his cousin Pentheus, who now rules Thebes, because he refuses to acknowledge his divinity or to pay respect to his rites. As Dionysus enters the city at dawn, his wild Asian women followers (the Bacchae) accompany him. While he disguises himself as a human and prepares to confront Pentheus, he gloats that he has already seduced all the women of Thebes into his ecstatic mysteries and driven them temporarily mad.

As the play unfolds you the audience member sit in awe, knowing yourself to be a participant in a profound communal mystery. It becomes apparent that Euripides is presenting an archetypal conflict between the principles of law and order, represented by Pentheus, and mystical transport, embodied in the god. Most alarming is that, in his brutal vengeance, Dionysus uses the very gifts of enthrallment for which the Greeks so love him. Listen to him give instructions for Pentheus's undoing:

> Women, our prey now thrashes
> in the net we threw. He shall see the Bacchae
> and pay the price with death . . .
> Punish this man. But first distract his wits;
> bewilder him with madness. For sane of mind
> this man would never wear a woman's dress;
> but obsess his soul and he will not refuse.

> After those threats with which he was so fierce,
> I want him made the laughingstock of Thebes,
> paraded through the streets, a woman. Now
> I shall go and costume Pentheus in the clothes
> which he must wear to Hades when he dies, butchered
> by the hands of his mother. He shall come to know
> Dionysus, son of Zeus, consummate god,
> most terrible, and yet most gentle, to mankind.[8]

Dionysus drives rational Pentheus to insane behavior (causing him to dress as a woman in order to spy upon the women's secret rites) and traps him in a tree, from which the wild Bacchae tear Pentheus down and rip him apart. You in the audience gape at the sheer audacity of portraying a beautiful god who is also so pitiless, and you are swept away with the splendor and terror of it all. The lesson of *The Bacchae*, according to Greek scholar Gilbert Murray, is that

> reason is great, but it is not everything. There are in the world things not of reason, but both below and above it; causes of emotion, which we cannot express, which we tend to worship, which we feel, perhaps, to be the precious elements in life. These things are Gods or forms of God: not fabulous immortal men, but 'Things which Are,' things utterly non-human and non-moral, which bring man bliss or tear his life to shreds without a break in their own serenity.[9]

This ability to evoke the ineffable, ultimate Force beyond all morality accounts in part for why Euripides' work has endured for twenty-five hundred years as some of the most astounding literature in the Western world. Did *The Bacchae* cause a riot among its first audience in 406 BCE? We cannot know, but, as Richmond Lattimore observes, "Plainly, [Euripides] wrote shockers. . . . Though the judges of Dionysus disapproved, there cannot be much doubt that the audience was fascinated even when it was not pleased."[10] Among the play's many ironies is that it won the prize for tragedy that year—all the more significant considering that, even though Euripides' plays were produced often, he won the great prize only four times during his life.

From this brief imagining, you may now be aware that the ancient Greek annual festival of plays contained enormous power. It was a ritual perhaps more similar to the fierce playoff games between rival football teams than to any theatrical performance today. Twelve thousand people crammed into rows of stone seats to see the dramatization of myths and stories that informed, guided, and sustained their civilization. Their great playwrights wrote terrible and beautiful versions of human beings' contention with their gods, as when the arrogant young ruler Pentheus comes face to face with a god he despises but whose power includes the immense force of Necessity. When Pentheus continues to attempt to rule over the god, the god destroys him without mercy.

Such intense confrontations between gods and humans, or between humans and the Inexorable, aroused profound feelings of terror and pity in the ancient Greek audience. In *The Poetics*, Aristotle tells us that by witnessing them, mediated through the skills of magnificent writers and equally magnificent actors, the audience could experience a profound *catharsis*, or deep, soul-level cleansing. The playwrights' task was to invoke the gods, present difficult or impossible situations, ask awkward questions, and raise painful shadow issues of the culture within the context of a communal ritual. The actor's task was to provide a satisfying imitation of the gods and humans in the play's unfolding. The audience's task was to "suspend disbelief"—as the famous phrase has it—and experience the performance with the greatest possible attention and good will. If everyone was up to the task, a mysterious conjunction occurred that allowed everyone to transcend ordinary life, if only for a brief, incandescent moment. And none of this could have happened had the audience not understood its power and engaged it fully by listening and responding from the deepest regions of its soul.

Hence the audience's role in traditional theatre has always been essential, from prehistoric campfires to the ancient Greek festivals to contemporary Broadway. That role involves listening and seeing with deep focus and the whole body, responding freely and appropriately, encouraging the actors with appreciation, and participating imaginatively in the story. Our task now is to use these qualities as a model for 1) understanding the importance of the audience for our own life play, and 2) being a good audience for the lives of the people around us.

## Relating to Our Own Audience

### The Long Table of Communion

In the great play of your life, you will find help, support, energy, and outright applause when you gather a sense of your personal sacred audience. First, you become aware of your obvious, overt audience: people and animals, trees, plants, and the elements of nature around you, such as brooks, rivers, rocks, forests, plains, oceans. All the forces and flowerings in your environment are witnesses to your life.

Even furniture can function as an audience. You may not want to explore the life in "inanimate" objects; to consider the aliveness of each and every thing can be confusing. But there is something nurturing in the thought that all the forms around you comprise a network of support. You can see your occasional trip-ups—a stubbed toe on the end of the coffee table, a broken vase—as reminders to be more alert. Otherwise, and as in the theatre when the audience laughs at the wrong moment, you may temporarily lose focus before you regain your balance.

So your friends and family watch and listen as you "play" your life. If they are good audience members, they support you even in your mistakes and encourage you when you try something new. On the other hand, they may resist the flow and insist that you play the part for which you are already famous in their lives. When, for instance, you step out of the role of nurturing mother or sturdy friend in order to try a different tack, they may become upset and want you

214

to return to being the character with whom they are comfortable. If their conditioned response is too negative, you may need to change your audience.

## *Pause, Please*

Consider your audience members in the physical world. Ask yourself.

Who in my family really supports the story the universe has invited me to play?

Who of my friends supports the fulfillment of my life play at the highest level?

What physical things—furniture, art objects, common tools—support me in this task? What parts of the natural world do I sense as supportive and eager to see how it all turns out?

How do my animal friends serve my play? Which invite me to play more and encourage me to move my body more, to see things differently?

Write a letter of gratitude to one of the audience members on your list.

### Ancestors: The Unseen Audience

We come now to the members of your audience of whose presence you may be less aware—your ancestors. Life is absolutely the gift of all those who have preceded you in your lineage, stretching as far back in time as you can imagine. What unique facets of this gift define you?

To consider this question, look first at the physical and psychological gifts you have inherited: the color of your eyes, the general health of your organs and your body, your emotional predisposition. Are you usually happy or more naturally depressed?

Dr. David Lykken and his colleague, Auke Tellegen, conducted a study in 1996 with thousands of middle-aged twins in Minnesota. They asked both identical and fraternal twins, representing a wide variety of schooling, occupation, and income, to score their sense of well-being. Findings clearly indicated that happiness has strong genetic roots, "that an identical twin's well-being now can be predicted from his cotwin's score years earlier, just as it can from the first twin's own score at that earlier time."[11] More recent studies demonstrate that our ancestors' gifts include what Dr. Lykken calls a "set point" for a sense of well-being or unhappiness. That point can be shifted through mindful practice, but, for most of us, it seems genetically predisposed.

But the world of ancestors goes deeper than their physical and psychological gifts. To explore it, I ask you to entertain my belief about the ancestors as mythic powers. The theatre is about making believe—so please make believe that your ancestors have entered an imaginal existence beyond our concepts of space and time. In the realm of myth, it is possible to share ancestors with everyone alive today. In fact, and according to Lucia Chiavola Birnbaum's beautiful book *Dark Mother, African Origins and Godmothers,* if we go back far enough we discover a single woman and man in Africa, the genetic mother and father of us all. [12]

In this imaginal homeland, I believe our ancestors want only the best for us; they want us to break painful, life-damaging patterns. This loving attitude is shared by our parents, who, no matter how they may have mistreated us in life, immediately become beneficent when they die. They join a powerful and supportive ancestral audience—millions strong—that wants only our healing and well-being. And not only are these ancestors passionately concerned for our own safety, they are also devoted to safeguarding the future of the race. They are asking us to change the patterns that are placing our children's future at such risk.

These ancestors may well be doing other work for the health of the planet or for the playing out of their souls' new experiences, but for our individual plays, they are the ideal audience. When we need fresh ideas or have momentarily forgotten our role, our lines, our light—they will help, if we ask. Indigenous tribal teachers in North America not only remind us that the ancestors deserve our honor; they also want us to invoke their presence and be ever aware of it. Further, they advise that in making any decision we consider its effect on the seven generations that will follow.

We want to be grateful to the ancestors, whose existence was much more tenuous than that of most of us living now in the Western world. Their survival depended upon being ever-alert to danger. No one has ancestors who were carefree, insouciant, and thrill seeking; such light-heartedness would have gotten them killed long before they could reproduce. Over time, and as chapter 7 discussed, their quicksilver responses to danger grew hardwired into their descendants' brains—*our* brains. Now, when our ancestors form an important part of our unseen audience, I imagine that safety is still one of their main concerns. Nevertheless, they recall that in life even they had to take measured risks in order to explore new lands or try innovative ideas. While they advise caution, they also ask us not to be so frightened for our security that we neglect the joys of adventure.

## *Pause, Please*

In a meditation, I saw crowds of every race and temperament billowing forth beyond my two parents, four grandparents, eight great-grandparents, and so on. I realized that my travels around the world have in some sense been guided by those ancestors, that every land I have visited and yearned for has been walked by them. When I arrived in their place, their spirits greeted my spirit, challenging me to claim a gift they had left. Looking back, I see that in some places I was only vaguely aware of that possibility. From now on when I travel, I will try to be consciously guided by the sense of ancestral call.

I now invite you to do the same: Imagine your parents standing before you, and behind them your grandparents, and behind them, ever more ancestors. See them spread out across the world.

Now remember your own travels to different lands, even if it has just been in an armchair with a good book. Imagine your ancestors' presence in those places. Do they offer a gift to you? If so, what is its nature? This gift might be a physical trait, an attitude, or a propensity for a certain talent. Or it might be simply a touch and a blessing. Can you describe it in a journal entry, poem, drawing, or song?

### Enter the Gods

We come now to the most vital members of your audience, again mostly unseen, though nonetheless potently present. My friend and teacher, the remarkable Robin Van Doren, says that the primary purpose of our lives is to entertain the gods. We have a responsibility not to bore them. These are the gods who are the members of our sacred audience. By *gods*, I mean the archetypal principles of primal energy that contain the essence of certain qualities—such as beauty, truth, joy, ecstasy, wisdom, enchantment, healing power, vigor, and justice—and that may well have given you focus for living the drama you have been offered. I do not mean the One God, however you may experience that Being; I mean those energy emanations from the One that have provided us with stories and myths and that form a rich part of our cultural psyches.

## *Pause, Please*

Who are the gods for whom you are enacting your life play? Who among them have you come here to entertain? Consider the holy ones you want to invite to witness, hear, feel, and support your play. From the Greeks, possible divine allies include the goddess of wisdom, Athena; the goddess of beauty and love, Aphrodite; the protector of marriage and family, Hera; and many others. From the Celts come Brigid, goddess of fire and art; Epohna, goddess of horses; and Angus, lord of love. You can find a myriad of others, or you may have a guide or angel unique to you. Write a few words describing the "gods" you might want as holy witnesses to your life.

## Inviting Your Sacred Audience to Your Play

Inviting a specific deity or energy pattern to be your audience day by day carries a gentle, intimate power. That is why it is so helpful to determine whom among the primal forces you want to ask to witness, mediate, inform, and help shape your moment-to-moment actions.

Knowing, for example, that you have asked the principle of beauty, perhaps as the Greek goddess Aphrodite, to witness your play today can shift events subtly and gracefully. When Aphrodite wafts her magic, even for an hour, you will slow down, perhaps stopping to appreciate a beautiful thing—a peach, a rose—that comes to your attention. Or you will spend a moment more on your clothes as you prepare for a meeting, maybe adding a piece of cherished jewelry. Or you might pay more attention to the beauty of your friends, or call a beloved one just to say, "I love you."

Formal theatre originated as a means of honoring the gods. We've discussed that in the ancient Greek theatre special seats were reserved for the representatives of Dionysus, to whom the festival of plays was dedicated. In later times that special seat became the king's. You can, in your mind's eye, invite the god to place her/himself there now for the purpose of attending your life play. This kind of friendly invitation is worlds away from the warning I received as a child that "God sees your every move." That statement was made to admonish the hearer into "behaving." But here the god becomes the supportive audience, delighted, encouraging, and joyful to be invited to participate in your life's enactment of its holy purpose.

If I invite the principle of Wisdom, whom I imagine as Sophia, to sit in the honored seat of my sacred audience, then my work pace immediately slows. If I am writing by hand, my penmanship grows clearer. I pause and listen between words. Ideas flow more clearly, and I realize again that my desire is to transmit ideas that may invite you, as reader, to hold your life in the light and arms of Holy Wisdom and to frame it playfully as a fascinating work of performance art in progress.

## *Pause, Please*

What is wanted or needed in your life today? More order? More care? More beauty? Awareness? Ideas? Courage? Consciously invite the principle of Order, Care, Beauty, or whatever to participate in your life play now. Notice what happens. It is wise to be appreciative of the exquisite work these energies can accomplish in your life.

## How to Be—And Not to Be— A Good Audience for Others

When you serve another as audience, be it a family member, friend, partner, colleague, or even a casual acquaintance, your work is to enter the same mind-set you would want for your own best audience. Ask yourself, in the popular phrase, "What would the kindest, wisest person on earth do?" Then try to do that.

A good audience enters the theatre with warm-hearted expectancy. As a theatre audience we want to enjoy the play; we want to be seduced, tantalized, intrigued, and challenged and to respond richly to its comedy, its tragedy, its intention, its nuance. We want to understand

and empathize with the people on the stage. And we want to feel awed not only by the profundity of the action but also by the skill of the actors. We want to listen so attentively that we pick up the things not said as well as those expressed. What a gift to the people in our lives if we were to approach every encounter with them in the same way. How validated, seen, and heard they would feel!

In the theatre, the task of audience members is always to participate in a state of what the Zen masters call "Beginner's Mind," meaning that they are to be alert, aware, and ready to view with fresh eyes the actions onstage. The term comes from the famed Japanese teacher Shunryu Suzuki Roshi, first abbot of the first training Zen monastery outside of Asia, whose first book is called *Zen Mind, Beginner's Mind*. For my introduction to it I am indebted to the Abbess Zenkei Blanche Hartman, who tells us that the Beginner's Mind "is the mind that is innocent of preconceptions and expectations, judgments, and prejudices . . . [a] mind that is free to just be awake."[13]

What a perfect way to view a theatrical performance! Innocent of preconceptions and judgments, just awake. Every student of Zen recognizes how difficult—but how essential—it is to encounter life freshly, asking with interest, "What is this?" and then cheerfully investigating without having to know and judge it as good or bad. And just as having a Beginner's Mind is vital for being a good audience member in the theatre, so it is with our friends' lives. Lack of judgment or expectation, innocent curiosity, an intimate tenderness: all are critical to maintaining good relationships. Seeing with fresh eyes and listening with fresh ears will sustain our friends and grant us the privilege of being a good witness to the sacred play each person around us is enacting.

## *Pause, Please*

Let us engage something of the Zen masters' concept of Beginner's Mind. Return to the practice of listening. Bring awareness to the sounds you hear. Without needing to identify any of them, listen eagerly with the question of "What is this?" Explore the sound for the kind it is, not comparing it to another, but playing with it.

Just now a cricket has begun to sing outside the window. If I listen to it afresh, not dismissing it with "Oh, that's a cricket," I can really hear it, noticing just the nature of the sound it makes.

Become curious about the sounds reaching you, awaiting the next, and the next, and the next. Also, notice how difficult it is not to draw conclusions about the sound and thus end your engagement with it.

So it is in the theatre and in life: we want to keep being innocent and curious. We want to keep responding authentically and asking the mind to suspend judgment.

## Beware the Critic

In being a sacred audience member, beware of becoming a critic. A critic is 1) someone who makes a judgment about something or somebody and gives comments; 2) someone, especially a journalist, who writes or broadcasts opinions on the quality of things such as drama productions, art exhibitions, and literary works; or 3) someone who finds fault with or who simply does not like something or somebody.

We have all been trained to admire cool, rational thought (or what appears to be cool, rational thought). We have all been taught to admire astute criticism. Massive bodies of work are written with the sole purpose of explaining other bodies of work. Vast teachings exist to help us understand other teachings. Scholars devote microscopic attention to the works of the Bible, Shakespeare, the ancient Greeks, and countless others. Careers are made from literary criticism. Without it, we wouldn't know as much as we do about the world's literature. Ideally, the critic serves as interpreter and opens our minds.

Unfortunately, we are also accustomed to a different kind of critic. These are the reviewers who report on trips, plays, movies, art exhibits, books, and restaurants, mediating between us and direct experience. At a basic level, their kind of criticism acts as an economic force, saying essentially, "Buy!" or "Don't Buy!" It also appeals to the aspect of human nature that wants to be ahead of another, if only slightly. Most of us feel a momentary jerk of satisfaction when reading about the peccadilloes even of people we admire, if we perceive them as the rich and famous. Whatever human littleness this quirk springs from, we find it fun to read gossipy critics making a tasty meal of someone else's mistakes. We can become infected with that same desire when we attend a play, dissecting each performance with the eyes of a forensic surgeon. And in the replay, we compete vigorously with others of like mind to see who noticed the most egregious errors. That's how we critics feel we've gotten our money's worth.

But it is one thing to direct the fierce power of one's critical mind toward a theatrical production and quite another to direct that same fierceness toward a friend. It is important not to become so negatively analytical that we see only the mistakes our companions make. That is murderous to friendship. And it's morally forbidden, unless a friend has explicitly invited us to critique her. In that case, it is imperative that we do so with care and humility: as a constructive critic, we must observe with great attention, listen with great respect, and report what we observe meticulously.

## The Chorus: A Noble Intermediary

Just as we sometimes do a disservice by being critical of others, we also often use the critic to hurt ourselves. I know of few people who never fall prey, at least now and then, to the harsh, belittling inner voice that says, "You should have done better" or, "You can't do that; you're too stupid!"

True, we need an inner observer with bright eyes attending to our actions. But it's important to find the appropriate characterization. We want a *helpful* internal voice, not a vicious critic. We want one who understands, reviews, perceives other possibilities, and proposes positive actions. For the role of this good inner critic, I suggest the creation of a noble intermediary, one that has existed since the theatre began: the Chorus.

In ancient Greek plays, the Chorus consisted of twelve to fifteen members who became one being. They were capable of speaking back and forth, one part to another, occasionally with a single voice sounding out, but together they embodied "the one in the many and the many in the one." The Chorus's job was to represent the audience onstage, but with heightened responsibilities. It provided interludes of dance and song when the action required a reflective pause, when it was necessary to indicate the passage of time, or when the actors and audience needed relief from the intensity of the action.

The Chorus offered physical and vocal responses to the onstage action but were never expected to intercede. It could plead with a character like Oedipus, for instance, not to act rashly in his determination to find the source of the disasters haunting the city, but it could not stop the tragedy from unfolding.

The finest Greek playwrights presented the Chorus as characters, sometimes even as the title characters. They were the old men of Argos (in Aeschylus's *The Agamemnon*) and Euripides' *Trojan Women*, for example. In other plays, the Chorus represented the daughters of Danaus, the citizens of Thebes, and, as we have learned, the Bacchae. They could portray either the forces of retribution or the energies of forgiveness.

Many generations later and a world away, Shakespeare varied the convention by designating a single actor to be the Chorus. This character speaks directly to the audience, inviting their imaginative participation; he also sets the stage, introduces the play, provides interim information, and encourages richer engagement by thickening the story. The Chorus in *Henry V* summons his audience's imagination in the opening lines:

> O for a muse of fire, that would ascend
> The brightest heaven of invention:
> A kingdom for a stage, princes to act,

And monarchs to behold the swelling scene. . . .
Think, when we talk of horses, that you see them.
Printing their proud hooves i' th' receiving earth;
For 'tis your thoughts that now must deck our kings,
Carry them here and there, jumping o'er times,
Turning th' accomplishment of many years
Into an hourglass . . .

(1.1.1–4, 26–31)

In the modern musical theatre, or even on MTV, there is often a Chorus whose primary task is inherited from the ancient Greeks. This Chorus is a group of highly trained singers and/or dancers who support the lead singer or dancer in many ways—supplementing her energy, interpreting her action, heralding the information she presents, and sometimes just giving her a break from the action. In the current Broadway revival of *South Pacific*, the sailors and nurses echo the emotions of the lead characters. In *West Side Story*, the Chorus of gang boys not only augments and restates the emotions of the lead singers but also mirrors the cultural diversity of Tony and Maria (Romeo and Juliet revisited) while inciting further conflict.

There is a particular joy in enacting a Chorus member, whether as intermediary, interpreter, or ally for a friend's sacred drama or your own. Just as we all have audience members, secular and sacred, we all need a fine and useful Chorus. The difference is that, while you invite your sacred audience, you *create* the Chorus. You get to choose its attitude and who or what it represents. The key quality in any case is *kindness*. It is useful to remember the analogy of the Chorus as beneficent inner observer—one who, even when evaluating, holds the potential of the actor's highest well-being in mind.

## A Training in Kindness: Enacting a Chorus for a Friend

Sometimes this noble intermediary, the Chorus, steps onto the stage of a friend's life to play the role of gentle observer. Rather than simply watching and listening as a good audience member, the Chorus becomes one of the actors. This action may be of two kinds: Internal and External.

## The Internal Chorus

Internally, you as your friend's Chorus speak to you as his audience. For instance, when I'm having a hard time with George's life play and I want to tell him how to fix it, it is helpful instead to create a Chorus that dances out on the stage in my mind's eye and speaks to me as his audience, as in:

> I, George's Chorus, am here to speak about his life. I come to honor the choices he has made throughout it and to allow you, his audience, to gain insight into his difficulties. Given his beginnings, the fact that he is alive at all is cause for rejoicing. So watch while we now sing a praise song to George. Notice that he is who he is and not necessarily who you want him to be!

Just imagining that process frees my heart and mind and gives me time to make choices about how to react to the latest self-destructive thing George has done. Visualizing a Chorus of people in top hats and tails dancing on the stage is such a treat it makes me smile. It changes the chemistry inside my brain so that instead of telling George off for making another stupid decision, I can stay quiet and realize that all my telling him off in the past has not made us happier or easier together. It is possible that this change in me will affect George favorably; he may become less defensive and feel able to confide the distress that is causing him to consider such a negative action. It could even be that his speaking freely to an encouraging Chorus might help him make a better decision.

Notice in this case that I have not said a word to George; I have only spoken to myself internally to shift my dangerous tendency to become a critic instead of a good audience member.

## The External Chorus

A good Chorus can, though, speak aloud in a friend's play, if it does so with kindness, clarity, and interpretive skill. This can be done in two ways, imitating the Greeks.

One way is to create an interlude of beauty and peace, wherein a choral ode is offered to remind the friend of past glory or achievements. I can do that with George in his present crisis by reminding him of how elegantly he has served as a volunteer at the Food Bank and taken care of his neighbors' cat while they were away. It's helpful to remember as many good things as possible to enrich this choral interlude.

The second way the Chorus can overtly participate in a friend's play is to speak directly about the issue at hand, encouraging him to remember his better nature. So might I gently give George my insights about his actions and voice my care and concern for him. Doing this as a Chorus lifts the emotional tentacles I might have were I either to enter his play as an antagonist, challenging his actions, or to remove myself permanently as good audience and become only a silent but firm critic.

# MORE KINDNESS:
## CREATING YOUR OWN CHORUS

In creating an internal Chorus for your own life play, the advantage is that you can step outside the immediate action and introduce it kindly to your imagined, or real, audience. Instead of falling into self-blame or self-defense, you, as your own Chorus, feel compassion for the lead character (yourself) and tell your story from a place of empathy.

Here's an example: Recently I felt the need to call upon a Greek Chorus to address both the friend who was my immediate audience and my own inner critic, who happens to be a harsh, demanding entity. The Chorus I selected was a group of kindly grandmothers. Over gentle background music, these are the words they spoke:

You may have noticed that Peggy on this afternoon did lose her short and somewhat tried hot temper. Notice, too, how easily she perceives as a criticism what was declared an innocent question and then translates it into an attack. When that happens, she reacts immediately, fiercely, and totally. How close she must be all the time to stark fury at feeling she is only noticed when being attacked!

So whatever the intention of what was said to her, it touched a deep wound. Her response to such situations in lo! these many years has always been blind rage and the equivalent childish reaction of, "I'm taking my toys and going home!"

Thus my grandmotherly Chorus mirrors my actions to me and reflects on them to my friend who, because of my angry response to his "innocent" question, is also feeling hurt and waspish. The Chorus's kind comments give me time to breathe and consider. After this quiet interlude, I can talk reasonably to my friend and he to me about what his question really meant. My Chorus further explains of this holy work:

As Peggy's Chorus, I offer her an opportunity to collect herself and respond more clearly when she can. If need be, I can create an ode to rage that allows her to see the effect it has. The trick is for me to be activated enough within her psyche that I can step in before she reacts impulsively. So I say to her privately, "This adrenaline-fueled response may have saved your life in earlier years. Certainly it saved your ancestors. Being able to hear a knife being drawn is a real advantage when you're in a knife culture. But right now you're driving in a car with a dear friend. So could you allow me to help you calm down and reflect on your feelings?"

By inviting my inner Chorus to keep watch this way, I train myself not to lash out thoughtlessly, and at the same time I avoid stifling my feelings. The latter usually has the effect of slamming a lid down on a boiling pot—pretty soon there's a messy explosion. The Chorus relieves the pressure by recognizing my feelings and then gently reminding me that expressing them violently, or *suppressing* them violently, is hurtful to everyone. "They're simply feelings," my Chorus says, "and, as you know, sometimes just acknowledging them provides the juice they need to change." Hence the Chorus helps me back to clarity. I become able to sit with my emotions and, if appropriate, express them in ways that deepen my friendships rather than damage them.

## *Pause, Please*

In working with the inner Chorus, we first describe the nature of the role. It is an observer, yes, and can represent your sacred audience. It can provide an interlude of peace and remembrance, and it can persuade you to a kinder, calmer course. There is delight in imagining who makes up this Chorus and allowing it to change with circumstances. Sometimes, for example, mine needs to be a huge, beneficent figure powerful enough to stop me in my tracks, not unlike an angel. At other times, I imagine my inner Chorus as a group of motherly priestesses paying attention to those things I have done well. When I'm happy and out walking, it's fun to bring in my inner tap dancers, including Fred Astaire and Gene Kelly, to keep me going.

But the guiding impetus for training the inner Chorus is to become aware of the hotspots in your life. Consider what angers or depresses you. What happens just before you drop into sorrow or rise into rage? For example, my Chorus says: "My task is not to allow Peggy to fall into fruitless self-blame or self-defense, stances that entrench her more deeply in such harmful behavior. Before that happens I intervene, giving her time to think and to avoid reacting carelessly, either to herself or to the other."

Consider also those times when you have accomplished something and no one has noticed—or noticed sufficiently—leaving you to feel that something is unfinished. It is your Chorus's magnificent job to notice, to announce (if only inwardly), and to sing praise. This way, your work is honored formally and the energy of it will feel complete, so that you can proceed to your next accomplishment with a whole heart and mind.

Write a short ode to yourself in the voice of your Chorus that would have been helpful during a recent upset. Remember that the inner Chorus is a kind observer who wants only your highest good. Use it to allow some healing balm to enter the space that was damaged. Recite the ode aloud.

Now compose a choral ode that praises an achievement you feel good about. Describe it to your sacred audience in fresh terms, acknowledging its trials and triumphs. Invite this accomplishment to provide an opening for embracing the final Power of Sacred Theatre, the reason for it all: The Power of Celebration.

*The time will come*
*when, with elation,*
*you will greet yourself arriving*
*at your own door, in your own mirror,*
*and each will smile at the other's welcome*
*and say, sit here. Eat.*
*You will love again the stranger who was your self.*
*Give wine. Give bread . . .*
*Sit. Feast on your life.*
                                        — Derek Walcott

# Nine

# The Power of Celebration

Derek Walcott's lovely poem opposite this page helps us answer the question, Why? Why have we come so far in reviewing our lives, looking at powers that can lift us to clarity, provide fresh understanding for life's twists and turns, and suggest practices for maintaining ourselves with sweetness and generosity? It's been a long journey. Why have we bothered?

We have "bothered" in order to meet this final power gallantly, eager to embrace its energy and open to its ecstasy. I believe the Power of Celebration is primary to existence; it is in the delight with which the universe throbs with wonder in the mystery that is life. Engaging this power awakens us. We remember it as the reason we came into being in the first place and recognize that it provides the holiest of reasons to stay alive.

When we speak of celebration, we commonly think of family or communal ritual occasions, some of which we greet with glee and some with groans. We celebrate birthdays, holidays, festivals, accomplishments; we host or attend parties to mark such events; we may decorate our homes and offices to announce a special season; we routinely send messages of congratulations and gratitude. That's what celebration means for most of us—a slight, even desultory blip in the routine of the week or month or year.

But the *Power* of Celebration is a different matter entirely. Far from concerning just a few days of the year, it has to do with a state of being so vibrant that awaking to it shakes us into joy. I have said that theatre shouts a great *Yes!* to life; whenever we engage the Power of Celebration, life imitates theatre, rather than the other way around. The Power of Celebration invites us to confront all, explore all, reveal all, and dare all in order to participate fully in the miracle of being alive. It carries a precise and loving message from the Divine: make sure this miracle of life continues! It is the uncontainable life urge Dylan Thomas describes as the "the force that through the green fuse drives the flower." And more. It is "everything which is natural which is infinite which is yes," to quote E. E. Cummings. This power demands that we choose life no matter what—through pain, desolation, and sorrow as well as in joy. If you remember all the happy weddings you have enjoyed, all the births and birthdays, and—yes—all the deathbeds and wakes and funerals, and then add together the ebullient energy they all contain, you might come close to intuiting the force of the Power of Celebration. At its core is a deep sense of equanimity and affirmation, which stays serene even in the midst of life's most severe challenges. Tapping into it will feed you riches beyond imagining. Invoke it, swear by it, live by it. It will never let you down.

To gain a sense of the all-encompassing dynamic of this power, we need only turn to some of the smallest of life's dramas—the making and breaking of molecules.

## HERE'S THE STORY

*Billions of years ago, a tiny light blinked on somewhere and has come to illuminate every nook and cranny of our earth's surface.*
—Mahlon Hoagland and Bert Dodson[1]

You may not realize it, but you and every other living creature are participating in a drama that seems absolutely contradictory to two fundamental laws of nature: *the laws of thermodynamics.* These laws state that 1) energy can change form, but it cannot be created or destroyed; and that 2) energy inevitably dissipates, and ordered structures become disordered. (This process is called *entropy.*) You may have observed the second law vividly at work: machinery wears out; the cream in hot coffee disperses; that same coffee grows cold; and, left to itself, a messy desk always gets messier.

We cannot escape the laws of thermodynamics, but we find that they (especially the law of entropy) provide ingenious ways actually to sustain our capacity to keep on keeping on. In fact, we owe our very existence to entropy, it being the dynamic that causes the sun to disperse energy in the heat and light upon which all life on earth depends. And not only does entropy thus sustain us, but by doing so it gives us the power to counteract its other effects.

This planet we live on is ever so conveniently located; we bask in the sunlight that we would find too hot if we were closer to it or insufficient were we further away. Not too hot, not too cold, but just right: that's the earth. And this perfect combination of comfort and energy accomplishes three things that allow life to continue seemingly *contrary* to the law of entropy. According to Mahlon Hoagland and Bert Dodson's enchanting book *The Way Life Works,* those three things are

1. the making of bonds,
2. the breaking of bonds, and
3. the easy transfer of energy.

We will consider these actions first in terms of how at the molecular level they ensure life's continuation and then as how at a much larger level they form the basis for engaging the Power of Celebration.

# CHAPTER NINE

## Making Bonds

Imagine your life at its most basic level: your atoms dance and move, swirl and crash into one another. Sometimes they are repelled in this movement (since the electrons hurtling around the nucleus of each atom all have the same strong charge and thus push against each other), but sometimes the collision is so hard that the atoms stick together and begin to share some of their electrons. These create a powerful bond called a *molecule*, and this process is the fundament for all building and growth that takes place in the body.

## Breaking Bonds

Your molecules pick up the same wild, kinetic dance, sometimes crashing into one another in a way that causes them to break apart and become separate atoms again, with your mixed-up electrons coming home to surround their original nucleus. When this happens, the energy inside the bond dissipates, pouring outward as heat.

## Transferring Energy

Certain kinds of your larger molecules, however, produce an extra kick of energy. When *their* bonds break, this energy can jump to another molecule instead of being released as heat, and a new bond is created. Hoagland and Dodson tell us, "Everything that happens in living cells is the result of various combinations of bond breaking, bond making, and energy transfer."[2] Life flows as these transfers are made. When you lift your hand, it's because billions of molecules are transferring energy to allow your muscles to move; likewise as your body makes proteins or sugar or stores information. You are a living being because these processes are going on with a kind of joyful ferocity all the time.

Hence we have two reasons to be grateful for the second law of thermodynamics. The first, of course, is that the energy sustaining life comes from the sun, busily dissipating its warmth and light in just the right quantities. The second is that, in the bonding that forms our molecules, while some of the energy required to make the bond stays with it, some of that energy disperses as heat. Thank goodness for that dispersal; otherwise, so much energy would be maintained that it would break the bond apart, and building (the work of the bond) could not last. And here's where the mystery and miracle enter: As Hoagland and Dodson explain, "The construction of bonds between molecules makes possible the creation of information. Information, in turn, brings order in its wake." So, even though the law declares that energy runs inexorably "downhill," the process of creating information *builds up*, "resulting in an uphill snowballing of complexity. . . . Running uphill requires no special tricks, but rather a dogged and persistent repairing and rebuilding at the molecular level."[3]

So you, as a living creature, simultaneously hold two seemingly opposing truths. On the one hand, life's processes assault you at every moment, or, as in "The Second Coming" the poet William Butler Yeats so poignantly says, "Things fall apart, the center cannot hold . . ." You are ineluctably subjected to the law of entropy. And yet, on the other hand, simply by virtue of being alive you have glorious forces within you constantly working to restore, remake, and regenerate every cell in your body—by making bonds, breaking bonds, and transferring energy. Moreover, facilitated by busy miracle workers in the form of enzymes, this complex interchange of biological elements happens millions of times inside your cells every minute. What a story!

Notice how the various powers of Sacred Theatre link into one or all of the three molecular actions—making bonds, breaking bonds, or transferring energy. Incarnation begins with a transfer of energy on a large scale between our parents and on a tiny scale with the ovum and the sperm coming together to make a new being. The Power of Story draws constantly on all three actions in plots of union, separation, and reunion, and so on. We could think of the Power of Conflict as reflecting bond breaking and of the Power of Audience as encompassing all three processes: bonds are made, bonds are broken, and vast quantities of energy are exchanged. And, as I've said, I believe that all of life is held within and expressed through the Power of Celebration.

Notice, too, how many of the rituals that mark our passage through life imitate this living process: family christenings and celebrations of birth or engagement or marriage are forms of making bonds; graduations, initiations, divorces, retirements, funerals are forms of breaking bonds; and all of them involve transfers of energy.

## MAKING A BOND WITH LIFE

This miraculous tale of energy that bonds, dissipates, and also transforms gave me an insight into a profound truth. "All life is suffering," said the Buddha, in teaching his first Noble Truth. "Suffering" in Sanskrit is *dukka*, and other scholars translate it as "dissatisfaction." Once I understood what Hoagland and Dodson were saying about bonds, I began to see the Buddha's words in a new light. Dissatisfaction— manifest, for example, in the constantly shifting process of being hungry, eating, being full (sometimes too full), and then being hungry again—is precisely what defines life. It is precisely what drives the never-ceasing action of our cells in busily transforming the energy packets of sun and food into nourishing other cells and performing the necessary constant repairs and adjustments throughout our bodies. If we didn't have to adjust to the temperature, or go to the bathroom, or sweat when we exercise, or feel pain when we cut ourselves, we would not be alive. Instead, we would be inanimate objects, like machines, and when the assaults of entropy knocked us down, we would stay down.

Hence, the physical conditions that often cause us irritation are the absolute and necessary gifts of being alive. What folly then to whine about them! What ungrateful behavior! Especially when whining about what our bodies ask us to do gets us into a whining habit, and pretty soon we find ourselves dissatisfied about everything.

But we can change that habit by wholeheartedly embracing the Power of Celebration. How? By celebrating each physical shift and bodily need as integral to the process of bond making, bond breaking, and energy transference essential for doing the uphill job of keeping us alive. Eventually, of course, entropy will win this magnificent contest. No matter how diligently our atoms, molecules, and cells pursue their noble task, we will begin to feel older; and when time and conditions finally dictate, we will die. But if we bring some measure of gratitude to these inner workings, thinking of them as embodying the celebratory power of life, then not only will we add to the general joy of the universe (one of the sacred responsibilities of being human), but I believe we will also enhance the functioning of the microscopic entities who serve us so gallantly in sustaining our lives.

## Pause, Please

Imagine the billions of molecular processes happening inside your body right now, fueled by one intention only: to build and regenerate, and nourish and guide, your cells. Consider their frenetic activity as they both utilize the dispersal force of entropy and counter it by building up a continuous stream of information. This molecular process resembles the practice of martial arts, in which we use the very energy coming toward us to turn it the way we want it to go.

Suggestion: stand now, put on some wild music, and let yourself move in imitation of your atoms and molecules, using energy and transforming it to your will. Sense the exuberance that resides within each atom of each molecule of each cell in every living creature on this earth. Can you feel it surging in your own body?

An elementary sense of connection with all that lives is the first bond we make when we incarnate. Can you now bring that bond to awareness again with a sense of celebration, so that you feel buoyed and jubilantly held in its energies?

Speak aloud a praise song to life, using the words, "I give thanks to life for . . ." Let the words come forth as you feel into the miraculous mystery that life is, from tiny atoms pelting into one another all the way to humpback whales swimming, breaching, and blowing. If you can, let your words express joy at the sheer improbability of it all, the daring, the audacity, and the wild courage of being—and staying—alive.

Feel your elemental bond with all of life as vividly as you can and express it, too, as part of your song. Then seal the song for now by writing some essence of what you have experienced or can imagine experiencing.

## MAKING BONDS WITH OTHERS

Moving now from the internal to the external world, it is easy to see the Power of Celebration at work on a large scale when we consider the making of bonds with others. Deep bonds with friends, lovers, communities, projects, and gardens cause us to thrive, giving us good reason to celebrate. Remember that, at the most basic level, bonds have a high purpose: to build, regenerate, and respond to other molecules to produce ever greater complexity. The bonds we make in the world can be experienced as having the same purpose. We come together to create or *re*create. (And in so doing we participate fully in the second power of Sacred Theatre, the Power of Story. Love stories, quest stories, adventure stories—all allow us to bond with others in imitation of the great bonding that is the story of life on earth.)

To image the process of bond making on the external level and endow it with the ecstatic Power of Celebration, here is my vote for a mystical symbol: the Knot of Isis. As Normandi Ellis, luminous poet and scholar of Egypt, describes it:

> At the ends of the universe is a blood red cord that ties life to death, man
> to woman, will to destiny. Let the knot of that red sash, which cradles

the hips of the goddess, bind in me the ends of life and dream. . . . I rise and walk. The sky arcs ever around; the world spreads itself beneath my feet. We are bound mind to Mind, heart to Heart—no difference rises between the shadow of my footsteps and the will of god. I walk in harmony, heaven in one hand, earth in the other. I am the knot where two worlds meet. Red magic courses through me like the blood of Isis, magic of magic, spirit of spirit. I am proof of the power of gods. I am water and dust walking.[4]

Isis reigned as goddess of heaven and earth in ancient Egypt for thousands of years and bequeathed many of her vital attributes to archetypes that succeeded her, especially those who embody the heart of love and of mother. I can see, for instance, how her knot—this cord of connection unifying everything—could have transmuted into another symbol of enormous beauty, the Girdle of Aphrodite, Greek goddess of love and beauty. Aphrodite's husband, the craftsman god Hephaistos, forged it for her and made it so irresistible that anyone who saw her wearing it fell in love immediately. Hera, the Greek queen of heaven and earth, borrowed the girdle when she needed to seduce her husband into agreement with her. Young women in Hera's service would weave a new belt for her every year and present it to her statue at her temple at Olympia on the land said to be her body, the southern part of Greece.

Just as the Knot of Isis reminds us of our bonds to all life and to one another, I like to think that wearing such a symbolic belt or girdle softens our hearts. It surrounds us with a field of beauty and provides the opportunity to make bonds with others gracefully and truly, guided only by love.

## *Pause, Please*

I believe that belly-dancing belts with their bells and fringes are modern versions of this magical symbol of connection. Traditional costumes worn by men and women alike in the Mediterranean worlds often display fringes or colorful woven threads in their own form of Hera's belt or Aphrodite's girdle, perhaps signifying their readiness and availability to make a bond.

Take drawing materials (or weaving threads) and devise your own representation of the Knot of Isis or Aphrodite's Girdle. (Other people's images are available on the Internet to inspire you.) On your belt, design your own symbols of connection with those to whom you know yourself bonded. Include them all in this image of the Power of Celebration embedded in the making of bonds with others.

## Breaking Bonds with Others

Once we understand that the breaking of molecular bonds is an essential part of the experiment of life, it becomes easier to recognize that breakups in the larger, outer world can also be necessary and held within the Power of Celebration. Some fierce collision tears the molecule of partnered atoms apart and restores the electron field back to its original atom; each atom then careens on its journey, available and ready to run into another atom and make a different kind of bond.

A gentle way of noticing this making and breaking of bonds in the realm of human interaction is to walk down the street, encounter an acquaintance, stop for a moment to talk, and then walk on whole and solitary again. The nature of the bond making and breaking differs with each meeting and the emotional content involved. Such daily greetings can become more celebratory seen in the context of life's basic processes. We might encounter, for example, a puppy, all awaggle; clearly his cells vibrate with life. Each swish of his tail requires millions of molecular connections imbued with rollicking vigor—making bonds, breaking bonds, and transferring energy. Imagining the complexity of interactions inside our own cells as well can fill us with awe, and we can move easily from this amazement to the celebration of all life, if we simply allow ourselves the moment it takes to do so.

Another occasion for celebration is when we manage to break a bond that has kept us mentally, emotionally, or physically stuck. When we feel trapped, it is helpful to remember the wild activity of our molecules and invoke a larger one to strike at just the right angle in just the right way to break that bond. Opening to the Power of Celebration as a primary life force can strengthen our resolution to break the unhealthy bond, release its energy, and move on.

Here's an everyday example: You find yourself on the phone with a friend; the conversation devolves into complaining; you begin to feel annoyed. Picture this little emotional disturbance as a series of molecules, bonding with one another and increasing your upset. Then imagine the Power of Celebration barreling into the room to remind you that, as a joyful life force, it can pelt into one of these molecules of annoyance. It can break it wide open, release the stored heat, and give you the wisdom to break off the conversation, hang up the phone, and use the released energy to start singing or clean the refrigerator.

When bond breaking occurs at the deepest level—when we lose someone or something to another love, or to death, or by the betrayal of trust—we need to invoke the Power of Celebration more intensely. Here I am suggesting, not that we pretend to celebrate when our hearts are breaking, but that we hold the generosity of this power as an ally in living through the heartbreak. We want its help in order to participate in the process instead of resisting it. It can keep us from feeling that we ourselves have been broken rather than the bond.

Developing this sensibility takes time and patience; it takes grieving and acknowledging the grief through appropriate and (if possible) beautiful expression. Here's an example:

One day the husband of a friend who had been married many years told her he wanted a divorce. My friend was devastated; the great bonds they had made with each other, and the bonds they had made with their children and others as a married couple, were broken. When the worst of her grief was assuaged (through the right expression of rage, fear, concern for the kids, etc.), my friend and her husband created a ritual of divorce, inviting their nearest allies to witness it.

In planning the ceremony, they reviewed their marriage vows and rewrote them, formally releasing one another. My friend reports that saying those words before witnesses brought a sense of true release from both the marriage and her suffering about its dissolution. This was the first time that she had felt such relief, and she experienced its power in a wave of joy. (Not that her sorrow was forever gone, but the occasion did mark the possibility to begin something new. Formerly, she had felt so burdened by the whole thing that she could not imagine anything fresh could occur out of it.)

During the ceremony, they spoke about their love and sorrow and acknowledged the great gifts of the marriage. They invited us to say what we needed to say. Several of us spoke of our sadness that this bond was broken, because it also meant that our bonds with the couple were broken and needed to be reconfigured, and that takes effort. Then they spoke of vows they had written—never to speak badly of the other to the children, always to support the other in the continuing unfolding of a rich and productive life—and consigned their wedding rings to a tiny wooden box, which they closed together.

This ceremonial acknowledgment of a broken bond left everyone moved and the couple themselves capable of embracing a new future. The Power of Celebration, as the essential power that supports life, was definitely present.

Reaching into mythology to find a symbol of the breaking of bonds, I come upon the discus or wheel, *cakra* in Sanskrit, of the great Hindu god Vishnu, whose task (like that of the Power of Celebration) is to sustain life. His discus represents the "constantly turning wheel of time, which inexorably destroys everything that has name and form."[5]

A guide in Calcutta once told me this story about Vishnu's discus: The creator/destroyer god, whose name is Shiva, felt his heart break when his beloved wife, the goddess Parvati, died. Mad with grief, Shiva began to race and turn and twist far above the earth, holding Parvati's body over his shoulder. He would not let her go; he could not bear the breaking of this love bond. Consequently, he neglected his duty as the god whose dance keeps the universe in a balance of creation and de-struction. Everything began to fall apart; all bonds were breaking. The other divinities were deeply concerned, but the situation was Vishnu's to handle since he is the one who sustains Shiva's creation. No amount of commiserating with the stricken Shiva, though, made any differ-ence. With great sorrow, Vishnu did the only thing he could think to do. He threw his discus across the sky toward the fleeing Shiva, intending it to cut the body of the goddess Parvati into bits, so that Shiva would have nothing left to hold. Vishnu reasoned that then Shiva would be forced to his senses and the universe set in motion again. The discus spun mightily in its flight from Vishnu's hand and sliced Parvati into little pieces that rained upon the earth. In every place where some part of the goddess landed, a holy city grew with a temple dedicated to her. Calcutta, said my guide, received one of her little toes. Thus Vishnu's terrible but necessary act restored Shiva to himself; it gave him the chance to mourn less madly and so continue the work of creation and destruction.

Vishnu's discus as the wheel of time is a powerful symbol for the breaking of bonds. The story reminds us that even seemingly eternal forces can die as time spins on. But it also reminds us that, with time, a broken goddess can come to life again, in this case in the form of beautiful cities and temples.

## *Pause, Please*

Sketch the wheel of time as it moves across your life and slices through bonds. Note the places where the bonds are easy, even pleasant, to break—such as in meeting and passing people on the street, leaving home to go to school, or quitting a job you were ready to quit in order to make a new bond with a new job.

Then sketch an instance when the wheel of time helped break a bond that trapped or enslaved you. Perhaps, for example, an abusive friend or lover, someone it seemed impossible to cast off emotionally, went away on a vacation. The hiatus gave you time to strengthen, so that when the friend/lover returned you could speak truthfully of your pain. You had the courage to set new guidelines for the relationship, which included the possibility of a formal break if the abuse continued.

Then draw one incident when time's slicing wheel broke a bond that tore your heart, as when a beloved parent or sibling suddenly died before their time. As you sketch a representation of this loss, notice whether you feel that enough time has passed to restore you to yourself again. Notice whether, in the breaking of the bond, energy was released that could be used to form new bonds. Even if you feel that the broken bond is still affecting you, draw a beautiful temple around your broken heart. Then invoke the Power of Celebration to move into that temple and bring you peace and a new sense of potential in the time to come.

Perhaps you might write something like this: "Great Power of Celebration, may the love I felt for my father who died so early in his life, and so painfully early in mine, be released as energy to bless all fathers and all children. And may my longing to talk with him one more time provide the energy for me to express my love for friends and family so richly that I never leave appropriate words unexpressed."

## TRANSFERRING ENERGY

We open our mouths to sing; that takes energy. The blue jay outside breaks a twig and flies it to the nest he and his partner are building; that takes energy. A yellow rose blooms; that takes energy. Each of these actions depends on the breaking of a bond and the transfer of energy from a large, high-energy molecule to a new molecule that now carries on in the work of singing, flying, constructing, and blooming. In the never-ending dance of this dynamic, some entity with strong energy offers that energy, not by dissipating it, but in a precise transfer to another specific entity; this action brings the two together and allows for new growth.

A healer, for instance, will direct her own strong energy to a friend in need, knowing that together they create both a bond and an opening for health to be restored. A powerful leader will communicate his high dreams for a whole country to his listeners so effectively that he ignites their own dreams, encourages them to organize new communities of engaged people, and persuades enough voters to elect him president. An actor will burst on the stage and electrify his audience, bonding them to him so that together they generate an unforgettable performance. Or a Tibetan lama will sit by the bedside of a dying man and by his training and wisdom generate the action called *Phowa*, the transference of consciousness at the time of death through the top of the head directly into a pure realm, so that the dying one bypasses difficult after-death experiences. And present as it is in the energy of every living being, I can imagine the Power of Celebration fully engaged in every such transfer, from the smallest to the most grand.

As a mythic representative of energy transference, I suggest one of the gifts brought to Ireland by the magical race called the *Tuatha de Danaan*, or "people of the goddess Danu." That gift is the Cauldron of Plenty given by Dagda the Good, their high god of abundance and agriculture, weather and harvests. This cauldron supplied enough food for Dagda's legendary appetite, and it was never empty; everyone was welcome to the feast and able to eat his fill at any time.

Celtic tradition is rife with magic cauldrons. Another appears as the Cauldron of Rebirth, sometimes said to be in the keeping of a hero called Bran the Blessed. Kings could place their dead warriors in this Cauldron of Rebirth at night, and they rose the next day as good as new, though not capable of speech. In one version, the cauldron emerged from the Lake of the Cauldron, carried by a huge man and woman.[6]

A third cauldron is the Cauldron of Knowledge. We know of it in the story of Ceridwen, queen, witch, and/or goddess—definitely a woman of power—whose son was born ugly. She wanted to make him beautiful, but that being impossible, she decided to make him wise. Learning a spell for wisdom, she began to concoct a magic brew in her cauldron that would require a year and a day to cook. She set two servants, an old blind man and a young boy, to stir the cauldron and keep the fire under it hot. They worked at it long and hard, all the while telling each other wonderful stories.

Just as the soup reached perfection, it boiled over and three scalding drops splashed on the servant boy's finger: he put it quickly into his mouth and instantly knew everything there was to know, including the future. When Ceridwen realized what had happened—those three drops, and only those three, held the wisdom elixir!—she began the famous chase. The boy ran from her and turned into a hare; she turned into a greyhound. He ran to the river and became a fish; she became an otter. He became a bird; she a falcon. In his flight he saw below him a heap of corn. He dived toward it and became a grain of corn. But Ceridwen became a black hen and devoured him. She became pregnant, and after nine months the boy was reborn as the magnificent, all-wise poet and "chief of bards," Taliesin.[7]

In a Welsh version of the cauldron stories, King Arthur captures the Cauldron of Ireland containing all the treasures of that land. And Taliesin is said to have been a member of Arthur's court, revered for his shamanic gifts such as the capacity to sing a lost soul back into its body. He could also celebrate his power as a shape-shifter with words like these, as Tom Cowan adapts in *Fire in the Head*:

> I have been in many shapes:
> I have been a narrow blade of a sword;
> I have been a drop in the air;
> I have been a shining star;
> I have been a word in a book;
> I have been an eagle;
> I have been a boat on the sea;
> I have been a string on a harp;
> I have been enchanted for a year in the foam of water.
> There is nothing in which I have not been.[8]

The eminent scholar, teacher, and writer Caitlín Matthews says, "The prime roles of the cauldron in Celtic tradition are to bestow nourishment, to confer status, and to govern the reception and dispensation of knowledge and inspiration."[9] All these cauldrons participate in a glorious, life-giving transfer of energy. This marvelous symbol has transmuted more recently as the chalice, or the Grail, whose magic properties include all those of the Celtic cauldrons: wisdom, abundance, and healing.

Mythic forebears of Dagda's Cauldron of Plenty are found in the Hindu tradition, especially in the Invocation to the Isha Upanishad, which tells of Fullness manifesting Fullness and leaving only Fullness. Hindu scholars believe this invocation inspired the poet Anne Sexton to write these beautiful lines in "What the Bird with the Human Head Knew." They contain the essence of the Power of Celebration:

> Then the well spoke to me.
> It said: Abundance is scooped from Abundance,
> yet Abundance remains.[10]

## Pause, Please

For you to read these words, millions of transfers of energy must take place in your cells. Can you ease into that thought, thanking the molecules that make it possible to bestow and to receive your energy from one to another in a way born of goodness and compassion, fueled by the Power of Celebration?

Draw or paint your version of the Celtic cauldrons. Looking at the Cauldron of Plenty, consider those times when you have received energy in the form of food, money, or gifts. Create a note of thanks for them. When have *you* made such an energy transfer? Create another note of thanks for the abundance of spirit that made it possible for you to celebrate by giving to others.

Now look at the Cauldron of Rebirth. When have you received a transfer of energy that brought you new life? Note such times. When have you given so generously that another was reborn, at least in some sense, through you? Note those occasions.

Consider the transfers of wisdom you have received from the Cauldron of Knowledge. Choose one to celebrate. In honor of the bard of bards, Taliesin, write and speak aloud a brief poem that tells of this gift. Now take the time to realize those times when you have transferred wisdom to another. Make a note of it.

Pour into all of these cauldrons the images that come to you as representatives of the Power of Celebration. Draw or paint them in. Feel the artwork you have created, the words you have written and spoken, and your whole body suffused with this generative energy. Notice that you have transferred energy to a page of paper and that, as you fill it with the Power of Celebration, it conveys energy back to you.

## A Story about All of the Above and More

A profound ritual can commemorate the making of bonds, breaking of bonds, and transfers of energy between the human world and the world of spirit. It can affirm the renewal of such bonds and perfectly illustrate the true nature of the Power of Celebration. Here's one I have experienced:

Loretta Cook, a friend and teacher, is a member of the Oglala Lakota tribe. Every year she and others of her family, descendants of the legendary leaders American Horse and Afraid-of-Bear, hold a traditional Sun Dance during the days immediately preceding the summer solstice at the Wild Horse Sanctuary in the Black Hills. One recent year I felt deeply called to attend as a witness. I asked for and was given permission to do so.

Loretta describes this well-known ceremony in awesome terms: A year-long preparation. Four days of dancing in the sun with no food or water. A time of intense call to spirit by spirit. A time of profound prayer for the people and for the earth. A ritual given by the legendary savior of the tribe, White Buffalo Calf Woman, who also gave them the sacred pipe and taught the holiness of its purpose.

As the months moved closer to the event, Loretta asked Betty Rothenberger, another friend who also felt called, and me if we would dance instead of serve as witnesses. I gulped, stammered, and said I would be willing to begin and dance as long as I could—if that would be good enough. Betty's response was beautiful: "Loretta, I feel like a child saying yes to something I really know nothing about." But we did both say yes, as did another friend, Emily Devine, who has much more experience in this tradition than either Betty or I.

Loretta's elders teach that their sacred rites should be shared with others, even non-natives. She assured us that the power of the ritual would consume us once we stepped out from the encircling arbor and entered the dance. That we never doubted.

Tom, Loretta's husband, suggested we might want to have a motel room to recuperate in if the dance proved too difficult. Not terribly reassuring, but we made our plans: fly to South Dakota, rent a car, drive to the little town nearest the location of the dance, find a motel room, and wait. We were jittery all the way, mostly with fear. What if we faint and fall down, what if we disgrace Loretta with our ignorance, what if what if what *if*? We knew full well that in many native places the very idea of Anglos joining this ceremony is both troubling and insulting. We had been told, in fact, that one reason the ceremony we were attending was to be held off the reservation was so that anyone who was a friend and felt called to dance could do so. We did our best to prepare spiritually. What were our prayers to be? In indigenous American tribes most of the prayers are of gratitude, with thanksgiving offered to all living things for their presence and blessing. We meditated and talked, pondered, and gave thanks for everything we could think of.

On arrival in South Dakota, we learned of delays. The people who were clearing the dancing ground of weeds and setting up camp for the support crew could not get onto the site yet; a Wells Fargo Bank commercial was being shot at the Wild Horse Sanctuary. So we had to wait. Loretta told us she was having Sun Dance dresses made for us. That was both a relief and a concern: What if they were heavy and beaded, like so much traditional dress? We would ruin them! Not to worry; they turned out to be simple white and red dresses, light and comfortable.

Loretta, who was suffering from back pains but was going to dance nevertheless, suggested that we each needed a pipe. We all knew the story of the gift of the pipe by White Buffalo Calf Woman, but none of us had connected that gift with the Sun Dance. All we had heard about the dance came from stories Loretta had told and from a few accounts by other past witnesses, whose descriptions were fascinating but grim.

But we needed to buy pipes. The thought alarmed us more than a little because we had always understood that one could carry a pipe only if one had done a vision quest and received a pipe dream. Not only were we a trio of white women, two of us in our sixties, showing up to take part in a Lakota ceremony and thus terrified of making gross mistakes and ruining it all with our ineptitude, but we were moving ever deeper into a mysterious spiritual space where we could only be seen as fools at best and crude invaders at worst.

Finally we realized that, having been invited by one of the leaders, we could simply trust her to lead us.

On the day when the film crew finally left the scene, we drove out, got stuck in mud (it had rained wildly, which was one reason the commercial had taken so long to shoot), felt lost, and watched others make preparations without knowing what we were supposed to do. So we wandered back into town, finally connected with Loretta, packed up our stuff, including our new pipes, and drove again to the dance ground. It had been freshly mowed, the traditional arbor surrounding the wide circular space refreshed, and a hole dug in the middle, with much ceremony. It would soon be filled with a young cottonwood tree, symbolizing the World Tree, on which we would tie our prayers in the form of small tobacco offerings.

We began to pick sage and wrap it into anklets, bracelets, and head crowns with red cloth. "Do we wear these?"

The answers came from those who had danced before. "Yes, the one around your head protects you a little from the sun. The ones at your wrists and ankles are there in case you faint; helpers will use them to pull you to the central tree. Once you set foot on the dance ground, no one should touch your flesh; you're sacred. And the sage provides protection; it's a holy plant."

"Oh," we gulped.

Helpers set up teepees, one for the musicians, one for the male dancers, one for the females. The driver with the porta potties arrived. Two sweat lodges were constructed—again, one for the men and one for the women. A huge fire pit was made, with a mountain of chopped fire logs, which, once lit, would be tended every hour. A sacred universe was created in one day.

Then it was time to get the tree. We set off in a caravan of cars and trucks over the countryside, through mud holes and ditches and almost roads to a particular spot where a tree had been selected. It was a young cottonwood, decorated and dedicated. The leader, a shaman and holy man, said the prayers, and each of the dancers hacked at the tree to bring it down, but not all the way. Without being allowed to touch the ground, the tree was passed on to a truck bed and carried back to the dance site. In procession with songs and prayers, we unloaded it from the truck and brought it in through the eastern gate (the gate the spirits enter) to the center, where the hole had been dug earlier and sacred food placed into it. People made offerings in cloth ties and placed them on the tree's branches. The dance being dedicated to the earth's environment, a huge shell was placed aloft on behalf of the oceans and an eagle feather on behalf of the air. After these offerings, it took all of us to get the tree lifted and planted in place securely.

Then it was time for feasting—our last meal for four days—and the first sweat lodge. Loretta led us in honoring the directions and all the ancestors (including the hot rocks that created the heat) and our animal relations. And we each spoke our prayers and hopes for the days ahead. At least three of us had no idea what we were facing. Finally, when we were preparing for sleep in the teepee, one of us gathered the courage to ask, "Loretta, what if I have to go to the bathroom?"

"You can't," she answered. "The agreement is that once you step out from the arbor, you do not leave the dance, you are there unto death." We exchanged wild and terrified glances. "Of course, you can use the bathroom during a break."

"We get breaks?" we asked incredulously.

"Certainly. The musicians need them. And I've asked Willard (the shaman) to allow us medicine during the breaks; so many of us are diabetic or borderline diabetic that we need sustenance of some kind. Strawberry water; perhaps even a peach."

When the ceremony began, we did indeed dance. And we participated in morning and evening sweat lodges, drank one dipper of water in the morning and evening, slept on cots in the women's teepee at night, filled and dedicated our pipes with sacred tobacco, approached the tree to offer prayers, witnessed the sacrifices of flesh made there by many of the men, and watched Loretta and tried to do what she did. We made it through the four days, supported and protected by all the other dancers and the singers, drummers, and witnesses. Emily, a dancer all her life, remarked that she felt what it was to be a sacred dancer. She subsequently joined the Sun Dance for two more years.

The mystery of this ceremony speaks about the Power of Celebration at the deepest possible level. A people—whose bonds with their beloved land, with one another, and with the world of spirit have been broken by murderously invasive outsiders in a long and painful (and ongoing) piece of American history—nevertheless affirm and reaffirm those bonds with fervor, intensity, and magnitude of heart. They seek to acknowledge what has been broken, to rebuild, and to celebrate what will emerge in a new form. They perform sacred dance in a context of respect, beauty, caring, high service, sacrifice, and belonging. They show that bonds can be made at the human level by dedication, willingness, and love. They make this affirmation not only for themselves but also for us and for the world. The men and women of the American Horse, Afraid-of-Bear lineage who perform the Sun Dance in the sacred Black Hills of South Dakota exquisitely embody the Power of Celebration.

When my friends and I joined something about which we had only heard stories, we too embraced that power, called—as we all are—to participate in life as a celebration. What calls us is unknown, perhaps unknowable. We agree; we want to do it. We don't know what it will be like, or whether we can do it right, or what our purpose is. We feel terror, uncertainty, fear of ridicule, and exhilaration.

But once we step out from the arbor, we are dancing.

## No Matter What

I can find no better way to end this chapter on Celebration, and this book, than with two beautiful thoughts of contemporary American poets. The first is by W. S. Merwin, who is also a playwright. His poem "Thanks" reminds us to keep making bonds, and breaking bonds, and transferring energy—to keep on playing the great performance piece that is life, no matter what. I urge you to speak it aloud:

### Thanks

Listen
with the night falling we are saying thank you
we are stopping on the bridges to bow from the railings
we are running out of the glass rooms
with our mouths full of food to look at the sky
and say thank you
we are standing by the water thanking it
standing by the windows looking out
in our directions

back from a series of hospitals back from a mugging
after funerals we are saying thank you
after the news of the dead
whether or not we knew them we are saying thank you

over telephones we are saying thank you
in doorways and in the backs of cars and in elevators
remembering wars and the police at the door
and the beatings on stairs we are saying thank you
in the banks we are saying thank you
in the faces of the officials and the rich
and of all who will never change
we go on saying thank you thank you

with the animals dying around us
taking our feelings we are saying thank you
with the forests falling faster than the minutes
of our lives we are saying thank you
with the words going out like cells of a brain
with the cities growing over us
we are saying thank you faster and faster
with nobody listening we are saying thank you
thank you we are saying and waving
dark though it is[11]

If enough of us say thank you "faster and faster" and live our lives as dedicated sacred players, then perhaps it will be our privilege to hold back the dark a while, and even to create and sustain a world that honors everyone. With that thought, the incomparable Diane Ackerman provides us with a pledge:

**School Prayer**
In the name of the daybreak
and the eyelids of morning
and the wayfaring moon
and the night when it departs,

I swear I will not dishonor
my soul with hatred,
but offer myself humbly
as a guardian of nature,
as a healer of misery,

as a messenger of wonder,
as an architect of peace.

In the name of the sun and its mirrors
and the day that embraces it
and the cloud veils drawn over it
and the uttermost night
and the male and the female
and the plants bursting with seed
and the crowning seasons
of the firefly and the apple,

I will honor all life
–wherever and in whatever form
it may dwell—on Earth my home,
and in the mansions of the stars.[12]

# Epilogue

*Our revels now are ended.*
—Prospero, in Shakespeare's *The Tempest*
(4.1.148)

In Shakespeare's *The Tempest*, the magician Prospero conjures a glorious pageant to celebrate the engagement of his daughter, Miranda, to her beloved Ferdinand (and to divert the lovers from sexual temptation). He calls forth goddesses in exquisite temples and palaces to bless the pair. Suddenly he interrupts the scene; he has remembered another, more urgent task he must perform.

Beginning with "Our revels," Prospero describes life as "such stuff as dreams are made on" and assures his children, who sit mesmerized by the pageant (as do we in the audience), that ultimately everything created will dissolve and vanish "into air, into thin air" (4.1.148–157), just like the magical phantom world he has created before them. In this speech and others, we lovers of Shakespeare hear overtones of his own magical powers as his life in the theatre began to wind down. Many of us believe this is his last play. A few works carry later dates, but they seem collaborations. So when Prospero bids farewell to his "rough magic," we can almost hear Shakespeare speaking in his own voice about his own life. My belief about this poignant confluence between Shakespeare and his character Prospero underlies any production of *The Tempest* that I see. I want it to be true.

As we come to the end of our work together, I realize that I also hold an underlying desire for you, the reader, as you move through your world, creating your own kind of magic. I see you standing on your sacred stage, beautifully accomplishing your incarnational task

259

as you move toward realizing the great gift you carry in this lifetime. You enact a holy and unique story, in the mystery of this present moment, with all your powers of expression, acknowledging your special way of seeing the world, noticing when you need to change or enlarge this point of view. You gallantly engage in authentic conflict in order to grow; you perform your great play for a sacred audience, seen and unseen; and you do it all as a miraculous celebration of life.

Here is the Prospero/Shakespeare mystery: you too are the playwright of your life, and you have created this amazing character/person—yourself —in a truly memorable play. In my imagining, you as playwright and you as magnificent star merge into one playful, joyful, infinitely creative person. I have two great desires for you: I want you to love your life; and I want you to love the theatre. Go to plays, make plays, act in plays, form a play-reading group, volunteer at your local theatre, enroll others in realizing the sacred plays of their lives. Use the material you have written and designed throughout this book to write a one-person show; present it to anyone who will watch and listen. Encourage others to do the same. Theatre matters.

Once each summer since 1988, the Oregon Shakespeare Festival has presented an AIDS benefit called the Daedalus Project, which grew out of an idea of James Edmondson (remember him from the chapter on Incarnation?). He concludes the evening with these magic words about love and life by Thornton Wilder from his short novel, *The Bridge of San Luis Rey*, which won the Pulitzer Prize in 1928: "But the love will have been enough. All those impulses of love return to the love that made them. Even memory is not necessary for love. There is a land of the living and a land of the dead and the bridge is love."[1]

Your life as a sacred player matters. And your living it fully will build bridges of love that will make a difference to the world.

## Here's a Story

The brilliant actress Helena de Crespo carries her legacy well from strong and visionary women. Her parents met through their deep interest in Theosophy. Before they were married her mother, an English woman, rescued her father, a refugee from Franco's Spain. And when Helena was born, they named her for Helena Petrovna Blavatsky, the fiery nineteenth-century Russian mystic who traveled the world in search of ancient esoteric knowledge. Author of *Isis Unveiled, The Secret Doctrine*, and many other works, Blavatsky is known for being the first to connect the spiritual wisdom of the East with the new science of the West, and hence for launching the New Age.

Helena de Crespo, the actress, who is particularly known for her one-woman shows, has also traveled the world to fulfill her life's mission, performing in many countries. While in Singapore a few years ago, she realized how close she was to Angkor Wat, the huge Buddhist temple complex in Cambodia she had always wanted to visit. So she flew in, rented a car with a driver and an interpreter, and drove to see the miles and miles of temples.

Returning to the airport, Helena stopped the car because she saw a building that was clearly a theatre standing somewhat back from the road. As she tells it,

the construction was impressive and indigenously Cambodian in design. My interpreter accompanied me, and we crossed the open space, where the audience would sit later that night, and I introduced myself to the actors who were getting some food together on the grass. After the usual formalities and a great demonstration of hospitality on their part, I told them what I did. How I had toured like them and had taken shows to the hinterland of several South American countries as they were doing now. And what was their story? That opened the floodgates and they poured out their astonishing and horrifying stories, how actors were the first Pol Pot ordered to be assassinated (not with bullets—they wouldn't waste expensive bullets on them—but bludgeoned to death), followed by other intellectuals in the country, and so on. The massacre of four out of five Cambodians had started.

Their intent now was to restore the ancient repertoire of the Ramayana (the dramatization of the legends of Rama and Sita, the core of Cambodian religion and culture) and train young performers in the highly skilled art of *Bassac* (Classic Opera). Their tradition goes back well over three thousand years, outdating the Greeks. As I had been brought up on these classic Indian stories in England, I could relate to their relevance. And so my adventure started of trying to contribute to the betterment of their life. They were starving when I met them, well belying the opulence of the stage construction. Tears were shed, first from my interpreter when he realized that the lady sitting humbly on the grass with us was a famous Cambodian actress who had escaped the Khmer Rouge by hiding in the jungles after everyone around her had been killed, and second from the troupe's director, Len Choeun, begging for help to feed his company.

Needless to say, Helena pledged her help. Since meeting this troupe, she has raised enough money for the group to buy a reliable truck for touring as well as a piece of land on which to build a permanent home for the company. She remarks, "They will still continue touring, navigating the land mines that the world has ignored, buried at Nixon's orders precisely when he was on American TV saying that such a thing would never happen."

Helena also has plans for a medical office and a small school. In addition, a new "Cambodian Treasures" website will export authentic Cambodian art such as silks, leather filigreed work, and shadow puppets. All proceeds will be used for the revival of the Cambodian theatre. "The project is already causing great interest," says Helena. "When completed, it will definitely be a stimulus to the local economy."

Many children come to the company's home because they are orphaned and have no other place to go. Others come because they have been damaged by land mines and the terrible years of war, but they have all found a center to care for, an art to practice, and important work to do—thanks to a remarkable woman of the theatre from the other side of the world.

Helena says, "If I believe anything, it is that my craft represents a vital and positive activity for the peoples of this planet, no matter where they reside or what society they come from. That I believe. I have seen it work wonders on the disenfranchised with low self-esteem as much as on the highly sophisticated. The image of us all writing our own scripts and performing on our own stage is exhilarating. It makes me feel that, even though there are times when it doesn't feel that way, we do have a say in our own destiny."

Just as I was finishing this epilogue Helena wrote about her recent visit to Cambodia: "When I actually walked on the site of the theatre and touched the walls in their present state, I realized that all the struggle has been worth it. We still have a long way to go, but it is happening."[2]

Theatre matters.

As a farewell reminder, I change one word of Jaques' speech in Shakespeare's *As You Like It*. He says,

> All the world's a stage,
> And all the men and women merely players.
>
> (2.7.139–140)

I say:

> All the world's a stage;
> And all the men and women *sacred* players.

The book ends. The play begins.

# Notes

All quotations from Shakespeare are from *William Shakespeare: The Complete Works*, eds. Stanley Wells and Gary Taylor (Oxford: Clarendon, 1986).

## PROLOGUE

1. *The Orphic Hymns: Text, Translation and Notes*, trans. Apostolos N. Athanassakis (Atlanta, Georgia: Scholars Press, 1977), 63. These are lines 5–7 in number 45 of 87 Orphic Hymns invoking many deities, thought to have been composed by different poets between the third century BCE and the second century CE.

2. David Sacks, *Encyclopedia of the Ancient Greek World* (New York: Facts on File, Inc., 1995), 244.

## CHAPTER ONE

1. B. Iden Payne devoted seventy of his ninety-five years to working in the theatre as director, actor, and teacher. He began at Dublin's Abbey Theatre, Manchester's Gaiety, and Stratford's Shakespeare Memorial Theatre. He then directed several Broadway productions and taught at Carnegie Tech, the University of Washington, and the University of Texas. In Washington he inspired Angus Bowmer with his revolutionary idea that Shakespeare should be performed on a "modified Elizabethan stage," so that the action could flow uninterrupted by cumbersome scenery changes. In 1935, Bowmer began the Oregon Shakespeare Festival, now in its seventy-fifth year. Mr. Payne's teachings, acting, directing, and relationship with Shakespeare remain among the most dynamic influences on my life and work. Yale University Press published his *A Life in a Wooden O: Memoirs of the Theatre* in 1977.

2. Rimpoche Nawang Gehlek, *Good Life, Good Death: Tibetan Wisdom on Reincarnation* (New York: Penguin Putnam, 2001), 164.

3. Bernard Shaw, *The Complete Plays of Bernard Shaw* (London: Constable, 1931), 746.

4. Ori Brafman and Rom Brafman, *Sway: The Irresistible Pull of Irrational Behavior* (New York: Broadway Books/Random House, 2008), 100.

## Chapter Two

*Epigraph*: Elie Wiesel is a writer, teacher, humanitarian, Nobel Peace Prize winner, and Holocaust survivor. This line is from the prologue of his novel, *The Gates of the Forest*, trans. Frances Frenaye (Austin, TX: Holt, Rinehart and Winston, 1966).

1. Nobody tells this story better than Dava Sobel: "As the stars enriched the heavens that had borne them, the heavens gave rise to new generations of stars, and these descendants possessed enough material wealth to build attendant worlds, with salt seas and slime pits, with mountains and deserts and rivers of gold." See her *The Planets* (New York: Viking/Penguin, 2005), 15.

2. My source for Bob Rauschenberg's idea is Emily Devine, the best dancer I have ever known, now a teacher of dance at Sarah Lawrence College. She thinks she first heard it from John Cage, who worked with Rauschenberg and Merce Cunningham.

3. The Internet Public Library (www.ipl.org/div/farq/plotFARQ.html) in "The 'Basic' Plots in Literature," describes one, three, seven, twenty, and thirty-six plots. And Cecil Adams, author of "The Straight Dope" newspaper column and the "world's most intelligent human being," will respond with his typical pungency to the question, "What are the seven basic literary plots?" on www.straightdope.com.

4. Denis Johnston worked as a playwright during the 1920s and '30s in Ireland, one of theatre's most fecund times and places. An award-winning BBC correspondent in World War II, he was also a lawyer, director, biographer, professor, and librettist and had a distinguished theatrical career in the United States as well as Ireland. His delineation of plotlines may be found at sismedia.wetpaint.com/page/Denis+Johnston's+7=plots.

5. Tom Cowan, *Fire in the Head: Shamanism and the Celtic Spirit* (San Francisco: (HarperSanFransisco, 1993), 175. Older versions account for Merlin's disappearance as a voluntary retirement to a magic island, or the forest of

Broceliande, or a house of glass, where he sleeps and dreams and waits to be called to serve the world again.

6. Charles Squire, *Celtic Myth and Legend* (Charleston, SC: BiblioBazaar, 2008), 339. (Orig. pub. 1905.)

## CHAPTER THREE

*Epigraph*: Thornton Wilder, *Our Town: A Play in Three Acts* (New York: Coward-McCann with Samuel French, 1965), 83. (Orig. pub. 1938.)

1. Ibid, 36.
2. From Thornton Wilder's essay "Some Thoughts on Playwriting" quoted in Susanne K. Langer, *Feeling and Form* (New York: Charles Scribner's Sons, 1953), 307.
3. Steven Johnson, *Mind Wide Open: Your Brain and the Neuroscience of Everyday Life* (New York: Scribner, 2004), 189.
4. Ibid., 192–193.
5. Bruce Lipton, PhD, *The Biology of Belief: Unleashing the Power of Consciousness, Matter, and Miracles* (Santa Rosa, CA: Mountain of Love/Elite Books, 2005), 166.
6. Ibid., 169.
7. Ibid., 164.
8. Ibid.

## CHAPTER FOUR

1. Alfonso Ortiz, quoted in *Earth Prayers From Around the World: 365 Prayers, Poems, and Invocations for Honoring the Earth*, eds. Elizabeth Roberts and Elias Amidon (New York: HarperCollins, 1991), 125.
2. Dylan Thomas, "The Force that through the Green Fuse Drives the Flower," *Norton Anthology of Poetry*, 4th ed., ed. Margaret Ferguson, Mary Jo Salter, and Jon Stallworthy (New York: Norton, 1996), 1460.
3. I heard this myth from the Aboriginal woman who was our hostess in the Walker River area of Arnhem Land. As the story goes, where I stood is the very place where Pelican, having accomplished his great work in forming various features of the landscape, paused to converse with King Brown Snake, who had his own story to tell. Then Pelican, deciding his life work was complete, went back into the Dreamtime by entering the earth there, while King Brown continued his journey toward the center

of the continent to meld into another mythic being, the fabled Rainbow Serpent.

4. Anthropologist Diane Bell provides rich information about Aboriginal women's stories and the responsibilities they carry for sustaining the land in two books, both by Spinifex Press in North Melbourne, Australia: *Daughters of the Dreaming*, 3rd ed. (2001) and *Ngarrindjeri Wurruwarrin: A World That Is, Was, and Will Be* (2001).

5. Oodgeroo Noonuccal, *Australian Legends and Landscapes* (Sydney, AUS: Random House Australia/Bow Books, 1990), 30.

6. Lynn McTaggart, *The Field: The Quest for the Secret Force of the Universe* (New York: HarperCollins, 2002), 23. Another relevant book by McTaggart is *The Intention Experiment: Using Your thoughts to Change Your Life and the World* (New York: Free Press/Simon and Schuster, 2007).

7. McTaggart, *The Field*, 23–24.

## Chapter Five

1. All quotations of Gay Luce taken from personal conversations and emails, May 1988 and September 2009.

## Chapter Six

*Epigraph*: Peter Brook, *The Shifting Point: Theatre, Film, Opera 1946–1987* (New York: Theatre Communications Group, 1994), xiii.

1. Ibid.

2. Ibid, 10.

3. James Bertolino's poem is the title work from a poetry chapbook entitled *Like a Planet* (Cincinnati, OH: Stone Marrow, 1993). His poetry has been recognized internationally for over forty years and won him several fellowships and awards. His most recent of twenty-five books appeared in 2009. See http://jamesbertolino.com/.

4. Neale Donald Walsch, from a presentation at a Leadership Training course, International Institute for Social Artistry, Ashland, Oregon, 2007.

5. I cannot now find this quote of Mother Teresa's, but for a similar one see www.brainyquote.com/quotes/authors/m/mother_teresa.html/.

6. "Love Changes Everything," from Andrew Lloyd Webber's musical *Aspects of Love*, lyrics by Dan Black and Charles Hart.

# NOTES

7. His Holiness The Dalai Lama and Howard C. Cutler, MD, *The Art of Happiness: A Handbook for Living* (New York: Riverhead/Penguin, 2009), 173.

## CHAPTER SEVEN

1. Aeschylus, *The Eumenides*, trans. Richmond, *The Complete Greek Tragedies, Volume 1* (Chicago: University of Chicago Press, 1953), 163, lines 780–792.
2. Ibid., 165, lines 868–869.
3. Ibid., 167, lines 922–925.
4. Robert Kegan, *In Over Our Heads: The Mental Demands of Modern Life* (Cambridge: Harvard University Press, 1994), 320–321. Kegan's note on this passage reads, "This 'union of opposites' Jung called 'enantiodromia,' depicted by the snake who eats its tail, the joining of the poles making a single whole. Interestingly, Jung associated the union of opposites with midlife" (383).
5. As with most things Balinese, not everything is as it seems; this ceremony has several layers of meaning. In one back story, *Rangda* ("widow" in high Javanese) was once a queen of East Java, married to an eleventh-century king who exiled her to the forest for practicing black magic. Rangda wanted her daughter to marry well, but few takers vied for the honor. She turned her energies to destruction; finally a brave man married the daughter in order to learn Rangda's secrets. He killed her with magic, then revived her, then killed her again as a human.
6. Fred B. Eiseman, Jr., *Bali: Sekala & Niskala, Essays on Religion, Ritual, and Art, Volume 1* (Berkeley, CA: Periplus, 1989), 293–321.
7. David Patten, a spiritual teacher and student of all things Balinese, wrote to me recently that the Rangda and Barong drama is "deeper than the notions of good and evil." His Balinese teachers define *Rangda* as "space" and *Barong* as "thing" or "matter." They belong together. In David's understanding, Rangda is an incarnation of Uma, wife of the great Hindu god Shiva. Lonely for her, Shiva sends the Barong to lure her playfully home again. The conflict is within the Barong's followers who have fallen into the mental trap of believing that one is good and the other evil.
8. Adapted from Euripides, *The Trojan Women* in *Three Greek Plays*, trans. Edith Hamilton (New York: Norton, 1937), 81–86.
9. Ibid.
10. Josephine Hart, *Sin: A Novel* (New York: Knopf, 1992), 164.

11. Rainer Maria Rilke, "The Man Watching," in Robert Bly, comp., *News of the Universe: Poems of Twofold Consciousness* (San Francisco: Sierra Club, 1980), 121–22.

12. Sophocles, *Oedipus at Colonus*, trans. Robert Fitzgerald, *The Complete Greek Tragedies, Volume 2*, ed. David Grene and Richmond Lattimore (Chicago: University of Chicago Press, 1959), 79, lines 7–8.

## CHAPTER EIGHT

1. Alfred A. Tomatis, *The Ear and the Voice*, trans. Roberta Prada and Pierre Sollier (Lanham, MD: Scarecrow/Rowman and Littlefield, 2005), 86.

2. John Medina, *Brain Rules, 12 Principles for Surviving and Thriving at Work, Home, and School* (Seattle: Pear, 2009), 240. Medina is Professor of Bioengineering at the University of Washington School of Medicine. His delightful book not only tells us what our brains need and want but provides elegant accounts of many current brain studies with suggestions that can enrich our living and learning processes.

3. Tomatis, *The Ear and the Voice*, 61.

4. Ibid., 63.

5. Thich Nhat Hanh, *The Miracle of Mindfulness: A Manual on Meditation* (Boston: Beacon, 1975), 20.

6. Euripides, *The Bacchae*, in *The Complete Greek Tragedies, Volume 4*, ed. David Grene and Richmond Lattimore (Chicago: University of Chicago Press, 1960), 539, line 861.

7. See David Sacks, *Encyclopedia of the Ancient Greek World* (New York: Facts on File, 1995), 93: "Euripides' contemporaries clearly found his religious irreverence to be disturbing. Although he competed 22 times at Athenian festival drama competitions, he was awarded first place only five times (as compared with Aeschylus' 13 and Sophocles' 24 in their lifetimes). Yet he was always considered thought-provoking enough to be allowed a hearing. The Athenian officials never rejected his application to compete."

8. Euripides, *The Bacchae*, 581, lines 846–848 and 850–861.

9. Gilbert Murray, *The Literature of Ancient Greece*, 3rd ed. (Chicago: Phoenix Books/University of Chicago Press, 1956), 272. (Orig. pub. 1897.)

10. Richmond Lattimore, in Euripides, *The Complete Greek Tragedies, Vol. 3*, ed. David Grene and Richmond Lattimore (Chicago: University of Chicago Press, 1959), vi.

11. David Lykken, PhD. *Happiness: What Studies on Twins Show Us about Nature, Nurture, and the Happiness Set Point* (New York: Golden Books/Random House, 1999), 2. Lykken did, however, come to disagree with his statement in an earlier article that read, "It may be that trying to be happier is as futile as trying to be taller." (D. T. Lykken and A. Tellegen, "Happiness is a Stochastic Phenomenon," *Psychological Science* 7, (1996)): 186–89. In fact, he considered his book *Happiness* a "chance to set the record straight," meaning that although our genetic inheritance provides a basic "set point" for happiness or misery, it is not the only determining factor in our capacity for delight and joy.

12. See Lucia Chiavola Birnbaum, *Dark Mother, African Origins and Godmothers*. (Lincoln, NE: Authors Choice, 2001). In it, she cites the findings of geneticist L. Luca Cavalli-Sforza, who concludes that, "Our species, homo sapiens sapiens, appeared in east and south Africa around 100,000 years ago, long before appearing elsewhere . . . modern humans, replacing earlier human types, originated in Africa," and that "after 50,000 BCE, Africans expanded into Asia, Europe, Australia, and North and South America" (4). Dr. Cavalli-Sforza utilized DNA research into mitochondrial DNA, carried only by women. Since those early, somewhat controversial studies, tracings of the Y chromosome, carried only by men, have led to similar conclusions. Today the National Geographic Society is conducting a genographic survey that allows us to trace our individual DNA back to our original ancestors in Africa and then to follow the ensuing pathways they took to people throughout the whole world.

13. See page 1 of Zenkei Blanche Hartman's lecture at www.intrex.net/chzg/hartman4.htm.

## Chapter Nine

*Epigraph*: Derek Walcott, "Love After Love," in *Collected Poems 1948–1984* (New York: Farrar, Straus and Giroux, 1986), 328.

1. Mahlon Hoagland and Bert Dodson, *The Way Life Works: The Science Lover's Illustrated Guide to How Life Grows, Develops, Reproduces, and Gets Along* (New York: Times Books/Random House, 1995), 122.

2. Ibid., 41.

3. Ibid., 42.

NOTES

4. Normandi Ellis, *Awakening Osiris* (Newburyport, MA: Phanes, 1988), 180, in Normandi's glorious evocation of Hymn 55 in the ancient Egyptian The Book of the Dead, more accurately known as The Book of Coming Forth by Day.

5. *In Praise of the Goddess: The Devimahatmya and Its Meaning*, trans. Devadatta Kali (York Beach, ME: Nicholas-Hayes, 2003), 50.

6. Miranda J. Green, *Dictionary of Celtic Myth and Legend* (London: Thames and Hudson, 1992), 58. This is one of many sources on Irish and Welsh magic cauldrons.

7. Jean Markale, *The Celts: Uncovering the Mythic and Historic Origins of Western Culture* (Rochester, VT: Inner Traditions, 1993), 227–230.

8. From Tom Cowan, *Fire in the Head: Shamanism and the Celtic Spirit* (San Francisco: HarperSanFrancisco, 1993), 29.

9. Caitlín Matthews and John Matthews, *Encyclopaedia of Celtic Wisdom: A Celtic Shaman's Source Book* (Rockport, MA: Element Books, 1994), 219.

10. Anne Sexton, *The Complete Poems* (Boston: Mariner Books/Houghton Mifflin, 1999), 458.

11. W. S. Merwin, "Thanks," from *The Rain in the Trees* (New York: Alfred A. Knopf, a Division of Random House, Inc., 1988), 46.

12. Diane Ackerman, "School Prayer," from *I Praise My Destroyer* (New York: Random House, 1998), 3.

## Epilogue

1. Thornton Wilder, *The Bridge of San Luis Rey* (New York: Perennial Classic/Harpers, 2003), 109.

2. All quotes from Helena de Crespo come from conversation and email correspondence in August through November, 2009, along with the Oregon Stage Works' program notes for its 2009 production of *Shirley Valentine*, one of Helena's many memorable creations. For further information about her remarkable work with the Cambodian Theatre Troupe, visit helenadecrespo.com.

# Bibliography

These books and their authors have challenged, enchanted, and deepened my life and way of experiencing the world. They, and others like them, comprise a debt that cannot be paid but that enriches me beyond measure.

Aeschylus. *The Complete Greek Tragedies: Volume 1.* Edited by David Grene and Richmond Lattimore. Chicago: University of Chicago Press, 1959.

Aristotle. *Poetics.* Translated by S. H. Butcher. New York: Hill and Wang/Farrar, Straus and Giroux, 1961.

Barasch, Marc Ian. *Field Notes on the Compassionate Life: A Search for the Soul of Kindness.* Emmaus, PA: Rodale, 2005.

Berendt, Joachim-Ernst. *The Third Ear: On Listening to the World.* Translated by Tim Nevill. New York: An Owl Book/Henry Holt, 1992.

Birnbaum, Lucia Chiavola, PhD. *Dark Mother: African Origins and Godmothers.* Lincoln, NE: Authors Choice/iUniverse, 2001.

Boleslavsky, Richard. *Acting: The First Six Lessons.* New York: Theatre Arts, 1933.

Brizendine, Louann, MD. *The Female Brain.* New York: Morgan Road Books, 2006.

Broersma, Patricia. *Riding into Your Mythic Life: Transformational Adventures with the Horse.* Novato, CA: New World Library, 2007.

Brook, Peter. *The Shifting Point: Theatre, Film, Opera 1945-1987.* New York: Theatre Communications Group, 1994.

Burstyn, Ellen. *Lessons in Becoming Myself.* New York: Riverhead/Penguin (USA), 2006.

Campbell, Don. *Music: Physician for Times to Come.* Wheaton, IL: Quest Books, 2000.

Chekhov, Michael. *To the Actor: On the Technique of Acting.* New York: Harper and Row, 1953.

# BIBLIOGRAPHY

De Beauport, Elaine, PhD. *The Three Faces of Mind: Developing Your Mental, Emotional, and Behavioral Intelligences.* Wheaton, IL: Quest Books, 1996.

Doidge, Norman, MD. *The Brain that Changes Itself.* New York: Viking/Penguin, 2007.

Eden, Donna, with David Feinstein, PhD. *Energy Medicine: Balance Your Body's Energies for Optimum Health, Joy, and Vitality.* New York: Tarcher/Putnam, 1998.

——. *Energy Medicine for Women: Aligning Your Body's Energies to Boost Your Health and Vitality.* New York: Tarcher/Penguin, 2008.

Euripides. *The Complete Greek Tragedies, Volume 3* and *Volume 4.* Edited by David Grene and Richmond Lattimore. Chicago: The University of Chicago Press, 1959 and 1960.

His Holiness The Dalai Lama and Howard C. Cutler, MD. *The Art of Happiness: A Handbook for Living.* New York: Riverhead/Penguin, 2009.

Hodge, Francis, and Michael McLain. *Play Directing: Analysis, Communication and Style.* Needham Heights, MA: Allyn and Bacon, 2009.

Houston, Jean, PhD. *The Possible Human: A Course in Enhancing Your Physical, Mental, and Creative Abilities.* New York: Tarcher/Putnam's Sons, 1982.

——. *The Search for the Beloved: Journeys in Sacred Psychology.* Los Angeles: Tarcher, 1987.

——. *A Mythic Life: Learning to Live Our Greater Story.* New York: HarperCollins, 1996.

Johnson, Steven. *Mind Wide Open: Your Brain and The Neuroscience of Everyday Life.* New York: Scribner, 2004.

Kegan, Robert. *In Over Our Heads: The Mental Demands of Modern Life.* Cambridge, MA: Harvard University Press, 1994.

Lipton, Bruce H., PhD. *The Biology of Belief; Unleashing the Power of Consciousness, Matter and Miracles.* Santa Rosa, CA: Mountain of Love/Elite Books, 2005.

——. and Steve Bhaerman. *Spontaneous Evolution: Our Positive Future (and a Way to Get There from Here).* Carlsbad, CA: Hay House, 2009.

Lykken, David, PhD. *Happiness: What Studies on Twins Show Us About Nature, Nurture, and the Happiness Set Point.* New York: Golden Books/Random House, 1999.

McTaggart, Lynne. *The Field: The Quest for the Secret Force of the Universe.* New York: HarperCollins, 2002.

# BIBLIOGRAPHY

——. *The Intention Experiment: Using Your Thoughts to Change Your Life and the World*. New York: Free Press/Simon and Schuster, 2007.

Medina, John, PhD. *Brain Rules: 12 Principles for Surviving and Thriving at Work, Home, and School*. Seattle: Pear, 2008.

Pearce, Joseph Chilton. *The Biology of Transcendence: A Blueprint of the Human Spirit*. Rochester, VT: Park Street/Inner Traditions, 2002.

——. *The Death of Religion and the Rebirth of Spirit: A Return to the Intelligence of the Heart*. Rochester, VT: Park Street/Inner Traditions, 2007.

Rockwood, Jerome. *The Craftsmen of Dionysus: An Approach to Acting*. Glenview, IL: Scott Foresman, 1966.

Rossi, Alfred. *Astonish Us In The Morning: Tyrone Guthrie Remembered*. Detroit: Wayne State University Press, 1980.

Shakespeare, William. *The Complete Works*. General Editors Stanley Wells and Gary Taylor. New York: Oxford University Press, 1986.

Singer, Michael A. *The Untethered Soul: The Journey beyond Yourself*. Oakland, CA: New Harbinger and Noetic Books, 2007.

Sophocles. *The Complete Greek Tragedies: Volume 2*. Edited by David Grene and Richmond Lattimore. Chicago: The University of Chicago Press, 1959.

Tomatis, Alfred A, MD. *The Ear and the Voice*. Translated by Roberta Prada and Pierre Sollier. Lanham, MD: Scarecrow/Rowman and Littlefield, 2005.

# Index

# INDEX

# INDEX

# INDEX

# Quest Books

encourages open-minded inquiry into
world religions, philosophy, science, and the arts
in order to understand the wisdom of the ages,
respect the unity of all life, and help people explore
individual spiritual self-transformation.

Its publications are generously supported by
The Kern Foundation,
a trust committed to Theosophical education.

Quest Books is the imprint of
the Theosophical Publishing House,
a division of the Theosophical Society in America.
For information about programs, literature,
on-line study, membership benefits, and international centers,
see www.theosophical.org
or call 800-669-1571 or (outside the U.S.) 630-668-1571.

# Related Quest Titles

*The Hero and the Goddess*, by Jean Houston

*Life Force*, by Jean Houston

*Music: Physician for Times to Come*, by Don Campbell

*The Song of Arthur*, by John Matthews

*The Song of Taliesin*, by John Matthews

*Sophia: Goddess of Wisdom*, by Caitlín Matthews

To order books or a complete Quest catalog,
call 800-669-9425 or (outside the U.S.) 630-665-0130.

# Praise for Peggy Rubin's
# *To Be and How to Be*

"For those who seek lives of awareness, passion, and purpose, Rubin has distilled a series of spiritual practices from her profound understanding of the theater and her knowledge of world myths and cultures. She provides us with a framework for sacred empowerment, a way to become creative directors in the narrative play of our lives. The challenge she presents is rigorous, wise, and deeply nurturing. It is an immense gift."

—**Karen Ellen Johnson**, artist/teacher, New York City

"There are times when something you read has the power to stop your life in its unconscious rush forward. This book does that, and then again and again, it coaxes something more genuine to take shape. To take seriously these often deceptively gentle instructions, to give them the real chance to do their great work, just may be to find oneself suddenly, and quite radiantly, at home in the moment. Read, in other words, only if prepared to loosen yourself from the tight grip of your old stories and know your birthright: the vast stage is always arriving right under your feet."

—**Sensei Bonnie Myotai Treace**, Gristmill Hermitage, founder of Hermitage Heart and Bodies of Water Zen

"From Sacred Theatre to sacralizing your life's story, Peggy Rubin takes you through an engaging process that will expand your perspective in a myriad of ways and enrich your journey forever. We love this book."

—**Donna Eden and David Feinstein**, authors of *Energy Medicine*

"This effervescent description of Sacred Theater should inspire us all as composers of our lives and caring actors in the world."

—**Mary Catherine Bateson**, author of *Composing a Further Life: The Age of Active Wisdom*

"This is a groundbreaking book in human and spiritual development. By transposing the nine elements of theater into a guide for human life, the author brings us not just the richness of theater but ancient as well as modern knowledge. From the first fires lit in ancient times, from Shakespeare to molecules, you are inspired to be the star of your own play, to recognize that your life is a sacred event necessary to you as well as the planet. This book is wisdom; don't miss it."

—**Elaine de Beauport, Ed.D.**, author of *The Three Faces of Mind*, Director of the Mead Institute for Human Development

"Peggy Rubin's brilliant elucidation of the nine powers of Sacred Theatre propels us away from any impoverished tunnel vision about our lives into which we may have slipped. We find ourselves in a vast new landscape, where we recognize our lives for their full power and wonder."

—**Trish Broersma**, author of *Riding into Your Mythical Life: Transformational Adventures with the Horse*